More-Than-Human Literacies in Early Childhood

Feminist Thought in Childhood Research

Series editors: Jayne Osgood and Veronica Pacini-Ketchabaw

Drawing on feminist scholarship, this boundary-pushing series explores the use of creative, experimental, new materialist and post-humanist research methodologies that address various aspects of childhood. *Feminist Thought in Childhood Research* foregrounds examples of research practices within feminist childhood studies that engage with post-humanism, science studies, affect theory, animal studies, new materialisms and other post-foundational perspectives that seek to decentre human experience. Books in the series offer lived examples of feminist research praxis and politics in childhood studies. The series includes authored and edited collections – from early career and established scholars – addressing past, present and future childhood research issues from a global context.

Also available in the series
Feminist Research for 21st-Century Childhoods: Common Worlds Methods,
edited by B. Denise Hodgins
Feminists Researching Gendered Childhoods: Generative Entanglements,
edited by Jayne Osgood and Kerry H. Robinson
Theorizing Feminist Ethics of Care in Early Childhood Practice:
Possibilities and Dangers,
edited by Rachel Langford

More-Than-Human Literacies in Early Childhood

Abigail Hackett

BLOOMSBURY ACADEMIC
LONDON • NEW YORK • OXFORD • NEW DELHI • SYDNEY

BLOOMSBURY ACADEMIC
Bloomsbury Publishing Plc
50 Bedford Square, London, WC1B 3DP, UK
1385 Broadway, New York, NY 10018, USA
29 Earlsfort Terrace, Dublin 2, Ireland

BLOOMSBURY, BLOOMSBURY ACADEMIC and the Diana logo
are trademarks of Bloomsbury Publishing Plc

First published in Great Britain 2021
This paperback edition published 2022

Series design by Anna Berzovan
Cover image © Steve Pool

A catalogue record for this book is available from the British Library.

Library of Congress Cataloging-in-Publication Data
Names: Hackett, Abigail, 1980- author.
Title: More-than-human literacies in early childhood / Abigail Hackett.
Description: London ; New York, NY : Bloomsbury Academic, 2021. |
Series: Feminist thought in childhood research |
Includes bibliographical references and index.
Identifiers: LCCN 2020046674 (print) | LCCN 2020046675 (ebook) |
ISBN 9781350144729 (hardback) | ISBN 9781350144736 (ebook) |
ISBN 9781350144743 (epub)
Subjects: LCSH: Children–Language. | Language arts (Early childhood)–Great Britain. |
Child development–Great Britain. | Educational sociology–Great Britain.
Classification: LCC LB1139.L3 H2193 2021 (print) |
LCC LB1139.L3 (ebook) | DDC 372.6/049–dc23
LC record available at https://lccn.loc.gov/2020046674
LC ebook record available at https://lccn.loc.gov/2020046675

ISBN: HB: 978-1-3501-4472-9
         PB: 978-1-3502-1518-4
       ePDF: 978-1-3501-4473-6
      eBook: 978-1-3501-4474-3

Series: Feminist Thought in Childhood Research

Typeset by Integra Software Services Pvt. Ltd.

To find out more about our authors and books visit www.bloomsbury.com
and sign up for our newsletters.

Contents

Illustrations

Figures

Tables

Acknowledgements

This book seems like it has been a long time in the making, a slow piece of thinking, fiddling and fraying the edges of some things that never quite seemed to hang together when it came to everyday life with toddlers in communities. It is grounded in my long-term thinking-with-place in one local community in northern England, and I am enduringly grateful to the families, children, staff, organizations, places, buildings and spaces that have welcomed me and taught me so much over the years.

I want to offer many thanks to Maggie MacLure, Christina MacRae and Kate Pahl, colleagues who gave me so much time, advice, mentorship and encouragement, for months on end during the writing of this book, including reading countless draft chapters. And also special thanks to Rachel Holmes, an inspirational researcher and exemplary manager who championed my work and supported and encouraged it all the way through. Steve Pool collaborated with me as artist in residence for some of this project, and I want to thank him for his fresh and thoughtful contributions. I am honoured that this book is part of the *Feminist Thought in Childhood Research* book series, and am so grateful to Jayne Osgood and the rest of the editorial team who provided space for this book as well as many important suggestions. I also want to acknowledge the wisdom of several anonymous reviewers, of both the proposal and final manuscript, who challenged and improved my thinking probably more than they realize. Finally, I wish to acknowledge the Naming the World collective, and particularly the mentorship of Margaret Somerville and Pauliina Rautio; this project would never have unfolded the way it did without our many conversations. To all of you, the generosity of your comments has been the thing that kept the words flowing much of the time, and your thoughtful and critical prompts have shaped the manuscript and strengthened it in so many ways.

I got a 'Facebook' memory on my phone last week that is has been six years since I submitted my PhD thesis. At that time, Isla had not long started school, Nancy was a toddler, and Ol and I were frantically juggling too many things. Our two girls are bigger now but the juggling between careers and family life has not changed. Ol, Isla and Nancy, thank you three so much for juggling this with me, for the cuddles, coffee, space to work and times you distracted me and reminded me work is nowhere near everything. Love you three xxx.

Thank you to the British Academy for funding this research as part of a Postdoctoral Fellowship award. In a context in which early career academic life is precarious, competitive and vulnerable, the difference such an award made in terms of space and time to think was invaluable.

This book is dedicated to Lisa Procter, who inspired me when she was here, and still inspires me now.

Series Editors' Introduction

The series *Feminist Thought in Childhood Research* considers experimental and creative modes of researching and practising in childhood studies. Recognizing the complex neo-liberal landscape and worrisome spaces of coloniality in the twenty-first century, the *Feminist Thought in Childhood Research* books provide a forum for cross-disciplinary, interdisciplinary and transdisciplinary conversations in childhood studies that engage feminist decolonial, anticolonial, more-than-human, new materialisms, post-humanist and other post- foundational perspectives that seek to reconfigure human experience. The series offers lively examples of feminist research praxis and politics that invite childhood studies scholars, students and educators to engage in collectively to imagine childhood otherwise.

Until now, childhood studies has been decidedly a human matter, focused on the needs of individual children (Taylor, 2013). In the Anthropocene (Colebrooke, 2012, 2013), however, other approaches to childhood that address the profound, human-induced ecological challenges facing our own and other species are emerging. As Taylor (2013) reminds us, if we are going to grapple with the socio-ecological challenges we face today, childhood studies need to pay attention to the *more*-than-human, to the *non*-human others that inhabit our worlds and the *in* human. Towards this end, *Feminist Thought in Childhood Research* series challenges the humanist, linear, and moral narratives (Colebrook, 2013; Haraway, 2013) of much of childhood studies by engaging with feminisms. As a feminist series, the books explore the inheritances of how to live in the Anthropocene and think about it in ways that are in tension with the Anthropocene itself.

The latest edition to the book series is authored by Abigail Hackett and entitled: *More-Than-Human Literacies in Early Childhood*. This volume makes an important contribution by inviting readers to think afresh about early childhood literacies; not so much in the sense of trying to define what they might be but rather to be open to what they produce; and the invitation that a feminist, post-humanist framing offers to contemplate literacies as inherently more-than-human. It is a book that invites wonder at what else might be learnt about language and literacy practices in early childhood when we start with the everyday in local communities. Hackett offers intricate and carefully woven stories that draw upon her close and long-standing connections to a specific urban community, and her sensitive attunement to the complexities of childhood as they are formed and play out in the neoliberal context of contemporary Britain. The attention to the significance of place, materiality and the body in the literacies of young children conjure a sense of the ways that very young children (between the ages of one and three years) participate in, and are entangled within, literacies and language in the contexts of their everyday lives. Through the experiential knowing of parents and communities Hackett mobilises 'body-place knowing' and 'ordinary affects' as a conceptual means to illustrate that young children's literacies are always more-than-human, and are consistently shaped by sounds, gestures and movements between humans and nonhuman places and things. It is by paying close attention to the more-than-human nature of literacies - that rely on bodies, places, animals, humans, objects and atmospheres for their ongoingness - that the book makes a persuasive case for decentring young children, and troubling notions of individualized human agency, to arrive at complex accounts of early childhood literacy practices.

The book proposes a more generative and generously non-anthropocentric notion of young children's literacies, in which more-than-human bodies, places, things and affective forces are central. In dialogue with other books in the *Feminist Thought in Childhood Research* series, this volume stresses the significance of situated knowledge, and is invested in interrogating the politics of hierarchies of knowledge in relation to families and young children. Hackett asks: *whose knowledge, expertise, lived experience counts and why, with regards to what very young children require in their daily lives?* Following Hodkins' (2019, p.6) insistence that 'it matters which stories we tell' Hackett makes clear that the decisions made about the stories that get told and the voices that are amplified, is a deeply political undertaking with far-reaching consequences. Her investments in telling different stories, differently, about families, communities, early childhood and literacies lay bare the importance of this mode of enquiry to imagine childhood otherwise.

In concert with other books in the series, this volume advocates for a more-than-human ontology in order to challenge global-North, developmental and anthropocentric frames, with a particular interest in the intersection between feminist new materialist, indigenous and affect theories. Hackett's work contributes to an emergent and growing post-developmental movement, which directly challenges claims that early childhood development is either neutral or universal.

Rather, developmentism must be understood an inherently, and persistently political and situated. This book contributes to this movement by specifically focusing upon young children's language and literacy practices to argue that:

> "Young children's language, vocabulary, and emergent literacy competencies sit near the heart of anxiety about young children's development, believed by many to evidence their ability to rationalize, problem solve, make abstract connections, empathize with others or hold their own views. Young children's literacy and language practices unfold amidst the smells, sounds, scattered toys, sticky fingers, anxieties, hopes and frustrations of everyday life of families in communities. The lives of young children and their parents in these communities are ordinary. Not in the sense of being obvious or self-explanatory, but in the sense of being unpredictable, contradictory, specific, illogical, in the sense of meaning everything and nothing all at the same time."

The book takes up the invitation offered by the series to rethink not only the politics of what counts as knowledge, but the kinds of research processes and practices that might be required in order to attend to both the problemisation of discursive taken-for-granted 'truths' and the affective and material actualisations of these in everyday life. In the first book in the series the authors (Osgood & Robinson, 2019) proposed that feminist researchers should "immerse [them]selves more fully in the intensities, flows, rhythms, affects and forces of children's entanglements with space, place and materiality (p.8). Hackett's book does precisely this by offering a rich and deep engagement that attends to the affective and curious in early childhood. It is through practices of deep hanging out that start with the situated and lived knowledge of families in communities, and goes on to trace the (extra)ordinary of lived experiences in more-than-human worlds, that the book arrives at a set of lively, compelling and important insights that push the field of childhood studies in new directions.

Part One

Starting with Community and Place

More-Than-Human Literacies in Community Spaces of Early Childhood

At singing time, H picks a dead piece of leaf off the floor and pops it in his mouth, lightning fast. She[1] sees it sitting on his bottom lip and, like a reflex, stretches her hand to grab it away. For a split second, she feels the softness of his bottom lip, a strange kind of inappropriate intimacy for a small boy she has just met. She wipes his saliva on her trousers as the group begins the nursery rhyme singing.

> [Children and families] live in a universe that has not been accurately described. The right words have not been coined. Using habitual vocabulary sends us straight down the same old much-trodden paths. But there are other paths to which these footpaths do not lead. There are whole stretches of motherhood that no one has explored.
>
> Stadlen, 2005, p.12

This book is grounded in the community spaces of early childhood; community playgroups in particular, but also parks, streets, day care, a local museum, in small urban community in northern England. It attends to small moments, bodily experiences and sensations, things that can be known through the body and partially articulated in writing. These aspects of lived experience with babies and toddlers are rarely articulated and often hard to explain; as Stadlen (2005) writes above, it is a universe that often goes undescribed (Figure 1.1). Concerned with the experiences of being and being with very young children, experiences which are marked by both ordinariness and exceptionality, this book wonders; what we might learn about language and literacy practices in early childhood by starting with the everyday in communities.

This question is particularly pertinent at time of increasing global anxiety around young children, their families, their early experiences, the rate of their

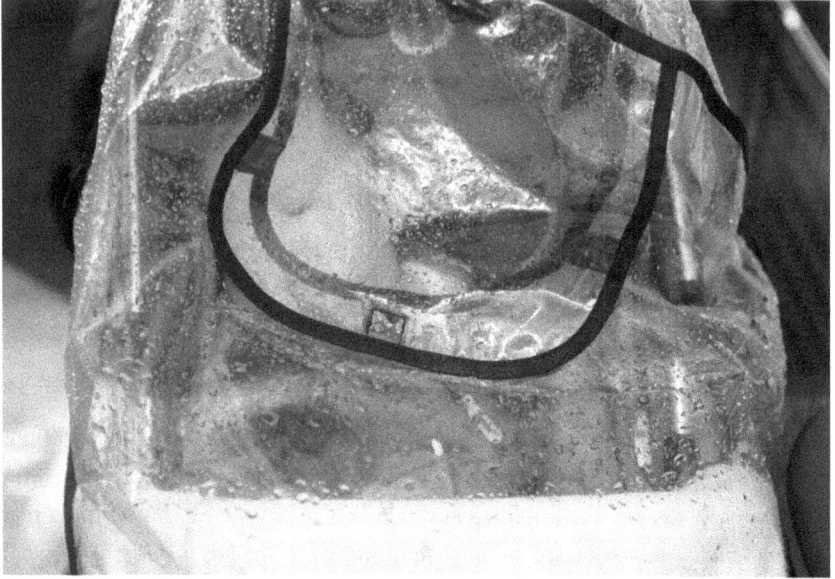

Figure 1.1 Pushchair at Playgroup. Photo credit: Steve Pool

development and the implications for their future schooling and success. Intensifying interest in 'the first 1000 days' of young children's lives leads to increasingly prescriptive, instructional and instrumental recommendations for parenting and pedagogy for children aged under three years (Figure 1.2). In such a context, academics (re)search for a model, a solution, to identify 'what works', and in doing so, it sometimes seems necessary to generalize, reduce, quantify and work with correlations (Jones et al., 2014). Yet, despite reams of 'evidence-based' parenting advice and policy interventions, parents don't always seem to 'do what they are told'. Something is lost in translation; parents, particularly from marginalized communities, seem to refuse to take the medicine, to follow the instructions, to act in ways that are 'proven' to most effectively socialize young children into a certain way of being.

Generalized, rational, universalized ways of describing young children's development, what toddlers are like, what they need, how things might unfold, whilst not wrong, somehow seem to miss something crucial. Perhaps reading these descriptions at a desk in my office, they seem plausible, reasonable. Then I return to playgroup, swing open the door, step over some items on the floor, into a particular kind of soundscape, smellscape, some place filled with hopes and anxieties, humour and extreme sleep deprivation. And then, those neat, reduced, demystified accounts no longer seem thinkable.

Every Child a Talker (ECAT) is designed to help practitioners and parents create a developmentally appropriate, supportive and stimulating environment in which children can enjoy experimenting with and learning language. Through everyday, fun and interesting experiences which reflect children's interests, ECAT encourages early language development right from the outset, extending children's vocabulary so that before they start school, children are confident and skilled communicators.
Department for Children, Schools and Families, 2009

Language; speaking
(8-20 months) I can use single words like "cup" or "daddy" that are important to me.
(16-26 months) I can use words that I have heard you say, such as "Oh dear" and "All gone".
Extract from a poster display at a community playgroup

Developmental Language Disorder (DLD) is a condition where a child has difficulties understanding and/or producing language and these difficulties impact on their everyday life. Approximately 5 to 8 per cent of children may have DLD.
Levickis et al, 2017

TOP TALKING TIPS
2 years old
It helps me if you;
- Repeat any unclear words back to me, this will show me the right way to say them.
- Turn off the tv when we are talking, playing or eating. I can't listen or concentrate with all that background noise!
- Point out any sounds you can hear outside. This will help develop me listening skills.
Extract from a display for parents at a day care

CLASS is an observation tool used to gauge teacher effectiveness with a focus on adult-child interactions. It measures the emotional, social, organizational, and instructional supports educators provide that contribute to social, developmental, and academic achievement. The tool is used to assess interactions and provide feedback to educators for professional development, performance evaluation, or research.
Early Learning Coalition of Escambia County, 2018

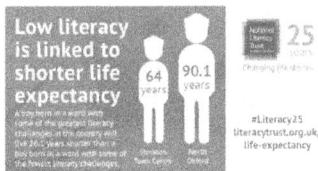

Figure 1.2 Children's Literacy Practices as Neat, Rational and Generalizable

> They miss how someone's ordinary can endure or can sag deflated … how it can become a vague but compelling sense that something is happening, or harden into little mythic kernels.
>
> Stewart, 2007, p.4

Stewart offers the notion of the ordinary as a way of interrogating how forces that make up systems are not already set, but rather they are alive, immanent and unpredictable. Thus, the ordinary is 'a shifting assemblage of practices and practical knowledges, a scene of both liveness and exhaustion' (p.1). By attending to ordinary affects, Stewart's work traces how flows of energy and intensity between people, things and places 'pick up densities and textures as they move through bodies, dreams, dramas and social worldings of all kinds' (p.3).

Tracing how the ordinary is constituted by these affectual circuits and flows helps to understand the singularity, or specificity, of a particular moment, place and time. Where might ordinary affects go *right now*? What thoughts and feelings does the ordinary they make possible or impossible *right here*? Models of thinking that work at the level of large structures, seeking to abstract, generalize and simplify, are unable to recognize or begin to describe ordinary affects, and so miss something important about how and why people act, feel, react and make sense of their lives.

> At once abstract and concrete, ordinary affects are more directly compelling than ideologies, as well as more fractious, multiplicitous, and unpredictable than symbolic meanings.
>
> Stewart, 2007, p.3

The shadow of reason haunts the judgements made against both parents and children in communities. If research shows a correlation between x, y and z parenting practices and certain kinds of advantageous school outcomes, why don't parents comply? Perhaps in order to make sense of this seeming mismatch, we firstly need a deeper acknowledgement that specific visions for how children should be socialized and recommendations for parenting practices are far from neutral or apolitical. Secondly, conceptualizations of being and being with young children require a consideration of the idiosyncronicities of lived experience, and particularly the way in which what unfolds in communities with young children transcends a rationale of logic and intent. Attending to ordinary affects offers the possibility of breaking away from the hegemony of the rational subject, the subject who says what they mean, means what they say, and would always act in their own best interests according to a reasoned logic. Parents who do not follow the prescribed instructions for how to interact with and stimulate their children 'correctly'. Children who seem to refuse to compliantly play their role in processes of socializing them into being certain kinds of 'literate subjects.'

Young children's language and literacy competencies sit near the heart of anxiety about young children's development, believed by many to evidence their ability to rationalize, problem solve, make abstract connections, empathize with others or hold their own views. Yet, young children's literacy and language practices unfold amidst the smells, sounds, scattered toys, sticky fingers, anxieties, hopes and frustrations of everyday life of families in communities. These bodily and affective aspects of everyday life are frequently under-played or erased by universalizing and abstracting accounts of literacies. Re-conceptualizing early childhood literacies as more-than-human offers the opportunity to explore and acknowledge the materiality of language (MacLure, 2013a) and literacy practices, as they emerge from and between leaky, porous, unbounded human and non-human bodies.[2]

The lives of young children and their parents in these communities are ordinary. Not in the sense of being obvious or self-explanatory, but in the sense of being unpredictable, contradictory, specific, illogical, in the sense of meaning everything and nothing all at the same time (Stewart, 2007). Two parents with children of the same age living in the same community have both everything and nothing in common. This ordinariness is the starting point if we are to begin to understand young children's literacy and language practices. Thus, this book begins with the singularity of place and community, aiming to attune to ordinariness and affective flows as a starting point for a different way of knowing. It does this by attending to, and remaining with, details and intensities of everyday decisions and experiences, even when they seem unhelpful, illusive, uncodifiable. In addition, it acknowledges the political and resistant nature of an insistence on this kind of describing (Rautio, 2013).

Universalizing Lines of Child Development

Gallacher (in press) describes how the metaphor of 'milestones' in child development offers fixed points of orientation, which 'enable development to be assessed according to their timekeeping within the universal developmental plan'. Line drawings commonly used to illustrate developmental milestones, such as those in the 'red book' given to all new parents in the UK (Figure 1.3), offer a visual example of the kind of reducing, discarding and omitting that is necessary for a rationalized and universal account of child development.[3] The kinds of children depicted in these images are individual, bounded, abstracted

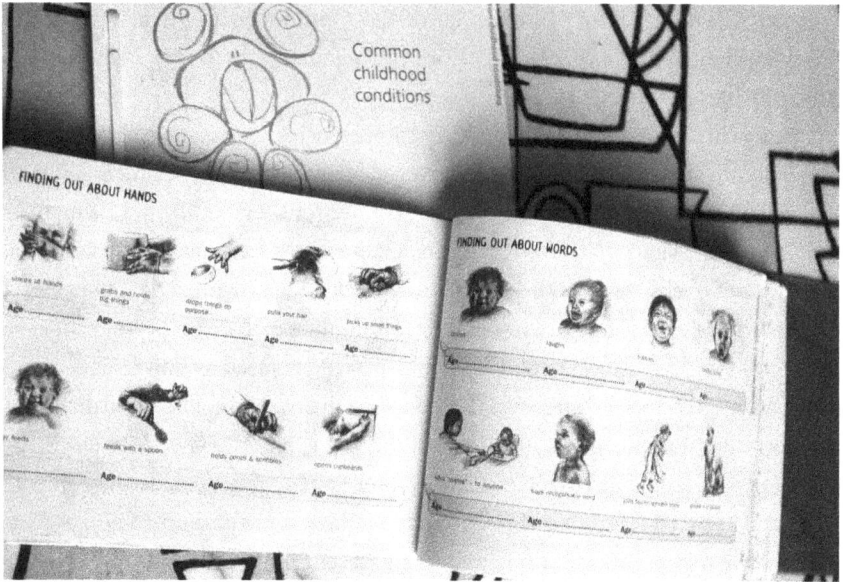

Figure 1.3 Developmental Milestones Visualized. Photo credit: Steve Pool

from their communities, separated from the more-than-human, free of emotion, performing various competencies such as stacking bricks or crawling, in their preoccupation with moving competently through their milestones.

In the everyday, ordinary experience of parents, carers and practitioners who spend time with young children, there is much that seems to divert from, exceed and disrupt these universalized lines of development. Yet the integrity of these lines must be maintained. In order to compare, to chart a generalized line of progress, it is essential to discard that which is not deemed relevant to the comparison.

> Complexity, the 'thick of things', is not only lost, it becomes fundamentally threatening as it undermines the imposing edifices constructed from comparative data.
>
> Jones et al., 2014, p.64

There is a politics, then, to what must be overlooked or played down in order to maintain the integrity of the universalized, all encompassing, line of child development, and the policies and interventions that can accompany such a line. As Trafi-Prats (2019) points out, early intervention policies, in their intention to making parenting practices objective and auditable, explicitly aim to separate practices from the material conditions of parenting. The ordinary experiences of those who spend time with children, particularly women, particularly women in powerless positions, must often therefore be disregarded, in order to maintain the truth and power of the line.

> A line becomes what you have a duty to follow. A line becomes a bond, a line as direction and directive; a line that leads you to where you must go, who you must become.
>
> *Ahmed, S. (21 May 2017), Snap! Retrieved from*
> *https://feministkilljoys.com/2017/05/21/snap/*

Parents and carers have a different way of knowing their children (Hackett, 2017). They can be collaborators in research, providing context or extra information about the child. However, beyond this, they *know* in a different way; they know within their aching muscles, in their guts, from the inside (as Ingold [2013] would put it). This kind of (material, bodily, intuitive) knowing is far away from mastery (what parent ever feels like they have mastered the art of parenting?) and difficult to articulate in words. It is inchoate and powerfully affective. Perhaps it is a way of knowing that early childhood researchers could also attend to better; after all, parents or not, most researchers have had everyday, ordinary experiences of young children in some way, including memories of their own childhood (James, 1993; Lively, 1994). This kind of childhood research would attune to knowing from the gut, from a tiny funny incident or a powerful fear that the worst might happen, from a frustration, a victory, an arm ache from pushing a pushchair up a hill, from the smear of a child's saliva on your sleeve. Is it possible to remain with this kind of knowing, and resist codifying the knowledge into something reducible, logical, easily explainable? Perhaps. Certainly, if we are to try, we first have to let go of our attachment to, our investment in, the truth of the universal line.

Community Places as a Way of Knowing

She takes to writing fieldnotes in a local café after group, rather than driving home first, and it seems to make the fieldnotes different. A voice, a description of a child, a well meant piece of guidance on child rearing, perhaps seems perfectly appropriate in the place it was written, then seems to be a different thing when it is transported into another place.

We urge readers and colleagues to reconsider place and its implications, not because it offers a generalizable theory or universal interpretation, but because generalizability and universality are impossibilities anyway, in no small part because place matters and place is always specific.

Tuck and McKenzie, 2015, p.21

Watts (2013) points out that Western social science research, even when attending to place, continues to consider knowledge and place as capable of being separated from each other. In Indigenous ontologies of place-thought as described by Watts (2013), Tuck and McKenzie (2015) and Todd (2016), amongst many others, knowing and place could never be separated; place should shape methodology, as well as being inseparable from what it is possible to think or to know. There is much then, for researchers interested in community and place-based ways of knowing early childhood, lives and literacies, to learn from Indigenous scholars of place-thought. The question of how to think with place, how to understand the materialized and spatialized nature of social inequity, and the relationship between humans and place, are always political questions; as Nxumalo and Cedillo (2017) write, 'it is important to continually interrupt the benignity of place stories' (p.101). One of the ways in which a commitment to the specificity of place and genealogy of ways of knowing is political lies in the question of what forms of knowledge become powerful. Somerville (2013) makes a distinction between two processes of coming to know through research; rational processes of logic and order and body/place knowing, a way of coming to know through the body, involving 'a necessary unravelling of the self, of certainty and prior knowledge' (p.27). This kind of knowing relies, writes Somerville, on a mutual entanglement between body and place and an investment in ways of knowing that emerge slowly and uncertainly, and can be difficult to pin down with words.

This rejection of the possibility of extracting knowledge from place (or of knowledge ever being abstract), acts as a powerful form of refusal (Tuck and Yang, 2014). Rather than offering a new, innovative way of articulating young children's emergent language and literacy practices, for example, it points to the impossibility of ever doing so. Instead of a theory that can be generalized, we are left with slow, particular describing (as advocated by Tuck [2010] below), coupled with an awareness of the politics of how this kind of description rubs up against other, more powerful claims to knowledge. Grappling with this 'unravelling of the self' (Somerville, 2013, p.27) as the body-in-place responds to ways of knowing that come before sense-making and neatly organized arguments, relies on listening to places and thinking with and through the logic of that particular place.

The ideas in this book were developed everywhere and nowhere. They owe a particular genealogy to three sites I worked with throughout the study; two playgroups and a day care in a small town in northern England (see Chapter 2 for more detail). My research in this particular community has happened over a long period of time. Experiences, relationships, fieldnotes and video data accumulate in overwhelming quantities; three years of ethnographic research funded for this research project, ten years since I first started doing ethnographic research in this community, nearly twenty years since I first arrived in this town, as community heritage officer for the local museum. Still I return again and again, despite having plenty of 'data'. I find it possible to think differently when I am there.

Description

> To describe *is* to value, Carini tells us Describing I pause, and pausing, attend. Describing requires that I stand back and consider … Describing makes room for something to be fully present. Describing is slow, particular work. I have to set aside familiar categories for classifying or generalizing. I have to stay with the subject of my attention. I have to give it time to speak, to show itself.
>
> Tuck, 2010, p.648

In the above quote, Carini offers close, slow description as a response to the 'manyness' of the education system, a kind of complexity that can make us feel overwhelmed, tempted 'to distance ourselves, to make some space, to detach or disengage' (Carini in Tuck, 2010, p.647). What is difficult to articulate runs the risk of slipping from view. This applies to everyday life in communities with families and young children just as much as it applies to experiences of schooling. As Stadlen (2005, p.12) writes in the quote that opens this chapter, parents 'live in a universe that has not been accurately described'.

Ingold (2013) draws a distinction between telling and articulating, arguing that using articulated, specific speech 'assembled in the mind of the speaker prior to its vocal expressions' (p.111) to describe bodily experience, is difficult or impossible. Telling, in contrast to articulation, is a mode of communication that offers pointers, or gestures towards meaning, without pinning it down. In valuing rather than trying to 'fix' what it is not possible to express in words, this kind of description (this kind of 'telling') is the opposite of the kind of generalization, or categorization, or articulation, that points to a full knowledge of or mastery of a subject. There is a particularity and slowness to this kind of describing. Similarly, for Stewart (2007), the 'intensities of the ordinary' can be approached through close attention and writing, through 'continuous, often maddening, effort' (p.5). To give attention to what gets overlooked is inconvenient, and difficult to put into words. It involves attending to complex, elusive and constantly reforming assemblages of inchoate elements (Nxumalo et al., 2011). Importantly, this kind of description values the irreconcilable (Tuck, 2010) in the sense that there will always be something significant that exceeds what can be expressed in the words, no matter the slowness, care, particularity with which the words are crafted. 'The struggle to explain how this came to be, to herself, to others, throbs' (Tuck, 2010, p.648).

The Politics of Early Childhood Literacies

Child development often presents itself as apolitical (Millei and Kallio, 2018; Nimmo, 2008). Yet, perhaps, the 'common-sense, interests-of-the-child' nature of much early years rhetoric is where the power of these deeply political acts of socializing children lie (Canella and Viruru, 2012; Nxumalo and Brown, 2020; Pacini-Ketchabaw et al., 2014). What is known, what is described, and what must be disregarded in order for a neutral, apolitical version of early childhood to endure? The intense and insurmountable affects around which the experience of caring for young children circulate; the tiredness, the mess, the judgements, the worry and the contradictions have to be cut away from the image of the developing child, in order to offer a universal and rational picture. This kind of cut is a political act, silencing community ways of knowing and the specificity of knowledge to place. 'The very absence of considering children as political agents is a political act in itself,' write Millei and Kallio (2018, p.43).

Language and literacy practices have a long history of being tied to notions of human exceptionalism and mastery (Finnegan, 2002; Sheets-Johnston, 1981; Tarc, 2015). Kuby et al. (2019) argue for a more expansive view of what 'counts' as literacies, grounding this argument in critiques of Western secular humanism as a project that has set up hierarchies of the human (Braidotti, 2013; McKittrick, 2015). Wynter's concept of epochs of 'Man' outlines a Western colonial project that positions white, adult, Western, cis, heterosexual, able-bodied humans as a benchmark, as a 'the measuring stick through which all other forms of being are measured' (McKittrick, 2015, p.3). The further an individual diverges from these categories, the less humanity they are accorded. To what extent does the valuing or encouraging of particular kinds of literacy and language practices in early childhood work to shape young children increasingly in the direction of 'Man' (white, adult, Western, cis, heterosexual, able-bodied etc)? In describing early childhood literacies, assumptions and hierarchies are always at play. In early childhood education, necessarily partial accounts must be given of young children's language and literacy practices; perhaps energies are focused on describing the vocabulary a child knows, their willingness to speak clearly and individually to an unfamiliar adult, or whether their story telling has a beginning, middle and end. In each case, what is valued, counted or described as 'progress' is always deeply political, according to the ways in which such practices reproduce, uphold or resist particular ways of being a child, a human, a literate subject, of being in the world (Truman, 2019a). In trying to express in words what unfolds in a place, processes of reducing and generalizing seem unavoidable to a certain extent. Instead of striving for completeness then, we might respond with a careful attuning to who or what is excluded or marginalized, to how some families are positioning as more or less human, than others. As Truman (2019a) writes:

> We have to be very careful when we advocate for new kinds of literacy, if at the core they still operate based on bringing 'outsiders' into a particular world-view rather than expanding what counts as 'legitimate' ways of knowing and being and representing the world … The proliferation of different kinds of 'literacies' that profess to attend to varied ways of reading-writing-knowing the world don't undo the basic truth that the prevailing idea of a universal 'literacy' is a colonizing project.
>
> Truman, 2019a, p.9

Leaky, illiterate, uncontrollable, young children can be regarded as particularly resistant to the hierarchy of language over other representational systems (MacLure, 2016). Whilst, certainly, all young children frequently diverge from the rational, predictable, 'mastery' model of 'Man', young children from marginalized communities in particular, making sense of literacy and language practices in a variety of ways (Burman, 2008; Heath, 1983), can be seen as falling far from the 'measuring stick' of 'Man' to greater or lesser extents. To give just one example, Gillies (2007) describes how middle-class claims to their children's brightness or exceptionality rely on constructions of unexceptionality or lack in working-class children. Deficit discourses ensure that the designation of 'bright' constantly eludes children of colour (Dyson, 2015) or working-class children

(Gillies, 2007), who, if they stand out, are more likely to be recognized as trouble makers or a threat than as special or gifted. This perception of lack in young children from communities that are not white, Western and middle class, is described variously in the literature as a language gap (Avineri et al., 2017), a word deficit (Kuchirko, 2019) and a threat to early brain development (Gillies et al., 2017). *What gets overlooked, who gets silenced and how must knowledge be re-arranged or erased in order to begin to account for young children's literacies?*

In asking what we might learn about early childhood literacies by starting with the everyday in communities, this book is in dialogue with a rich body of work in which scholars have written about everyday literacies that seem to escape narratives of progress (Tsing, 2015) and function. A child twirling in a homemade super hero costume (Thiel, 2015a), or prayer beads spread out as shapes on the bedroom floor (Pahl, 2002), or passionate discussions about EastEnders (Maybin, 2013) or a boy reading Manga in his bedroom whilst wearing an appropriate headband (Leander and Boldt, 2013).[4] For Rautio (2013), 'practices that bear no economic or otherwise measurable significance are political statements' (p.405). Attending to those aspects of the ordinary affects of young children's lives that seem particularly dense or textured (Stewart, 2007), even when (or especially when) they disrupt or refuse to contribute to logical and reasoned sequences of skill acquisition, is a political statement about what young children's literacies should or could encompass. A call for a re-conceptualization of young children's literacy and language practices as more-than-human is an insistence on the value of literacy and language practices that operate beyond human intentionality, beyond reason and rationality, that are specific to place and community, and unfold according to unpredictable and powerful affective forces. It is a call to reimagine literacies in a way that does not merely work to uphold dominant and oppressive hierarchies.

More-Than-Human Literacies

Re-conceptualizing young children's literacies as more-than-human requires attending to bodies (human and non-human) sounding and moving in place (Hackett and Somerville, 2017), even when this sounding and moving seems to evade easy capture, function or signification. Thus, this book will interrogate these processes of bodies moving and sounding in place, attending through close description to densities and textures of flows of affect (Stewart, 2007) that seem to shape and drive them. As a starting point, I offer three propositions for more-than-human early childhood literacies.

Literacy and Language Are Bodily Practices

The children eat snack enthusiastically. Cheese, apple, toast, crackers and spread
– all go apart from the large bowl of cucumber! M sits on the floor eating cheese.
His legs are spread wide. He vocalises a lot, and squishes the cheese in his fist and
puts it into his mouth. He makes eye contact with her, and when she responds
he vocalises some more, and stretches up his arm, showing her his fist of cheese.
Squished cheese is smeared on his hand and cuff. Cheesey dribble also drips out
of his mouth. A few moments later, M has tipped his (lidded) cup of milk upside
down; white drips splash all over the brown wood floor. They blend with the
cheesey dribbles. She asks the staff if there is a cloth. M tries to splash the milk
with his hand. He is also sitting on it. 'Oh look you've split your milk and now you
are playing in it!'

As others have pointed out, language (MacLure, 2013a; Martín Bylund, 2018a), mark making (de Rijke, 2019; Trafi-Prats, 2019b) and other forms of meaning making (Hackett and Somerville, 2017; Jokinen and Murris, 2020; MacRae, 2020; Thiel, 2015a) are bodily practices. Bodies jiggle and spin, arms and hands stretch and sweep, breath must be thrust through throats and vocal chords in order for vocalizations of any sort to emerge. Lips and tongues must move and flex to make words that can be understood by adults.

> Is not the acquisition of speech based on the ability to put the words in one's mouth? To push the lips this way and that, shaping breath into particular forms? To handle all sorts of materials and issues, desires and commands, by way of the oral?
>
> LaBelle, 2014, p.7

Thus the first proposition of this book is that early childhood literacy and language practices are thoroughly bodily activities, relying as they do on a physical body moving and responding in place, perhaps most obviously (though certainly not exclusively) through the manipulation of mouth, tongue, throat, arms and hands (see Figure 1.4).

That young children frequently make vocalizations whilst also thrusting food into their mouth is an ordinary observation, although it is rarely discussed in relation to language and literacies. Perhaps this is because in our common imaginary eating and talking involve things moving in opposite directions; in eating inanimate materials move downwards from mouth to stomach, whilst in talk, ideas (animate, 'high level', a 'purely human preserve') are imagined to fly between lips and brain. During this flight, neural pathways are imagined to be

Figure 1.4 Objects Go in Mouths. Photo credit: Steve Pool

built, development and learning are imagined to be happening, as young children move from animal-like illiteracy to knowing, perceiving humanity. Similarly, the vocalizations young children make which are not recognizable words are rarely taken very seriously (Gallagher et al., 2018), but equated instead with not being fully human.

Literacy and Language Involve the More-Than-Human

J loves playing in the sand and water. He walks through the little streams created by the water, and walks to the pump and places his hands under the water stream. He stands in the midst of all the water, little streams flowing around his ankles, and vocalizes 'wwaaaaateeeerrrrr. Water. Wawawawawa.' His joy and elation make the adults laugh with delight.

A gesture, a vocalization, a word, a nod, a full body run across the space; as Kress (1997) outlined several years ago, young children employ different modes, using their bodies, voices and gestures (amongst other things) to make meaning (see Figure 1.5). Whilst the importance of recognizing and valuing young children's different modes of communication is well established (Flewitt, 2005), a more-than-human theory of early childhood literacy extends this work

Figure 1.5 Walking through Little Streams of Waaaaateeeeerrrr

by rethinking the processes of emergence that underpin literacy practices, as well as who or what might drive and contribute to these processes.

Children's gestures, words, movements, sounds, interactions with objects (such as a pen or a toy or craft materials) all involve a mixture of sounding and moving in place (Hackett and Somerville, 2017). Understanding modes of communication as sound and movement is useful for rethinking early childhood literacy, because whilst essential to meaning making, sound and movement also transcend the human and the representational (Gallagher, 2016). At a molecular level, sound is vibrational movement, and these vibrations have 'the potential to affect and be affected by another aspect of everything' (Gershon, 2011). Thus, sound and movement are never purely human endeavours; they exist above and beyond human perception. To understand, for example, the talk of a young child, it is necessary to consider the vibrational movement of vocal chords in relation to other human, non-human and environmental sounds, as well as the way these different sounds and the place in which they occur affect each other.

Whilst some readings of early childhood literacies emphasize the agency and competency of the individual child in choosing modes of communication or designing multimodal signs, a more-than-human understanding of literacy and language practices understands the agency required for any kind of communication to occur as always distributed between human and non-human participants (Kuby et al., 2015; Nxumalo and Rubin, 2019; Olsson, 2009). To put it another way, sound and movement can be understood as world-forming practices. This is not to assign authorship of the world to human children, but to understand sound and movement as more-than-human practices through which the world forms itself, and young children's sounding and movement, including their literacy practices, happen in relation to this (Hackett and Somerville, 2017).

Literacies as Collective Not Individual

The children run up the hill, slowly and with difficulty as their leg muscles encounter the steep angle of the hill. T ascends the hill. Once at the top, T pauses, a moment of stillness, before dropping to the ground and beginning to roll down. T goes faster and faster as she rolls, losing control of her body and of the process. The children roll together, some are half way down the hill, some at the top, some lie at the bottom, as if unconscious for a couple of moments, before getting up and repeating. Their coats are getting wetter as they roll over and over again.

To speak, to gesture, to establish a certain way of moving in a space (like rolling down a hill), or a certain system for interacting with and arranging objects, is a collective act with human and non-human others (Hackett and Rautio, 2019). Bodily interactions in place, in which children become caught up in flows of affect, in more-than-human soundings and movements, happen all the time. Some of these soundings and movements might lead to shared meaning or significations glimmering in and out of view; provisional, possible literacies (an argument I will expand in Part 2 of this book). In the vignette above, movement began spontaneously between children's bodies, a hill, gravity. Yet over time, shared meanings and ways of knowing and doing 'the hill' emerged from this collective more-then-human movement.

The notion of language and literacies as collective, not pre-designed, pre-intentional, or a solely human act, stands in contrast to most dominant thinking about young children's language, in which individual children are assumed to be autonomous, bounded, drawing in experiences and words through sight and sound to be stored in brains and utilized in the future. Whilst language in early childhood is usually assumed to be an expression of an *individual's* viewpoint or desires, as well as a direct index of what that individual knows or has learnt (e.g. Avineri et al., 2015), a notion of language as more-than-human collective emergence might pay attention to the inchoate, impersonal murmur of the 'collective assemblage of enunciation' (Deleuze and Guattari, 2013, p.93) that precedes language. In this sense, words, ideas and language are already 'out there', and in the singularity of a given moment, they might move through bodies, or be taken up within the sounds, movements and actions of individuals and groups.

Conclusion

Starting with everyday observations of children and families being in and moving in places, young children's language and literacy practices can be understood as occurring as a result of people, places, objects and things being caught up together in particular ways, through affective flows and circuits. Bodies (human and non-human) move, respond, act, vibrate. Little of this is intentional, or designed ahead of the moment (Kuby et al., 2015), it rarely coheres with a logic of reason, and what takes place does not follow a linear or universal path of progression. During this research, as adults and children in the playgroups, we were all caught up in these processes, as 'something throws itself together in the moment' (Stewart, 2007, p.1).

In the midst of all of this, the vision of the ideal, abstract, generalizable child, parent, community never matches the reality. That those without power are the ones blamed for this illustrates the incommensurability of sticking with the 'ideal' in the hope children and families will benefit from approximating it as closely as they are able. Women, people of colour, those with few material resources, those suffering the effects of physical or mental ill health; the further outside the category of 'Man' (Wynter) they fall, the more responsible it seems they are for socializing young children within the logic of Man.

Stephanie Jones writes about the damage the dehumanization of education has caused.

> While we see the carnage produced in current conditions of schooling every single day all day long, we continue on and go to work. Perhaps with a grimace, or even complaints and protests, but no one is stopping to weep together with a soft and clean piece of fabric to tend to the wounded and disfigured.
>
> Jones, 2019, p.109

Scholars interested in posthumanism and literacy studies point to the way in which theories such as New Literacy Studies or multimodality get us 'so far' yet in others ways can feel inadequate, as though something important is missed (Kuby et al., 2019; Leander and Boldt, 2013; Lenters, 2016). However, beyond this, viewing literacies as more-than-human, driven by ordinary affects (Stewart, 2007) and approachable through body/place knowing (Somerville, 2013) might offer 'ways to disrupt and break free from the narrow-ness of rutted paths' (Kuby et al., 2018, p.14). These rutted paths force us into seemingly non-negotiable accounts of early childhood as generalizable, measurable, *describable*; accounts that do not serve children, families or communities well. To be clear on the distinction here, I am not proposing new theories of early childhood literacies in order to get us further down the same path (towards a more complete or comprehensive account of early childhood literacy). Instead I am hoping for a chance to sit down in the mud and refuse to go one more step, to then get up and stray off the path, and perhaps to stumble upon the 'whole stretches … ….that no one has explored' (Stadlen, 2005, p.12).

I see the carnage described by Jones (2019) playing out every day. This is not just about material access to healthy food, heating, safe housing, ways to keep children entertained during the summer holidays, although in the current period of austerity in the UK, amidst global movements towards reduced free movement and the rise of the far right, these issues are urgent and of the utmost importance in the communities I worked in. It is also about entitlement, positioning, knowledge, power. It concerns how it feels to be in a space, to account for a child, to answer the questions, to feel the tension, shame, stress, apathy. There is plenty for early childhood academics to be angry about. Accounts of early childhood that dwell in the cuteness/competency/progress/learning of the child are no longer enough. They were never enough. This book starts from this position; early childhood literacies are a deeply political project playing out through the ordinariness of the more-than-human in communities.

Acting Like an Ethnographer, Thinking with Posthumanism: Notes on Methodology and Method

As I described in Chapter 1, this book draws on long-term thinking, being and doing in a particular place. This approach to knowledge production relies on a rich lineage of feminist scholarship that values ways of knowing which are situated, political, derived from being in the world, and informed by the rhythms of everyday life (Haraway, 2016; Harding, 1987; Hodgins, 2019; Osgood and Robinson, 2019; Somerville, 2007). In this chapter, I share a little more about the processes of doing the research that informed the arguments in the book. I am grateful to The British Academy for funding a three-year postdoctoral fellowship that enabled the fieldwork and writing of this book to take place. Three years of funding for ethnographic work felt significant, because, after a series of short-term and precarious contracts, it meant I was able to commit to one space, to one set of communities, for a relatively long period of time.[1] At the same time, doing ethnographic research whilst drawing on post-qualitative and feminist new materialist scholarship presented a number of interesting shifts and dilemmas that I will discuss in this chapter.

The Fieldwork

The study was an ethnography located in two close-by urban communities in northern England, Northwood and Hill View/Bay Tree. Across a pilot phase and two main phases of fieldwork, I spent time in a day care centre and two community playgroups, and working collaboratively with children, families and staff, arranged a series of trips, experiences and visits for the children. Adding variety and difference to the places the fieldwork encompassed, whilst working with and building trust with small groups of families, was central to this work, as I attended to the role of bodies, places, animals, children, familiar and unfamiliar adults, material objects and affects in very young children's literacy practices. The study combined conventional qualitative data, such as video recordings, still photographs, fieldnotes and informal interviews, with a post-qualitative focus on affect, sensation and relations among human and non-human participants. Children's and place names are pseudonyms throughout the book.

Table 2.1 summarizes the dates and locations of fieldwork during each phase of the study. The pilot phase of fieldwork involved three months of fortnightly visits to Bay Tree day care. The first main phase of fieldwork involved visits once or twice each month over a seven-month period to two different community playgroups, Northwood and Hill View. The second phase of fieldwork involved eleven months of visits, firstly returning to Bay Tree day care, and then working intensively with Northwood playgroup. I worked alone for most of the fieldwork; however, I collaborated with visual artist Steve Pool as 'artist in residence' during phase 2 of the fieldwork in Northwood. He attended eight of the sessions there with me, bringing open-ended materials and other provocations to add to the activities regularly set out by the staff running the group.

Sharing findings of the research with participants in different forms was an important strand of the work throughout. I produced single-page visual reports for parents and staff in each community at the end of each phase of fieldwork, and delivered a sharing event for early years practitioners in the local museum towards the end of the project. I also collaborated with Steve Pool to create an exhibition in the local museum in the third year of the research, as a way of sharing the ideas coming out of the research in a different way with children and families (Figure 2.1).

Table 2.1 Summary of the Fieldwork

Pilot phase: March – July 2017	First phase Jan–July 2018	Second phase Sept 2018–July 2019
7 visits in total to Bay Tree day care	11 visits in total to Hill View playgroup 11 visits in total to Northwood playgroup	Sept–Dec 2018: 6 visits in total to Bay Tree day care March–July 2019: 12 visits in total to Northwood playgroup
7 sets of fieldnotes, 7 still photos, 10 videos	22 sets of fieldnotes, 116 still photos, 57 videos	17 sets of fieldnotes, 66 still photos, 34 videos[2]

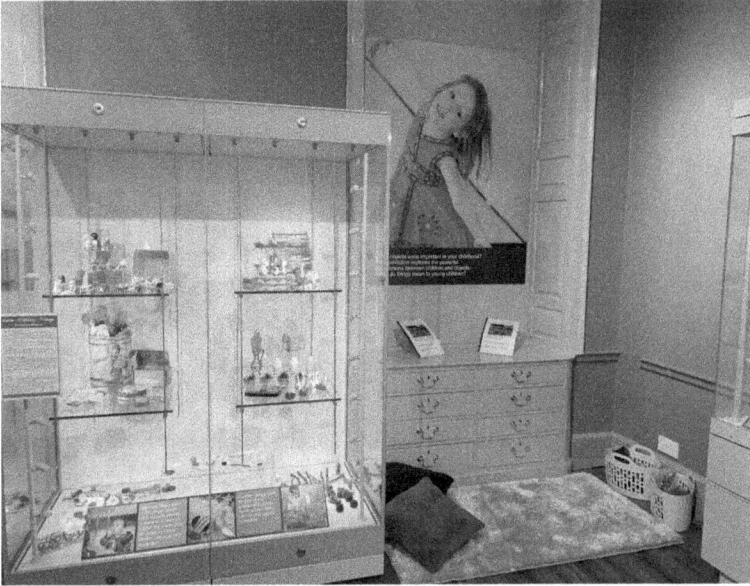

Figure 2.1 Community Exhibition

Northwood playgroup is in a very diverse community, at a walking distance to the town centre. Families attending the playgroup included African, Afro-Caribbean, South Asian and white British heritage; some of these families were several generations living in this community, whilst others had arrived more recently. There is also a well-established Roma community in this area, although these families did not tend to engage with the playgroup in a regular-enough fashion to end up as participants in the research.

Hill View playgroup and Bay Tree day care were run by the same organization, and were just five minutes drive out of town compared to Northwood. However, the difference between the communities was striking, in that Hill View/Bay Tree was almost entirely white. A former coal mining area, this community continues to live with the impact of closure of the mines and challenges for employment opportunities locally.

Communities

One of the reviewers of the proposal for this book pointed out that I referred to 'community' frequently without defining it. Community is a slippery term

(Wargo and Oliveira, 2020) often defined by what it is not, for example, the commitment to community in Facer and Enright's (2016) notion of creating living community knowledge is a statement of things happening 'not in/for the academy' (Facer and Enright, 2016). Similarly, in the most simple sense, what I mean by community spaces of early childhood in my book is 'not nursery/early years classrooms', which is where the vast majority of early childhood research tends to take place. For me, 'community spaces of early childhood' are ones where adults as well as children from the community enter freely, stay and shape what unfolds there (e.g. playgroups and parks).

The definitions of community are multiple and contested (Facer and Enright, 2016). However, many definitions are notably anthropocentric, defining a community as groups of humans who share common interests, identities or affinities. What does it mean then, when I talk about doing research in a more-than-human community, and particularly my responsibilities to that community? I think the notion of place/body knowing (Somerville, 2013) is important here. Having worked in this same community for a decade, I feel a love or kinship with it, and a responsibility to it, that is not attached to particular individuals. In that time, families have moved on, organizations have been restructured, key staff members have left to work elsewhere. Therefore, I would argue that the notion of community research can transcend individual humans, and instead refer to something more shifting that is created by the relations between place, geography, architecture, individuals, stories, histories, together with how these things are positioned in and relate to the rest of the world.

The Children and Ethics

When I began work at each fieldsite (having negotiated permission from the organizers of the group), I attended regularly and joined in whatever was going on. I also struck up conversations with parents and carers, played with the children and tried to get to know people. Only once people knew who I was and we had spent some time together, would I broach the idea of them participating in the research. In this sense, something that shaped who participated in the research was which families attended the group regularly enough for me to get to know them. The children attending the playgroup were aged from babes in arms to thirty-six months, and the day care catered for children between their second and third birthdays. The children participating in my research were all aged between ten and thirty-six months at the start of their participation.

The children who came to be participants in the study attended one of the three fieldsites involved in the study (see Table 2.2). At Northwood playgroup, eleven children became formal participants in this study, and feature in the vignettes in the book. I visited Northwood playgroup in years 1 and 2 of the study, and some of the children attended playgroup all the way through this time. Others left after year 1, mostly because they were taking up the offer a funded nursery place. When this happened, it was unusual for the children to attend nursery and playgroup, if it fell on the same day, as it made the day too busy and tiring for most children. Seven children at Hill View playgroup came to be participants in the research during phase 1, and four from Bay Tree day care during phase 2. When I visited Bay Tree day care during the pilot phase of the research, fourteen children became participants; observations from the pilot informed the conceptual frame and methodological approach of the main study, but the pilot-phase children are not included in the vignettes throughout the book.

When I talk about children 'coming to be participants' in the study, it seems an appropriate choice of words, because of the emergent nature of who was and was not part of the study. This is because of the way I slowly got to know families before broaching the invitation to be included in the research, and also because of tensions I note with the notion of consent as a fixed and stable category, as I will outline below.

The study followed my institution's guidelines for informed consent, utilizing a leaflet, information sheet and consent form for parents to sign. Whilst the children were too young to give informed consent in a meaningful way, I did seek to ascertain their assent (to participate in the group, to be observed, to interact with me, to be photographed or recorded) through verbal and non-verbal modes, which might include their silence, turning away, gaze, facial expression, moving away or so many other things. I tended to ask their permission verbally if I wanted to take a photograph or video of them or something they had made/were playing with, knowing, however, that the reply to this might be verbal or non-verbal. In adopting this approach, I followed the existing scholarship on young children's participation in research (Cocks, 2006; Dockett et al., 2009; Flewitt, 2006; Smith and Coady, 2020) located in a qualitative methodological field, and particularly concerned with the children's agency and participation in research. There are, therefore, tensions between this approach and my own position, which I do not know how resolve. I have argued in this book, for example, that children's multimodal literacies often contain multiple, contingent or unclear meanings (Chapter 6), yet this undermines my position above that, to be ethical, I sought children's moment-by-moment assent through multiple modes. Equally, when I write about parents giving consent to participate in the study, I summon up the image of a rational, objective individual who holds opinions that they stand by. How to square this with Tuck's writing on desire, malfunction and instability, on which I rely heavily in Chapter 5? Tuck and Ree (2013, p.648) write of 'promising myself one thing at night, and doing another in the morning'; what does it mean to think of this contradictoriness alongside the neat file of signed consent forms that underpin 'informed consent' in this research?

Turning to scholarship about ethics in post-qualitative research does not make any of these dilemmas much clearer, as ethics becomes something much bigger and more complicated. In collapsing binaries between knowing, being and doing (or between ontology and epistemology) posthuman theory tends to open up conversations about ethics to a broader range of considerations, effectively 're-orientating how researchers conceptualize the matter of ethics and the extent to which conceptualizations take root' (Schulte, 2020, p.2). Zylinska (2014), for example, writing about the need to rethink ethics in the Anthropocene, points out that we need to consider scale differently; that acting ethically in one space might cause damage in another. Our ability to act in or even to understand the world is severely limited and that ethics mostly involves intuitive and necessary responses to the world.

> If we then continue to philosophize, proselytize or moralize about the world, we will have registered that we are doing it from a uniquely situated (even if inherently unstable) standpoint, on a certain selected, historically legitimized scale.
>
> Zylinska, 2014, p.28

The meaning of being involved in the research seemed to unfold slowly between myself, children and families in particular places and at particular times. I frequently struggled to 'give an account of myself' to parents, that is, to adequately explain who I was, what the research involved and what I was seeking to investigate. Particularly when planning the museum exhibition, which Steve and I sought parents' views on, the conversation constantly seemed to be confused, unclear, as if parents and I were passing each other along parallel tracks. Over time, I came to understand that this was not a symptom of my incompetency as a researcher or community outreach worker,[3] but rather these mismatches had something to teach me about the way in which ideas can be more or less concrete or abstract; the way they can make sense at my desk and dissolve into something much less clear once I am in the community (Chapter 1). Hence, communicating about my research and seeking participants' consent/ assent became an ongoing and experimental process. Material artefacts, such as the interim research reports I provided, mock ups of the museum panels, and Polaroid photos Steve took of the children in playgroup and handed to them immediately (Figure 2.2) all played useful roles in an agreement between myself and my participants which was never quite fixed down.

Key directions for thinking about ethical research methodologies then, as I do ethnographic research with post-qualitative theories, include knowing that ethics involves embodiment and emotions, it is not just discursive (Davies, 2016; Zylinska, 2014), that consent and participation are always emergent, provisional, and quite possibly contradictory (Tuck, 2010), and that there are no positions of unquestionable virtue for a researcher. I cannot keep myself pure of the messy, implicated, power infused and world-making-story-telling nature of research by following a certain number of key principles or processes.

Figure 2.2 Polaroid Photos in the Assent Process. Photo credit: Steve Pool

Table 2.2 Summary of the Children Participating in the Study

Children	Involvement in the study
Northwood playgroup	
H⁴, Z, P	Phases 1 and 2
G, J, E	Phase 1
L, A, F, K, V	Phase 2
Hill View playgroup	
M, O, D, N, W, S, C	Phase 1
Bay Tree day care	
T, Y, R, B	All start of phase 2

Doing the Fieldwork: Acting Like an Ethnographer, Thinking with Posthumanism

Daniel Miller (1997) has suggested, ethnography is a 'particular perspective' constituted by the following 'commitments':

1.   'to be in the presence of the people one is studying, not just the texts or objects they produce' (p.16);
2.   'to evaluate people in terms of what they actually do, i.e. as material agents working with a material world, and not merely of what they say they do' (pp.16–17);
3.   'a long term commitment to an investigation that allows people to return to a daily life that one hopes goes beyond what is performed for the ethnographer' (p.17);
4.   'to holistic analysis, which insists that … behaviours be considered within the larger framework of people's lives and cosmologies' (p.17).

Macdonald, 2001, p.72

Radical alternative methodologies as the only way to respond to the postcolonial questions and research conditions in which I find myself.

Somerville, 2008, p.209

From its origins in anthropology and sociology, ethnography has become one of the biggest influences on qualitative research, taken up and adapted by numerous disciplines (Jeffrey and Troman, 2004; Macdonald, 2001). The post-qualitative methodological turn offers a serious challenge to the question of knowledge production through systems of data extraction, collection and analysis. Entwined as the development of ethnography is in colonialism, subjugation and domination (Gullion, 2018), and with ongoing unresolved debates around voice, reflexivity and othering, the question remains: *What is to become of ethnography in the post-qualitative turn?* Rautio (2020) describes the post-qualitative turn as a 'phase that takes its form both from and against what preceded it' and I find this a helpful way to think about the methodology within this project, which bridged ethnographic fieldwork with post-qualitative and posthuman approaches.

Trained as an ethnographer, I continue to do fieldwork that *looks* a lot like ethnography, according to Miller's description above (unstructured long periods of time spent as a participant observer in communities, coupled with production of fieldnotes and visual materials). At the same time, I am working intensively with post-qualitative and feminist new materialist perspectives on research (Osgood and Robinson, 2019). My project, it seems, works with what Springgay and Truman (2017) call 'the tensions between new empirical methodologies and existing phenomenological methods'. In this way, my approach might have something in common with Springgay and Truman's (2017) call not to invent new methods ('We have plenty of methods already'), but rather to 'approach methods propositionally, speculatively, and experimentally and maintain that it is the *logic of procedure and extraction* that needs undoing' (p.211). For Youngblood Jackson (2016), this might mean conducting '"traditional" qualitative fieldwork in a different ontological arrangement' (p.191).

What this different kind of ontological arrangement might mean for ethnography (or does it just completely dissolve it?) is a question that is still in the early stages of being explored by researchers. Thinking about ethnography beyond human-centricity has resulted in calls to attend better to non-human animals (Hamilton and Taylor, 2017) and other entities (Gullion, 2018) in ethnographic observation. Advancing a notion of diffractive ethnography (informed by the post-qualitative turn), Gullion (2018) proposes that rather than describing people and things, we need to ask questions about how assemblages work, 'mapping entanglements and investigating interference patterns' (p.122). Addressing the human-centric and logocentric nature of much previous early childhood research (Hultman and Lenz Taguchi, 2010) was certainly a driver for my own study, particularly as I noted the almost exclusive focus on the role of adult humans in young children's literacy practices in dominant policy rhetoric in the UK. Beyond attending to the more-than-human goings on within practices of observation and creation of data records, I believe there are several other important shifts my ethnographic work is making as I continue to grapple with the disruptive and generative thinking of the post-qualitative turn.

1. Being There

My research practices during this study still foregrounded the importance of 'being there' with communities. I believe several things are intertwined with 'being there' for the long term in community research, such as fitting in, building relationships and looking for ways to help out, making friends and building trust, and an ethical commitment to the well-being of people and places, including actively looking for ways to give something back. At the same time, I am mindful of Schneider's (2002) caution against the tendency for ethnographers to adopt 'being there' as an inscription device, that is, a way in which authority of scientific knowledge is built. I notice myself at points in this book walking this fine line when, for example, I appeal for a re-conceptualization of what children do with objects or with their voices by pointing out that the dominant accounts bear little resemblance to what is happening in the community. What am I trying to convey when I write that? 'You weren't there in that playgroup and I was, so my point must be more valuable'? One thing I believe is that often when I describe the ways infants and toddlers are in community spaces, it will resonate with, rather than surprise, many readers. Readers who work with, research with, or live in communities with young children, may well have noticed something similar. This is a knowledge that is present in practice and in communities, yet perhaps not always acknowledged or foregrounded (Hackett, 2017). I hope that by describing the mess, contradiction and complexity of everyday life with young children in this book, I open up an invitation for others to join the conversation, rather than inscribing my own account as an authority.

2. Time and Hanging Out

Time often seems central to any claims to knowledge ethnographers might make. In a traditional ethnographic approach, time spent at a fieldsite would equate with a claim to mastery, to saturation, to knowing the other better than they can know themselves. I see long-term commitment to communities and sites as an ethical position; the relationships I developed with staff, families and children at the research sites were essential, unique and relied on trust built over time. How, though, can I think about time and ethnographic research beyond chronos time, beyond the linear and predictable passing of a sequence of bounded progressive moments, and the tendency of these to be equated with progress (Chapter 9)? Writing about quantum time, Gullion (2018) writes, 'An interesting ontological question to consider is how we deal with the problem of a future state causing a past event' (p.66). As a partial response to the question of how to think about long-term commitments to a fieldsite beyond notions of progress and mastery, I turn to the notion of deep hanging out.

Somerville and Powell (2018) develop Geertz's notion of deep hanging out by bringing into dialogue with Haraway's discussion (drawing on Despret) of a curious practice to emphasize an approach of humility and fascination with both human and non-human others. Powell and Somerville (2018) describe a methodology of deep hanging out with young children, which involves 'sitting in the sandpit and in the dirt with children' (p.12), being implicated and absorbed in the moment and waiting with humility and curiosity to respond according to 'whatever the moment asks' (p.12). These research methodologies, in common with ethnography, have a commitment to 'being there', in places and with people and to time spent in the field. However, unlike ethnography, curious practice/ deep hanging out does not aim to collect increasingly detailed data in order to know more confidently, but to continually open up to possibilities for new thinking that might emerge through body being in place. This opening up is grounded in an ontology that accepts that knowledge cannot be extracted from place. I have come to realize that my continuous commitment to return to the same community is not about the accumulation of more data, the goal is not 'saturation' or mastery. Rather through deep hanging out over a long period of time, specific place/body memories accumulate (Somerville, 2013), enabling different ways of knowing to emerge, to become more tangible. Hence, Somerville's writing on place/body knowing has been an important influence for rethinking the implications of my ethnographer's body spending time being at and participating with fieldsites.

> The emergence of new knowledge is held in an image that has a direct relationship to my embodied experience of the place of the research.
>
> Somerville, 2008, p.212

3. Place

> Whilst there is a tendency to equate place with the here and now, it is always more than this.
>
> Tsing, 2015, p.50

Foregrounding place and lived experience carries the risk of becoming too literal, of describing only what children and families do and say in a place, and overlooking that which goes unsaid, that which importantly influences and shapes the action and gathers its power, perhaps from its taken-for-granted-ness or its slippery incohate nature (Hackett et al., 2015; Horton and Kraftl, 2018; Mitchell and Elwood, 2012; Robinson and Osgood, 2019). As Alaimo warns us, an over-focus on the immediacy of place risks squeezing out the space for "trans-corporeal mappings of networks of risk, harm, culpability and responsibility within which ordinary Western citizens and consumers find themselves" (Alaimo, 2016, p.3).

Whilst place is always political then, often people in those places (the participants of my research, for example) do not talk about the geographies, histories, discourses and past events that shape the politics of place. When doing fieldwork in communities, there is a need to ask whose knowledge, expertise, lived experience counts and why? The stories we, as researchers, tell and the voices we foreground are always political decisions, in which we are always implicated. A slow and careful tuning in to aspects of human and environmental history might reveal what is in danger of being overlooked or erased by a dominant narrative of, for example, childhood. What is most likely to be overlooked is often that which is unvoiced or inchoate – deeply consequential but not present in the data in a literal way.

Writing about the risk of posthuman research erasing relationships of power (Peterson, 2018), or reproducing the same findings with a different language (Gullion, 2018), Robinson and Osgood (2019) point out that new materialism needs to attend to and work hard at keeping its 'political edge' (p.53). One way to problematize taken-for-granted 'truths' and the affective and material actualizations of these in everyday life might be to 'immerse ourselves more fully in the intensities, flows, rhythms, affects and forces of children's entanglements with space, place and materiality' (Osgood and Robinson, 2019, p.8). It might involve an insistence on attending to that which is not functional, that cannot be easily and obviously appropriated for human convenience, and which cannot be mapped to intended outcomes (Rautio, 2013). Therefore, one way I have tried to respond to the challenge of 'edge' is to try to begin with the specificity of place, the particularity of children moving and living and making sense of their lives *at this time, in this place*. In doing so, increasingly, I notice glimmers and flashes of how past political decisions, inscriptions of power relations, community losses and trauma, environmental change, geology and geography, shape how children and place make each other, even in these seemingly neutral spaces in which daily life seems, at first glance, to be so exclusively concerned with the minutia of here and now.

4. Data (and Analysis)

During time spent in the field, experiences, relationships, fieldnotes and video data can accumulate in overwhelming quantities (Table 2.1). As several scholars have outlined, a post-qualitative approach to research involves a radical rethinking of data and its relationship with knowledge (Andersen and Otterstad, 2014; MacLure, 2013a; Rautio and Vladimirova, 2017). Writing about her long-term research with communities and places, Somerville (2007, 2013) describes the accumulation of ideas, experiences, memories, and the relationship between this and the physical data set she begins to accumulate.

> These images that I am working with are incredibly resilient; I can call them up whenever I choose, to focus on each experience. They have a relationship to the material I have collected in the box but they are not the box, nor are they in the box. The material in the box represents the structures, things like a research question, proposal, methods for data collection and analysis. The images represent the qualities of emergence. At the moment, these images want to develop into forms. These forms are poetic, sun-bleached, skeletal, bones stripped of extraneous matter, ideas coming into form.
>
> Somerville, 2007, p.231

Important here is the sense of something that always exceeds what can be recorded in the data set, and beyond that, perhaps the sense of something that cannot ever be fully captured in words. 'If I think they have to be anything, produce anything,' writes Somerville, 'they freeze, they die and lose their alive mobility. The only thing I can do with them is play, and even playing sometimes seems too serious' (Somerville, 2007, p.231).

Others writing from a post-qualitative perspective describe data that glows (MacLure, 2013c), that is sticky (MacRae et al., 2018) and that is companionable (Rautio and Vladimirova, 2017). Despite this, practical accounts of how post-qualitative researchers work across large sets of data using these concepts of glowing, sticking or companionship, for example, are rare (although see Caton, 2019 for one example). I did not code the date from this study, and I did not invent themes. Instead I trawled repeatedly through it, and made as much of it physical as I could (printed fieldnotes, printed still photos, printed selected frames from the video footage). I laid these things out of the carpet, I knelt on all fours and leaned over peering at them, I moved them, not so much creating groups (themes) but placing things in relation to each other. Sometimes I did this on a background of flip chart paper so I could draw arrows or write words inbetween them. Of course I noticed some instances of similarity between the data that could have become 'themes' (e.g. here is all the data when children vocalize), but instead I tried to stay with the notion of difference as well; 'here are different variations of something, here they might be arranged as an increasing continuum or a dispersed like sunbeams, or tell two sides of the same idea'. I find parallels here with MacLure's (2013d) description of coding as an embodied and immersive act which, if we resist the potential of coding being used merely to subsume difference and make datasets convenient and manageable, could instead operate as a 'long slow familiarisation with the details' during which 'some things gradually grow, or glow, in greater significance than others'.

I offer this account, not so much for transparency, but because I think these practical processes for working with data are something more post-qualitative researchers could be sharing and discussing. Central to this particular approach to data 'analysis' is that, like Somerville (2007), each piece of material data has a relationship with bodily and visual memories from my experiences of deep hanging out in these places. This particular approach would not be possible (I cannot imagine anyway), if the research design had involved one person collecting the data and someone else analysing it (Mauthner and Doucet, 2008).[5]

Fieldnotes and Visual Data

Accumulating, carefully recording and working with my ever-growing dataset seemed, on the one hand, essential to my research practice, and on the other, I was conscious of the way in which both written words (MacLure, 2013a) and video (de Freitas, 2016) can function to re-inscribe authority. Far from being inert representations of something that took place in the past, fieldnotes, images or video take on an energy of their own, recasting memories, experiences and what seemed to be significant in-the-moment anew each time I return to them. There have been some interesting experimentations in recent years with visual data that moves beyond representation, instead playing with imagery and effects in ways that seek to disrupt and unfix knowledge rather than reaffirm the truth (Caton, 2019; Elwick, 2015; Holmes and Jones, 2013; MacRae, 2020). Something I appreciated greatly in the still images Steve Pool took when he worked with me in Northwood playgroup during phase 2 of the fieldwork was the tendency of his photos to capture a feeling or a moment, rather than present a record of what happened in a space.

It would be exciting to see more researchers share similar experimentations with fieldnotes, a mode of recording my time in the field that I continue to use and continue to struggle with. I *hate* writing fieldnotes! When I come to write fieldnotes, I immediately sense my inadequacy and inability to capture what just happened with the families and children. I start by writing down locations and activity in temporal order – 'where did I go first and what did I see next?' Then I try to flesh out the detail. I wondered if one of the problems with my approach to fieldnotes is that linear time then becomes an organizer of the writing; memories and experiences do not naturally organize themselves into

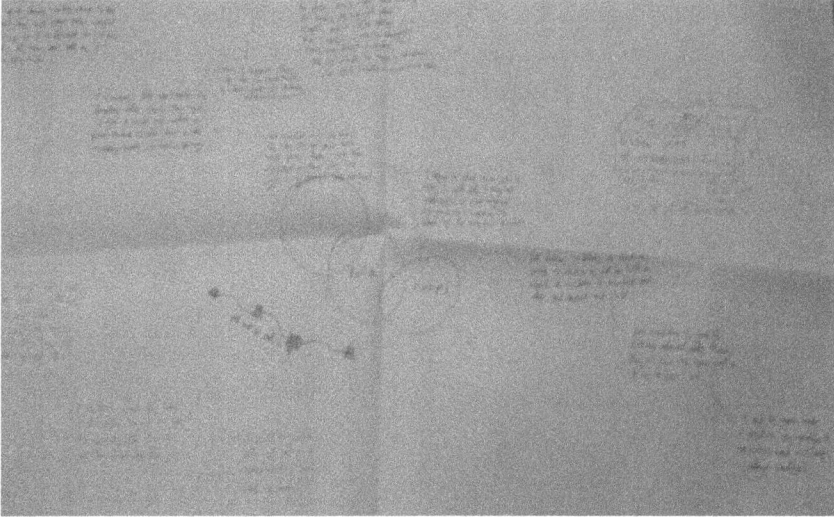

Figure 2.3 Spatial Fieldnotes (an Experiment)

linear time. I experimented with creating 'spatial' fieldnotes at the start of this project (Figure 2.3), trying to record what happened in terms of its location in space rather than time. This seemed only partially successful, and I did not keep the practice up throughout the study, but resorted back to typed fieldnotes half way through. I continue to wonder about the recording of events in writing, and what fieldnotes might become in the post-qualitative turn.

Further Questions

A pause is constituted when a particular assemblage of forms and meanings comes together as a moment of representation, a temporary stability within the dynamic flux of meaning-making in (re)search for new knowledge.

Somerville, 2008, p.209

Acting like an ethnographer whilst thinking with posthuman and post-qualitative theories has raised many questions for me about fieldwork, data and claims to knowledge. I still see great value in spending extended periods of time in community spaces, in 'deep hanging out' (Somerville and Powell, 2018) and in attending to 'intensities, flows, rhythms' (Osgood and Robinson, 2019, p.8). At the same time, the legacy of ethnographic and other Western social science research requires a constant grappling with questions of mastery, understanding, consent, data and researcher position within the work. I hope that sharing the details of how I did this study will be useful for some, and would appeal to other researchers, particularly those interested in pushing the boundaries of (post-) qualitative research to continue experimenting and to continue sharing, particularly sharing detailed, practical accounts about, for example, the doing of fieldwork, data collection and analysis.

The Politics of Describing the World

The pedagogy of order-words is not, of course, confined to school situations. Consider the following snippet of talk from a mother to her two-year-old in a restaurant queue, presented in Luke (1995):

> 'We're in a long line, Jason. Aren't we? There are lots of people lined up here, waiting for a drink. Look [pointing] they're carrying a Christmas tree with lots of things on it. They're moving it. Do we have a Christmas tree like that?' (p.21)
>
> MacLure, 2016, p.176

"It helps me if you:

- Repeat any unclear words back to me, this shows me the right way to say them.
- Add another word to mine, this will show me how to say a slightly longer phrase e.g. 'car' – 'daddy's car' and 'all gone' – 'apple all gone.'"

Text from a display board for parents about two-year-olds' talk.

Above, MacLure (2016) describes a kind of talk particularly prevalent in affluent Western societies, in which children are socialized to take up language in specific ways for particular purposes. The snippet example of white, Western, middle-class talk that MacLure (2016) offers will be familiar to many early childhood education practitioners and researchers because it is exactly the kind of talk many practitioners are tasked with encouraging parents of all backgrounds to use when they are with their children. For example, it includes direct parent–child dyad talk, pointing and naming, descriptive language, relating the situation to personal experiences and asking questions to encourage the child to respond with words. Avineri et al's (2015) anthropological work shows the specificity of these language socialization practices, which are only common in white, Western, middle-class communities, and thus reflect a specific view of the world, and the place of both humans and language within it. Language becomes a 'reflexive act of labeling that signals to the infant that the world is discrete and categorizable' (Avineri et al., 2015, p.73). In the context of my research, few families in the community fitted into the category of white-affluent-middle-class, yet, as is common in Western early years pedagogy, language and literacy practices like the ones described above were constantly and habitually promoted to parents and children as examples of good and responsible parenting practices. The *assumed superiority* of this kind of talk as natural, desirable or necessary for young children and families formed a constant background muzak for parents and children in community spaces. In this chapter, I trace how the dominance of this dogma might have skewed, silenced or overlooked other important aspects of young children's literacy practices in communities.

Blum (2016) argues that the over-representation of WEIRD (Western, Educated, Industrialized, Rich, Democratic) participants in research on language, childhood and learning has led the normalization of WEIRD child-rearing practices, including teaching children that learning, in preparation for school, is their job, and the embracing of 'wordism', that is, the assumption that more words are better. Particular aspects of white, Western child rearing have become so normalized as universal and necessary for child development, rather than a globally unusual, culturally specific choice, that the following statement bears repeating over and over again;

> Anthropological research shows, in fact, that addressing the youngest children as conversational partners is extremely unusual in the world. These linguistic exchanges have no communicative function except to reward children with parents' approval for passing the test.
>
> Blum, in Avineri et al., 2015, p.75

Drawing on Deleuze and Guattari to describe the kind of talk in the opening quote as a 'pedagogy of order words' (p.175), MacLure points out that talk of this kind communicates to children,

> what is normal and meaningful, and thereby demonstrates the very possibility of pinning meaning to the body of the world, and the body of

oneself .....[It invites children] to think in terms of the fixed relations of similarity and difference afforded by the logic of representation .... At the same time [indicating] that it is possible to stand 'outside' this world in order to observe and comment on it.

MacLure, 2016, p.176

Language from this perspective is not purely for communication in a neutral sense, but plays a powerful role in ordering and fixing an existing hierarchy within the world. Deleuze and Guattari (1987, in Martín Bylund, 2018a, p.25) describe how general standards of language normalize 'the average adult-white-heterosexual-European-male-speaking a standard language' as 'a majoritarian fact', that is, as the location of power. Thus, different kinds of language become understood as in hierarchical relationship to each other; speaking is seen as superior to not speaking (Viruru, 2001), monolingualism as superior to bilingualism (Badwan, 2020; Flores and Rosa, 2015), middle-class language as superior to working-class language (Heath, 1983; Ivinson, 2018). In each case, it is possible to trace movement from the concrete towards the abstract or from the bodily towards the cognitive (coupled with an assumption that these categories operate as binaries in some way). Approaches to language that rest on Western-centric ontologies manifest through the privileging of particular kinds of talk as standardized, more appropriate or higher quality (Flores and Rosa, 2015). Abstracted and explicated forms of talk, in particular, are privileged, meaning that styles of talk that rely on insider knowledge and the unspoken become pathologized and regarded as lacking (Ivinson, 2018; Viruru, 2001). When presented as natural and neutral, the *idea* of this kind of language (even when it does not exist in reality) works to reproduce and uphold whiteness and 'a racial status quo' (Flores and Rosa, 2015, p.168). In a counter move, scholars highlight the possibilities for difference, creativity, something new that could stray from what is expected, existing in the kinds of language and literacy practices that resist pinning meaning down too tightly, that leave some of what is significant unarticulated (Martín Bylund, 2018a; Olsson, 2009). Ivinson asks:

What happens if middle-class interactions codify and regulate what can be thought and done, to the extent that spontaneous imaginative flights of fantasy have less opportunity to take off?

Ivinson, 2018, p.546

Closing Down and Opening Up

'So, er, when the animal lady visits next week, would it be ok if I took some photos of E? For the research?' she asks E's mum.
Well you are welcome to, but don't expect her to say much
No problem. Actually, the study isn't just about words, I'm looking at gestures and things too. Cos often young children say a lot without words, don't they? E's mum immediately becomes animated. 'Yes!! Before kids have words, they use all these little gestures. And then, when they have the words, they stop using the gestures. And then you forget them, don't you.' says E's mum

As the words of E's mum (one of the participants of my research) clearly indicate, it is not the case that nothing is lost when young children take up language and literacy practices. New speaking and mark-making practices, for example, do not enter and fill an empty void (Figure 3.1). Between the ages of twelve and thirty-six months, changing ways of being in the world, different ways of moving the body, of flexing the vocal chords, each involve something being gained and something being lost, (as I will discuss in more detail in Chapter 9). 'Pedagogy of order words', in particular, runs the risk of closing down possibility, diverting attention away from the bodily nature of language

Figure 3.1 Children Have All These Little Gestures. Photo credit: Steve Pool

and emphasizing separation between human and more-than-human world and mastery of one over the other.

> Once one has learned a standardized version of language well enough to treat it as the only possible, or at least the only right one, listening to processes of literacies not only as already known but also as yet to become might be a bigger challenge.
>
> Martín Bylund, 2018a, p.38

Young children's vocalizations, gestures and other modes of communicating can hold open possibilities for multiple and varied meanings, in a way that very clearly explicated words (in line with the 'pedagogy of order words') cannot. Martín Bylund (2018a) embraces the possibility of not-knowing a language as affirmative and filled with potential. Similarly, Vladimirova (2018) speaks about the productive language gaps that can exist between human and non-human participants (children, teachers and researchers with different first languages, and the forest that they visit) as a space where something new becomes possible.

Those who work most closely with young children – parents, carers and practitioners – observe at an intimate detail the possibilities emerging from the contingent and complicated meanings young children's language and literacy practices enact. They witness the changes, and experience closer than anyone else the humour, frustration, creativity, wonder and inconvenience of the language gap (Vladimirova, 2018). Yet, as I outlined in Chapter 1, parents, carers and practitioners can be commandeered into the project of socializing young children as particular kinds of literate beings as quickly as possible, and any resistance to this is met with criticism and pathologization.

Separation and Entanglement

Young children, in particular, seem to employ a particularly wide range of modes such as gestures and movements of the body as a rich form of communication (Flewitt, 2005), which takes place in relation to the more-than-human world (Hackett and Somerville, 2017). Extending the notion of 'pedagogy of order words' to think about different forms of multimodal communication beyond language, we might ask: What kinds of relations between body and the world might different kinds of multimodal practices make possible? What is conveyed as 'normal and meaningful' by different kinds of multimodal literacies? And, in particular, to what extent do they cement a notion of 'stand[ing] "outside" this world in order to observe and comment on it' (MacLure, 2016, p.176)? If we recognize some kinds of language and literacy practices as creating a deeper connection between child and the world, and others as working like a 'pedagogy of order words' to reinforce separation and mastery, what new insights might this bring to analyses of young children's multimodal communication?

One community space of early childhood in which to think further about how different kinds of literacies make different kinds of relationships between bodies and the world (im)possible is during a visit to a farm.[1] I have focused on a farm visit in this instance because, as I will go on to discuss, points of encounter between children and other animals carry a particular significance with regard to the construction of the special nature of the human species.

> *The children and parents are ushered to the farm classroom, and seated on child-size seats in a semi-circle. There are a number of animals to be stroked, one at a time. The presenter tells us this is her first session. She introduces each animal with a series of clues (he is very soft, has large ears and eats carrots), and the children are shown a rabbit, a hairless guinea pig (skinny pig), millipede, tortoise, snail and dragon lizard. Each animal is carried around the semicircle so that children can take turns stroking them.*

When the playgroup visited a community farm (a funded trip as part of my research), families were first invited into a classroom, where they were introduced to one animal species at a time. As each animal was presented, the member of staff announced some facts about that animal, then allowed each child to hold or stroke the animal. Children were encouraged to use language to evaluate the animals ('What colour? What size? How does it feel? Do you like it?'). Certain appropriate ways to touch animals were conveyed. (Use only hands to stroke the back, place a palm of a flat hand on certain parts of the animal that are not too sensitive. Keep away from orifices. Wash your hands afterwards.)

This way of 'meeting' animals during the animal handling session conveyed a particular kind of relationship between human and non-human. As Birke et al. (2004) argue, different kinds of discursive regimes and material choreographies serve to either reinforce or disrupt the culturally constructed divides between humans and other animals. In particular, discursive and material aspects of human–animal encounters can render animals as more or less passive, more or less separated from the human species. Duhn and Quinones (2018) describe these differing relations as 'vertical' or 'horizontal' ways of children relating to animals; children can either stand apart from and objectively examine, or they can engage in practices that are about 'attuning to and becoming with her nonhuman companion'. Extensive recent scholarship has argued for more authentic, complex, respectful early years pedagogy when it comes to facilitating encounters between children and other animals (Born, 2018; Carlyle, 2019; Hohti and Tammi, 2019; Tammi et al., 2018). My interest here is in how specific kinds of multimodal literacy practices (words, gestures, body positions and so on) contribute to particular kinds of hierarchical ordering of the world. The purpose of a 'pedagogy of order words' is not so much to convey information, but to reinforce how the world is ordered and organized (MacLure, 2016). In the example of the children 'meeting' animals above, both language and other modes (such as seating and touching) seemed particularly to emphasize both an 'appropriate' physical separation between children and animals and a hierarchical arrangement in which children's role was to examine, know about, comment on and assess the other animals.

J really likes feeding the animals at the farm. He does this by offering his whole cupped hand up each time, meaning most of his hand disappears inside the goat's mouth, to be licked clean of food pellets, before emerging again slightly sticky, with his delighted face. It looks a little dangerous, like it might result in bitten fingers (she remembers having it drummed into her as a child to feed farmyard animals with a flat hand), but the system seems to work ok for him. His grandma places fresh little piles of food pellets on his hand. He holds out his hand for more food to feed, and says 'pease pease'.

Figure 3.2 Feeding the Animals

Language practices of labelling and categorizing the animals, coupled with specific rules about how children's bodies and animal bodies should encounter each other, work to emphasize the separation between the two species and the mastery of the latter by the former. In contrast, later during the farm visit, the families were free to explore the farm on their own (Figure 3.2). These less-mediated moments of encounter with the animals were often ones of very deep bodily engagement – faces were pressed against fur, hands and fingers disappeared inside animal mouths, hands and fingers stretched out to grab and poke. If language acquisition and child development are conceptualized purely as a project in which children ascend to greater levels of (white, adult, Western) humanity (see Chapter 1), encounters between animals and children present a particularly risky space. On the other hand, if as part of a project of more-than-human early childhood literacies, we were to seek out and celebrate moments in which literacy practices did something *other than* separate (human from non-human) and fix (meaning, hierarchies), perhaps child–animals encounters would be one productive place to start looking.

Unfixing Relations of Separation and Abstraction

> The more I spoke *about* other animals, the less possible it became to speak *to* them.
>
> Abram, 1996, p.25

Language and literacy practices have far-reaching consequences, creating certain kinds of relationships between humans and the rest of the world (Abram, 1996; Joks et al., 2020). 'Traditions and hegemony' (Viruru, 2001, p.32) come into play. Within a 'pedagogy of order words' approach to language and literacy ontology, which begins with language as the special preserve of humans alone, animals and places cannot speak, they can only be spoken *about*. However, many non-Western cultures understand animals and the land as possessing languages (Abram, 1996; Rasmussen and Akulkjuk, 2009; Todd, 2016); the notion of language as the special preserve of humans, as a sign of our superiority (Finnegan, 2002) is an assumption confined to Western culture.

Within Western early childhood education policy, young children are encouraged to take up the most valued literacy and language practices (those that support a 'pedagogy of order words') as quickly as possible. By speaking clearly enough for adults to understand, labelling and evaluating the world they can see or making marks that can be attributed a fixed meaning, young children are encouraged to enact a particular kind of being in the world as soon as possible. There is an unquestioned assumption that the faster these practices are adopted, the better. No negative aspects of a speedy uptake can be contemplated. I will return to the issue of progress and acceleration in Chapter 9. For now, I would like to make the point that the race towards particular kinds of literacy and language practices as quickly as possible is a political rather than a neutral choice, one that has profound consequences for emergent relationships between young humans and the world around us.

Mastering Language?

One way in which education perpetuates a colonial infrastructure is through the notion of ownership; knowledge is property to be tamed and commanded to benefit the learner (Patel, 2014). In *Unthinking Mastery: Dehumanism and Decolonial Entanglements*, Singh (2018) writes of the need for postcolonialism to go further, to rethink the logic of mastery itself. Mastery, in its need for something to be objectified (the object of the mastery), must always debilitate in order to be able to master.

> The most contentious claim of this book, then, and the one that cuts to its core, is that there is an intimate link between the mastery enacted through colonization and other forms of mastery that we often believe today to be harmless, worthwhile, even virtuous ..... mastery invariably and relentlessly reaches toward the indiscriminate control over something—whether human or inhuman, animate or inanimate. It aims for the full submission of an object—or something *objectified*—whether it be external or internal to oneself.
>
> Singh, 2018, p.19

A 'pedagogy of order-words' style of talk is particularly effective at dividing the world into signifiers and signified, promoting a separation between the child and the world, reducing the world to knowable, speakable categories, and fixing of these categories into place (MacLure, 2016). In other words, it promotes a mastery over the non-human world by the human child. The non-human must be debilitated in order for the human to master.

Given the substantial evidence against Western language socialization practices being universal or essential (Avineri et al., 2015) and the numerous, well-founded critiques of theories such as Hart and Risley's '30 million word gap' (cf. Kuchirko, 2019; Lareau, 2003), the level of confidence and surety in the essential nature of the WEIRD child-rearing practices seems surprising. Or maybe, not so surprising. As Patel points out, it is not just that research normalizing white, Western practices are misleading or incomplete, but rather that

> acritical and ahistorical educational research is complicit in the maintenance of these realities by consistently justifying its work through the lens of the achievement gap, rather than being grounded in the political, economic, and historical infrastructure of inequity (Ladson-Billings, 2006).
>
> Patel, 2014, p.366

Knowledge is always political, and continued investment in the myth that WEIRD child-rearing practices are superior effectively masks the structural inequalities at a national and global scale that cause suffering for families and children every day. It maintains the whiteness of the curriculum (Dernikos, 2018; Flores and Rosa, 2015), and the reproduction of colonial structures (Nxumalo et al., 2011; Patel, 2014; Phipps, 2019). I propose that certain aspects of young children's literacy and language practices have not been 'accidentally' overlooked or forgotten, but deliberately erased and discouraged in order to maintain certain hierarchies, normalize certain dominant practices, and in so doing, justify the kind of systemic inequalities described by Patel (2014).

White, Western middle-class parenting practices (we could begin a list; directly addressing pre-verbal children, repeating young children's vocalizations as words and attributing linguistic meaning to them, expanding young children's words into longer sentences and so on and so on) seem benign enough. Why not just promote them as 'the "ideal" in the hope children and families will benefit from approximating it as closely as they are able' (this volume, Chapter 1)? The issue here is that when any of these practices are taken up as *normal, preferred or essential* for child development and well-being, this is white colonialism in action within early childhood literacy.

I will return in Chapter 9 to the trauma the dominance of seemingly benign parenting practices being promoted as universal, preferred or essential can wreak. For now, the purpose of this chapter has been to argue for the importance of considering how separation and entanglement between children and the more-than-human world play out in language and literacy practices. I have started to make a case (which I will expand on in coming chapters) that children's acquisition of *more* literacy practices *earlier* is a not a neutral common-sense goal, but a political position in which 'different versions of what it is to know' are enacted (Joks et al., 2020).

Concluding Section

Just over twenty years ago, Kress (1997) asked the question of how to educate children for a digital and globalized future that adults have not themselves experienced. Today within early years scholarship, attention increasingly turns to the question of how to educate children for a globally uncertain and environmentally unsustainable future (Common Worlds Research Collective, 2020; Rousell et al., 2017; Somerville and Green, 2015). Human domination is at the heart of current global environmental problems (Schrader, 2012), named by some as the Anthropocene, a proposed geological epoch in which human activity has had a significant impact on the planet. Extensive scholarship has examined the implications of the Anthropocene for planetary futures including for childhood and education (Hodgins, 2019; Kraftl, 2020; Somerville and Powell, 2018), and I will take up these themes further in my discussion of the future of early childhood literacies in Chapter 10. Singh (2018) points out that Western humanity's goal of mastery has 'fractured the earth to the point of threatening destruction of its environment and itself' (p.19). What kinds of language and literacy practices, then, will young children require, in response to living in such an 'Earth to Come' (Rousell et al., 2017)?

In such a context, a 'pedagogy of order words' seems not only inadequate; it seems obstructive and dangerous to indicate to young children that 'it is possible to stand "outside" this world in order to observe and comment on it' (MacLure, 2016, p.176). Singh (2018) warns that ultimately 'human practices of mastery fold over onto themselves and collapse' (p.19), that is, a goal of mastery creates an illusion that it is possible to deny the dependency of the one who considers themselves master on (more-than-human) others. WEIRD society's almost exclusive privileging of language and literacy practices that are grounded in an illusion of the order of the world as natural, right, fixed and separate can be read, then, as an act of 'self-maiming' (Singh, 2018, p.10). I asked at the beginning of this chapter, what aspects of language and literacy practices are marginalized and overlooked by a 'pedagogy of order words' orientation to early childhood literacy? A further question: What alternative and potentially necessary ways of being-in-the-world are too quickly cast aside at such a young age in favour of fixing, reducing, separating, in the service of a goal of mastering both language and the world?

4

Literacies in Early Childhood as
Mundane Politics

The sand tray is back, despite her saying they might need to stop using it, as it makes too much mess. Several children play in the sand tray. Sand goes everywhere. J waves plastic toys with sand stuck to them around his head like a helicopter, whilst walking away from the blue plastic matting that covers the floor around the sand tray. Sand sprays across the wooden floor.

O and her mum sit at the craft table, so she sits at the end of the table. The activity is making robots. 'I've already made one – she just wants to take them apart!' says mum. Mum holds a cardboard tube, puts on glue, sticks on a pompom. Mum sticks on a feather, O pulls it off. O waves a felt pen. Mum tells her, 'she drew on the sofa and wall this morning – found her sister's marker pens and coloured all over it. It came off the sofa in the end, with spray.'

When the children and families arrived at community playgroup, things rarely went as planned. Staff took great care and effort to set up the playgroup spaces, to provide an appropriate range of stimulating and educational toys and experiences. Through this planning and arranging, a particular kind of engagement with the space and resources was envisaged, and in some cases, explicated through written aims and planning materials. It would be easy to dismiss this mismatch between planning and actualization as poor-quality planning/training on the part of the staff. Or to look to research to provide more fail-safe approaches to early years pedagogy, approaches where the planning, the uptake by the children and the expected learning outcomes and developmental aims, would all fall neatly into alignment. Such responses present generalizable claims about children's learning, development and 'quality' early years practice as hegemonic truths, seeking to blame those with little power (staff, parents, children) for the mismatch between these supposedly universal truths and lived experience.

As an alternative, it would also be easy to frame the mismatch between planning and actualization purely through humour, cuteness, 'sod's law' (and what happened in playgroup was frequently very humorous). Never work with children or animals. Millei and Kallio (2018) argue that political actions are frequently present in early childhood spaces, yet usually go unrecognized, rendering young children as innocent, vulnerable and apolitical. As Truman (2019a) points out, sometimes refusal can be generative, affirmative. Refusal can be capacious in the way in which it makes space for alternative possibilities (Truman et al., 2020). Drawing on Millei and Kallio's (2018) notion of the political in early childhood spaces, and Truman's work on generative refusal, this chapter asks how moments of subversion or disruption, such as those described above, demonstrate ways parents and children uphold or reject the roles, behaviours and literate practices that are imagined for them.

Mundane Politics in Community Playgroups

Political agency springs from contextual experiences with matters that appear particularly important to those involved, and is often connected with challenging and uncomfortable situations that invite people to act for or against something.

Millei and Kallio, 2018, p.33

Everyday politics, Millei and Kallio (2018) write, play out in early childhood spaces through the ways in which children and adults act in response to matters that are particularly meaningful or important to them (Figure 4.1). Within these 'intuitive politics' (p.40), political attitudes, awareness and activities in community or early childhood settings encompass 'fluctuating politics unfolding where people live' (p.33). Importantly, Millei and Kallio show that 'mundane political agencies involve different levels of reflexivity and intentionality' (p.33), including implicit gestures and performative elements. This recognition of the implicit and performative is important in the contexts described in this book, in which young children and their families rarely articulate a political viewpoint, yet frequently act in response to a political framing (to move either towards or away from it).

The constitution of the early childhood spaces can be seen as a particular kind of political positioning in themselves. At day care and in playgroups, children are extracted from the mess and ambivalence of life in communities, lived alongside people of various ages and various objects that carry different

Figure 4.1 Exploring at Playgroup. Photo credit: Steve Pool

meanings and purposes. They are inserted instead into a neutral and dedicated space in which people and objects are entirely focused on catering for the progress, learning and development of children of their particular age and 'stage'. Yet early childhood is never apolitical (Millei and Kallio, 2018); certainly not in a northern English town, thick with a history of de-industrialization that is not over (Campbell et al., 2018). Community and biographical histories and the ways of seeing the world these engender haunt (Bright, 2012) these spaces of early childhood.

In the community playgroups and day care where I researched, powerful claims to abstract knowledge about early childhood rubbed up against situated place-thought in stark ways. Practitioners, families, parents, children, objects and spaces came into dialogue with notions such as 'the needs of the developing child' 'a good level of development' 'every child a talker' and 'school readiness'. Each week at playgroup, and daily each morning in the day care classroom, the notion of the needs of the developing child is quite literally 'set up'. For the playgroups, which took place in multi-use community spaces, staff pulled their boxes and bags of resources out of the storage cupboard and spend a substantial chunk of time before families arrive preparing the space (Figure 4.2).

Figure 4.2 Setting Up the Playgroup Space

Dedicated, age-appropriate educational toys and resources mapped to the EYFS curriculum, and notions and categories of child development. The resources were carefully arranged according to different curriculum areas of development; role play, small world, physical development, sensory experience, mark making. There was a sensory area on a soft blanket for babies. Snack was a tightly regulated issue; only sliced fruit and vegetables, crackers and breadsticks were permitted, in order to 'model' healthy and affordable snack possibilities to parents. Sometimes a board detailed the expected learning outcomes for the session, or a flyer was provided with guidance for how parents can replicate these learning activities at home. There was some unspoken sense that if things were placed out with enough care, or precision, or quality, this would ensure a successful learning or engagement experience, for the families.

Setting up group before the families arrive, she carefully squirts shaving foam into the messy play tray, then adds small drops of food dye in different primary colours. She uses her middle finger to lovingly swirl and smudge each little pool of colour into the shaving foam, just the right amount.

She arrives before any of the children this week. The room is carefully set up – baby toys arranged at an angle on a soft blanket. Nearby scarves are laid out like sunrays, touching at one end and splaying out in different directions.

In this particular (and common) approach to early childhood education, there is a veneer of the apolitical. Dedicated spaces for young children's development draw on universalized notions of how children develop and what they require for engagement and learning. These notions start with a view of young children as vulnerable, incomplete and innocent (Nimmo, 2008) and do not take account of the messiness and singularity of children's daily lives in communities. If child development is a generalizable process, expectations for how children should play, communicate or be parented are assumed to be neutral, not ideological.

This chapter focuses in particular on community playgroups. These are interesting spaces, because they are prepared by practitioners, for parents and children to participate in together.[1] In the community I was researching in, community playgroups were seen as an important form of initial engagement with families, opening an opportunity to offer advice, signpost to other services, and encourage families to take up the offer a free day care places for their young children.[2] In this way, community playgroups are interesting spaces, because the hegemony of children's needs and development as sanitized, generalizable, separate in some way from everyday life rubs up against the everyday realities of the families who attend the group. Children attend playgroup *with* their parents, their clothing, their pushchairs, their mobile phones, their bags of shopping, and so the ordinary, messy, micro politics of daily life always somehow seeps in.

One time, a pack of 'Barney Bears' – highly processed sugary bear-shaped cake bars, which is definitely not on the recommended menu for playgroup snack time – peeks out of a shopping basket under somebody's pushchair. A few times during playgroup, children try to extract the Barney Bears pack from the shopping basket, only for them to be swiftly snatched back by parents or staff, and shoved underneath the other bits of shopping, outdoor clothing, drinking cups and other detritus that spill from this (and every) under-pushchair shopping basket.

She chats just outside the playgroup door with E's mum, who wants to hear more about the research and the planned book. It will be tidy up time soon, so as they talk, E's mum fills her vaping machine with fluid, ready for the walk home. E runs in and out of the playgroup room, and her mum tries to keep an eye on what she is doing inside whilst keeping the vape outside, and continuing to talk. Holding the vaping equipment low down by her thigh and slightly behind her body and E's mum peers through the door of the playgroup. 'E! Not in the water again! I don't have any more dry clothes!'

As the vignettes throughout this chapter indicate, children at playgroups frequently acted in unexpected ways, subverting the intended direction and

Figure 4.3 Mundane Politics

outcome for an activity. Both children and adults at playgroup often, either intentionally or implicitly, refused, circumvented or complicated the particular roles they were intended to play in playgroup-as-site-of-child-development. If mundane politics involve acting for or against something (Millei and Kallio, 2018), often it seems both adults and children acted against (or perhaps simultaneously, ambivalently, for *and* against) the pre-planned modes of engagement intended for them (see Figure 4.3).

Tuck and Yang (2014) point out that refusal can be an important way of demonstrating to those in power what is off limits. For Truman (2019a), refusal is a 'material force' (p.119) that can be productive and affirmative; resisting certain kinds of positions opens up possibilities for something else to emerge. Describing her work with Abida, a ninth-grade student in a writing workshop, Truman describes a kind of affective refusal in which Abida 'refused to perform "student writes poem" in a normative way – she refused to write during class time – although she continued to come to class' (p.118). Like many of the children and families described in this chapter, Abida refused to perform in a particular way, whilst continuing to attend the group. To continue to attend, whilst refusing to perform in particular way, can be hard work. Her 'refusal was work' (Truman, 2019a, p.118).

The denial of children as political agents is in itself a political act (Millei and Kallio, 2018). Similarly, parents from disadvantaged communities are frequently dismissed as disengaged, unreliable or uncaring when they refuse to follow dogmatic parenting advice, rather than being recognized as taking a political stance (Gillies, 2007). Writing in relation to 'hard to reach' families' reluctance to participate in early years music sessions, Osgood et al. (2013) suggest disengagement can be understood as an affective process, driven by a desire for 'the smooth, deterritorialised space of home' that might 'overturn hierarchical orthodoxies' (p.215) that pathologize those who resist performing certain kinds of parenthood and childhood. There is a marked tendency for those in power to dismiss resistance or refusal as a marker of the individual's mental capacity or morals, rather than a valid critique of the status quo (Weiss, 2016). Thus, to be recognized as political, is itself a privilege not afforded to everyone, and rarely afforded to young children (Millei and Kallio, 2018).

This chapter traces the political within early childhood spaces, looking in particular for the challenging or uncomfortable, and how this invites children and families to act for or against something. The dedicated age appropriate toys and resources, laid out each week at playgroup, created a sense of a space suspended from everyday life in communities. Children's engagement with these toys and resources, were to be read, at least officially, only according to the logic of the abstract, developing child.[3] Noticing moments of coherence and dissonance between children, adults, families, staff, things and places might help to understand refusal and recalcitrance within young children's language and literacy practices in new ways.

Interrogating the Underlying Scaffolding

During tidy up time, children stand in the frame designed to hold the sand tray. It is a series of blue curved tubes that lock together. They stand inside, looking delighted. One child steps onto the tube and allows their foot to slide off again, repeatedly, exclaiming with delight. Having put the sand tray away in the cupboard, she comes to dismantle the frame, and the children watch with interest.

At the end of group, the baby gate to the kitchen is open, as the staff are tidying up and washing the snack things. E walks inside the gate, and stays – seeming to revel in her body being in this forbidden place. She just walks inside a few steps and then stands for several moments. Then she spots a broom and tries to sweep with it. This is a struggle as it is too tall for her.

O walks to the craft table and immediately upsets a green plastic tub containing the crayons. Her mum sighs, and to try to help her not feel bad, she says, 'oh that

happens every week!' O's mum says 'she is really into that – does it at home too.'
Later, O upends a basket containing the wooden trains; her mum catches her eye,
rolls her eyes as if to say 'further evidence'.

A classic observation about young children is that if they are bought an expensive
gift, they spend all the time playing with the cardboard box it came in. Again, this
can be easily dismissed with humour. Yet when a certain kind of gift is enclosed in
box and wrapping paper, a particular kind of child, responding in a certain kind of
way, is imagined. A particular kind of being-in-the-world is proposed. The careful
design and preparation of the playgroup spaces also implied a particular mode of
being-in-the-world. Instead of falling into their designated place in these worlds,
children frequently acted in ways that exposed and interrogated the (physical and
conceptual) scaffolding underlying playgroup spaces.

A little boy patrols the room, seemingly looking for ways to be subversive. He bangs
the metal guards over the heaters so that they make a loud clanging noise. He tries
to open the doors and run out. Then he finds something that does disrupt the group
– scooping panfuls of rice and lentils mix from the sensory tray, and making piles
of them around the room. First she tries to laugh it off, saying 'he is just exploring'.
However, problems arise within a few moments. Rice and lentils piled on the hard
flooring create a slip hazard. Rice and lentils sprinkled on the rug with the baby toys
become a choke hazard for babies. First she laughs, then tries to distract, then coax.
Then she tells him no. They spend a long time sweeping up all the lentils and rice.

As Gillies (2007) points out, within educational and family intervention
policy, families are subject to a particular kind of liberal individualism, which
emphasizes both freedom and personal responsibility; a paradox in which
parents and children are free to choose, as long as they make the right choice.
Early childhood education activities offer a similar kind of paradox, suggesting
they can be engaged with in any number of ways, whilst at the same time, being
coded with a particular kind of 'correct' or preferred response. The lentils and
rice are a free play device, available to spark children's imagination and be
interacted with in any number of ways. *Just not like that!*

Depositing the lentils and rice around the room exposes the scaffolding
underlying the thing. Like a pushing a hand through the paper backdrop, Truman
Burbank bursts out of the show constructed for his benefit and pleasure.[4] As
I stated earlier, this is certainly not a critique of practitioners or parents; we
adults who find ourselves playing along with something as it unfolds, or faced
with impossible choices (as in the story above about lentils and rice), or swept

along by energies that contain or exceed us. Yet this is, also, not fall back into a well-trodden trope about young children's surprising social competency, the tendency of adults to underestimate the abilities of young children to participate in the world of human social interactions. In other words, this is not an account of young children's surprisingly adult-like (read – human) mastery of the social world, but instead about an affective response to a certain sense or feeling. As metal tubing encloses curious children, or lentils and rice create chaos through their out-of-place occupation of the playgroup space, such insynchronicities (Tuck, 2010) reveal a shared more-than-human curiosity for the political forces that we are all caught up in. For the way in which these forces might come together as 'something' (Stewart, 2007, p.2). For the ways in which adults and children might partially glimpse or express those forces in a certain moment. 'The ordinary is a shifting assemblage of practices and practical knowledges' (Stewart, 2007, p.1).

What Feels Like *Something*

She arrives at playgroup just after a disaster just happened – D got hold of the Sharpie pens unsupervised and drew all over the table. The table is the property of the parish hall committee, from whom we hire the hall. 'I nearly had a heart attack. But mum has scrubbed it all off'. D is sat at the craft table, hands covered in dark green Sharpie pen. There is a stone covered in the same pen on the side. She picks it up and shows it to D – 'is this one yours by any chance?'.

W slides halfway down the plastic slide, and then is stuck against the friction of the surface, sitting sideways, half way down. She shuffles down the slide using her black patent shoes. Stands upright at the bottom of the slide, and then tries to climb back up. Her patent shoes have red lights that flash as she does this.

Z fetches the grumpy-looking plastic baby doll. She loves that baby, Pushes it in pushchair, washes it in the water tray, places it on a high chair, (left over from snack time) in the sun to dry off. P and H want to play with the baby too, try to pick it up and take it somewhere else, but Z is firm – baby needs to dry. The high chair is right near the chalks, and H hovers with a chalk, eventually drawing a single line of blue on baby's head. Gradually, all three children begin to colour the baby, first using different coloured chalks on the baby's head, then working down over the baby's whole body. As she watches all this, Z tells her reassuringly ' we can just wash baby', and she agrees, 'yes, it is fine we can wash her'.

So how, out of the chaotic multiplicity, did an event unfold? Gather itself together in its singular just-so-ness?

MacLure, 2013b

Stewart (2007) writes against demystification and reductionism, instead seeking in her writing on ordinary affects to describe a curiosity about immanent forces. At points in time and place, a certain kind of atmosphere can seem to come together, and manifest itself either as a misfit, or as things falling into place. Sharpie pen covers table surfaces, and adults frantically scrub it away. A little girl sticks herself halfway down a slide, lights in her shiny shoes flash. 'Things that happen … that catch people up in something that feels like *some*thing' (Stewart, 2007, p.2). These events unfold, pulling and tugging on recent, close and distant feelings and sensations, creating a sense of how an action (including, for example, a word, or a gesture) makes sense and means something (Figure 4.4).

MacLure (2013b), drawing on Deleuze, describes events as not so much as happening *to* people as *through* people. 'Those involved are stirred up and carried along by currents that are not fully under anyone's control.' Whilst Stewart (2007) describes a certain kind of atmosphere, MacLure (2013b) proposes reading things that happen 'as a kind of mist, or vapour that hovers over early years classrooms'. Atmospheres, mists and vapours are not created by any one source, they penetrate and circulate everything, and are constantly

Figure 4.4 Just-so-ness

shifting and changing. No one can control or predict the outcome of a vapour event. It cannot be broken down into components, but instead exceeds the sum of its parts. In this way, such events always exceed 'the facts of the matter' – or what can be expressed or explained in words (MacLure, 2013b).

Millei and Kallio (2018) open up the possibility for mundane political acts of resistance to be implicit or intuitive. Understanding what unfolds in these moments, when certain propositions for how to act are either taken up or resisted, as being the result of immanent forces or atmospheres, in which people become caught up, illustrates the affective, more-than-human nature of mundane politics in early childhood community spaces. Mundane political acts, then, do not necessarily represent fixed positions or clearly articulated reasonings; instead they can throw themselves together in a moment, shaped by and (re)producing certain kinds of intensities and flows, sometimes in contradictory or illogical ways.

In the vignette above, D and the sharpies become a thrown-together event; something unexpected unfolds and creates a problem. Rocks and marker pens were present in the playgroup so that families could participate in a borough-wide craze involving decorating rocks and hiding them for others to find. This was incredibly popular at the time of the research; the local Facebook group on which people could record both the rocks they had decorated and were to hide, and the ones they had discovered and re-hid around the local area, had over 15,000 members. Introducing the activity at playgroup was a good idea that, somehow, did not work. Week after week, something did not quite click into place. Few children decorated the rocks. The weather seemed unseasonably bad every Thursday morning, meaning we never did get to hide the few rocks that had been decorated in the local area. There was no rational, fixed or clearly articulated opposition to the suggested activity, yet somehow human and more-than-human forces moved against the idea.

Stewart (2007) and MacLure (2013b), in different ways, urge a deeper consideration of the singularity of what unfolds in a moment. We cannot know, understand, master and control the immanent forces that Stewart (2007) is so curious about. As MacLure (2013b) points out, although these events seem to have some sort of significance, they will always elude the search for cause and effect, the desire for an explanation in which rational subjects hold explicable positions. However, perhaps attending to insynchronicity, refusal, mismatches between what is intended and what unfolds would give a glimpse at the layers of biography, community, place, material and bodily response that make up more-than-human literacies.

Being Silent

She sits at the playdoh table, where T is rolling the playdoh into cylinders. She sits companionably next to T, picks up a ball of playdoh, begins rolling and playing and trying to start a conversation.

'Oh look it's a sausage!' she comments
There it's a wiggly worm.
Do you like it?
Is it like a wriggly worm in your garden?
'It's a wriggly worm in your hand now.' She continues on.
Throughout all this chitchat, T continues to work silently, occasionally passing her playdoh, and refusing the respond to any of her verbal prompts. Much later, T shows her playdoh to another child and tells her 'I've got a wriggly worm in my hand!'.

This interaction between an adult and a child can be judged through a static lens of early childhood education quality or best practice (Holmes et al., 2015), in a number of ways. On one hand, it is of limited success, as it does not prompt spoken response from the child. If this continues, perhaps questions would be raised about the child's language development, their progress and the possibility of a speech and language intervention. At the same time, this approach involves an educator tuning into the interests of the child, and building on these with opportunities for further spoken interaction. In a context in which it is assumed children need to hear a great deal of words in their early years, particularly in rich and responsive dyadic interactions, perhaps even if the child is unresponsive in this moment, the words are 'going in' and supporting future brain language development.

However, thinking along the lines of mundane politics, and how children, caught up in events and atmospheres, might move towards or against something offers alternative readings of the above. As MacLure (2013a) makes clear, this kind of talk is a 'pedagogy of order words', in which a particular kind of way of orientating to or attuning to the world is being proposed. Those caught up in such a moment can respond, to move either towards or away from it. By narrating the playdoh play, and affixing representational labels to what emerges (as I do in the vignette above), words replace a more complex materiality, meanings become fixed, language works to create a hierarchy between humans and playdoh. Withholding words can operate as a kind of affective refusal (Truman, 2019a; Truman et al., 2020) which resists a fixing of the modes of engaging with what is unfolding, and instead holds open a space for alternative possibilities.

Becoming Willful; Unfolding Events and More-Than-Human Intensities

The children are ushered into the tepee⁵ by the staff. 'Find your tepee seat please!'
she calls. B enters last, silent and solemn, clutching her shoes (which she always
carries around with her outside, whilst wearing her wellies). There is the sound
of the wind, the rustling of the waterproof suits, feet on the wooden floor of
the tepee, very bright sun streams through the Perspex windows, causing eyes
to squint. She announces 'Boys and girls, we're going to say hello to everyone
today' – whilst waving her right hand in front of her body. During this time, B
*waves her hand and sings quietly to herself ⁶'**heelllooo e'one**'. '**Hello everyone**'*
*she sings '**How are you? Hello everyone, who's sitting next to you?**' At the*
end of the line, B becomes immediately animated – she is the first in the circle!
Sitting up straighter, making eye contact, jabbing her finger into the centre of
her own chest to claim her turn, exclaiming 'my name!'. She extends her arm
over B's head and says 'we're going to start with B. What is your name B?' B sits
in silence, swinging her wellie boots vigorously. Her arms are limp by her side,
her lips pressed shut. 'Want to tell everybody? Say I'm … …..' There is a silence,
which is filled by both a child and a member of staff from the other side of the
tepee, saying B's name. 'B – that's right' she says, and begins to sing the next
verse, seemingly giving up on B saying her own name on cue. As she begins to
*sing '**Hel……**' B says her own name under her breath. '**Hello B, how are you?***
***Hello B, who's sitting next to you?**'*

Figure 4.5 Entering the 'Tepee'

> To claim to be willful or to describe oneself or one's stance as willful is to claim
> the very word that has historically been used as a technique for dismissal.
>
> Ahmed 2017, p.77

Writing about her own memories of being a willful child, Ahmed (2017) describes writing an essay as a punishment at school, and including a paragraph within her essay about the injustice of the punishment. On reading that paragraph, the teacher 'could not understand why I would complete the task while protesting about the task' (p.73). Similarly, in the vignette above, B both participates in the task and resists it (see Figure 4.5). Why not say her name on cue? Surely she knows her name? And is capable of saying her name? B does not comply; she is supposed to participate in the song in a tightly defined way ('say I'm … … '), yet she does not take up her allocated role willingly. This disrupts the song and holds everyone up. Under her breath she sings the song, says her name. On cue, she is silent, causing a disruption and spoiling the flow of the song.

> You become a spoilsport. It is not only that we ruin their sport. To be called
> willful is an explanation of why we ruin things. We are assumed to cause our
> own ruin, as well as ruin things for others.
>
> Ahmed, 2017, p.73

Ahmed points out that willfulness can be read negatively (unwilling to obey) or more positively (strong willed). This reading is often gendered, with boys more likely to be defined as strong-willed, whilst the critique of willfulness tends to fall on women and girls. Those who are deemed willful are those who are not supposed to have a will of their own. Rather, they are supposed to submit happily to the will of others. 'Any will is a willful will if you are not supposed to have a will of your own' (Ahmed, 2017, p.78). Beard (2017) describes how the gendered nature of who is permitted to speak in public stretches back to the foundations of modern society; in ancient Greece, authoritative public speech, or mythos, was considered the defining characteristic of masculinity.[7] Whilst both Ahmed and Beard are writing about gender in these instances, the previous chapter has illustrated the ways in which all who fall outside the 'measuring stick' of white, able-bodied, adult 'Man' tend to be classified in similarly sub-human ways. Ahmed (2017) points out that those considered 'less human' are expected to willingly submit to the will of others. Class, race, gender and age thoroughly intersect in notions of who is permitted to speak out, to voice an opinion, to have a will of their own. Willfulness, then, is not an individualized character trait or a (necessarily) consciously selected position, but something that can unfold; within the singularity of a moment (MacLure, 2013b) bodies, spaces and atmospheres might 'get into and under one's skin' (Dernikos, 2018, p.2) depending on one's 'angle of arrival' (Ahmed, 2014).

The frequent situations during the research in which children refused to speak directly to adults, to speak on cue or to answer direct questions (even those with seemingly obvious answers) were typically read with concern, as evidence of poor language development. A child who does not answer is deemed not to have the capacity to answer. Whilst children's silence has been recognized in the childhood studies literature as a route to resistance and agency (Lewis, 2009; Markstrom, 2010), generally within the literature on children's language and literacy practices, silences is read as incompetency, shyness, an inability to speak and most frequently, a lack of knowledge of words. Dernikos (2018) describes willfulness as the refusal of rationality, shaped by surging affects transmitted across porous, unbounded human and non-human bodies that might gather in, for example, a classroom space. In their study of young children in classrooms, MacLure et al. (2010) describe children's refusal to speak as sites at which questions, emotions and ideas proliferate as adults 'rage for explanation' (p.494). Rage for a logical explanation is grounded in assumptions that young children should willingly take up language in their quest to become increasingly rational and 'adult' in the world. *What rational subject would reject the generous offer of progress and development? What kind of (in)human would resist attaining a 'Good Level of Development' by the time they start school?* Alternatively, situations of refusal and silence such as these could be more usefully read in terms of an intuitive politics (Millei and Kallio, 2018), in which events unfold (MacLure, 2013b) or are thrown together (Stewart, 2007) out of inchoate intensities and feelings.

Concluding Section

The politics of a certain kind of childhood, designed to orientate young children and their families towards the development of a particular kind of rational human, circulate around community early childhood spaces. Many of the prompts that children encounter for literacy and language practices in these spaces, such as tables of craft materials and crayons, or adults asking them direct questions or encouraging them to sing, sit within this logic. Children and families intuitively respond to this in different ways. Exposing the scaffolding behind early childhood spaces and how specific forms of engagement are sometimes quite tightly conceptualizing beneath a veneer of free choice and open engagement, is one way of creating a stutter in the narrative. Perhaps, as in the vignettes in this chapter, equipment is dismantled, objects are not used as intended or resources are scattered in out-of-place locations around the space. Affective refusal (Truman, 2019a), such as withholding words or not participating, is another strategy that can open up possibilities for something different to emerge.

It is important that an analysis of affective political responses of young children and families acknowledges the limits of intentionality or fixed and explicitly stated political positions. Such positions are rarely articulated, and moments of refusal and insynchronicity are rarely planned in advance, and are not in the hands of any particular individual. Instead, affective atmospheres catch people up in an unfolding moment, moving them to act. Nevertheless, willfulness is required in these moments. Will, as a more-than-human affective force, is required to persist with ideas, to speak against and about injustice, to be who you are.

Willfulness can carry a cost. Ahmed (2017) points out that a judgement of willfulness acts as part of a disciplinary apparatus, in which action to create a more willing subject can be judged as care, as being 'for your own good'. Frequently in community early childhood spaces, children who do not speak as required, do not use the resources as expected, and parents who do not perform as recommended are judged as lacking. Rather than seeing willfulness as childish, Ahmed draws on Walker's work to describe willfulness as womanish; having and expressing will can be 'responsible and serious' (Ahmed 2017, p.79), even for young children. Having a will, refusing, moving against what is proposed, or moving for and against it simultaneously, can hold open a space for alternative possibilities. Perhaps the continued existence of such spaces can have far-reaching effects.

Willfulness can be a spark. We can be lit up by it.

Ahmed 2017, p.83

Part Two

Re-conceptualizing Early Childhood Literacies as More-Than-Human

Wild Literacies: Re-conceptualizing Early Childhood Literacy through the More-Than-Human

She sits near the small world play items arranged on the grass; there are houses, swings, a merry go round. O approaches holding a handful of plastic bugs and snakes. She seems to be looking for a good location for them. She squishes them together in her hand. O carefully looks at the house, the merry go round, she walks across the grass and goes inside the play tent and the pop up tunnel, comes back out again. O returns to the small world area and ceremoniously places a snake in her palm. She feels genuinely pleased. Then O places a bug in each seat of the merry go round.

She helps to put the snack out – crackers, breadsticks, cheese cubes, apple, strawberries. D looks up at her, holding a half-eaten strawberry piece in front of his nose, vocalising and smiling. It is a joke. He places the strawberry on his nose and then over his eye, laughing. She laughs too. He says 'bei bei' many times. (She doesn't know if this is a word – berry? Strawberry?), and, like an adult, she finds herself trying to change the sound into a word and put the word into a sentence ('strawberries! Are they yummy? Do you like strawberries?'). D eats the strawberry, picks another, then a cube of cheese, doing versions of the same joke. They giggle together.

A call for a re-conceptualization of young children's literacy and language practices as more-than-human is an insistence on the value of literacy and language practices that operate beyond human intentionality, beyond reason and rationality, that are specific to place and community, and unfold according to unpredictable and powerful affective forces (see Figure 5.1). A mark-making table may be left abandoned, or be approached only to upend the crayon pot or rearrange the tiny chairs. A half-eaten strawberry can become a hilarious joke. In a context such as a community playgroup, where children aged 12–36 months

Figure 5.1 Bugs in the Merry-Go-Round

move between different activities, objects, spaces and possibilities, with either a frenetic energy or a slow uncertain intensity, what aspects of what is unfolding might offer clues about emergent literacy and language practices?

Literacy research tends to look for children's literacies in supposedly rational and intentional practices of ordering and labelling the world, or otherwise it looks to young children's attunement to the already-here literacy practices of adult humans. However, this chapter argues, that an account of emergent literacy that extends beyond adult socialization, and notions of humans as objectively acting on the more-than-human world, is necessary in order to account for some of the intense, creative, in-the-moment events young children are frequently caught up in alongside places, objects and things. Often young children's multimodal literacies occur in relation to, and in response to, places and things. These are not always modelled by adults, and do not necessarily even involve them. It is not often the act of a rational being marching in a predictable fashion towards mastery of certain adult skills.

Writing about the presence of literacy practices in homes and communities, Gillen and Hall (2013) note that 'young children are from birth witnesses to and participants in such practices' (p.7). Taking this proposition further, Flewitt (2013) proposes 'early literacy is viewed as beginning at birth and unfolding in babies' everyday experiences' (p.4). Yet despite this sense that the emergence of literacy is rooted in the lives of very young children, there are markedly few studies of the multimodal literacy practices of children between twelve and thirty-six months (notable exceptions include Hackett, 2014; Hancock and Gillen, 2007; Harrison and McTavish, 2018; Hvit, 2015; Lancaster, 2007; Lafton, 2019; Macrae, 2020; Olsson, 2013; Rowe and Neitzel, 2010). This is important, because the literacies of very young children, before school age, have a specificity. Young children's vocalizations tip into words in a messy and provisional way; perhaps a sound becomes a word because an adult hears it as such, or perhaps, as described in Chapter 3, children sometimes hold their vocalizations at a point where they could simultaneously mean multiple things, being both words and not-words. Young children's crafting or mark making is often described as about process over product (Bentley, 2012), or about the gesture in the air more than the mark on the page (Kress, 1997). However, this alone does not seem to quite account for the unpredictability, 'wildness' (Olsson, 2009) or multiplicity (de Rijke, 2019) of what happens between children and materials, sometimes with a great intensity and care, and sometimes with seemingly a complete lack of care and interest. A few marks made on a piece of paper can be preserved for weeks. Or they can be immediately discarded, happily left at playgroup to save parents the job of transporting them home. They can be treasured and revered for a number of hours, or days, or weeks, before everything changes in a moment and the item is cast aside without a second glance.

Emergent literacies scholarship frequently emphasizes young children's attunement to adult language and literacy practices, the competent ability of young children to notice, understand and potentially even participate in literacies (e.g. Gillen and Hall, 2013). Understanding emergent literacy purely in terms of young children beginning to participate in the literacy practices of adults, places literacy squarely as a process of socialization – a human-centric endeavour in which those who are 'more' human (educated, literate adults), improve or support the socialization of those who are 'less' human (illiterate, illogical toddlers). This also contributes to an over-emphasis on the role of adult humans in young children's literacy and language practices. Such an over-emphasis overlooks the way in which, when young children entangle with objects or spaces with little adult input, these are often the moments of most intense engagement, creativity and spark. Perhaps we need to pay more attention to these more-than-human entanglements, with all their intensity and vitality, if we would like to understand more about what drives young children's literacy and language practices and how these things emerge.

Re-conceptualizing Intent

New literacy studies scholars offered the radical proposition that, from birth, young children are 'participants in such [literacy] practices' (Gillen and Hall, 2013), which are 'unfolding in babies' everyday experiences' (Flewitt, 2013). Expanding on what this might look like in practice, Gillen and Hall write:

> It is not about emergence or becoming literate; it is about being literate and allows the literacy practices and products of early childhood to be acknowledged as valid in their own right, rather than perceived as inadequate manifestations of adult literacy.
>
> Gillen and Hall, 2013, p.14

The project to recognize young children's emergent literacies as something more than 'inadequate manifestations of adult literacy' has been powerfully taken up by Kress (1997) and the resulting field of multimodal early childhood literacies. Kress's theory of multimodality as a precursor to young children's reading and writing argues that young children's semiotic representation across diverse 'modes' such as drawing, making and arranging objects, can usefully be understood as a precursor to more formal literacy practices of reading and writing. Through this process of making meaning with diverse modes, children learn at an early age to separate form from meaning, and represent what is important to them to others. Kress states that 'in learning to read and write, children come as thoroughly experienced makers of meaning' (p.8) and therefore we should turn to 'how children themselves seem to tackle the task of making sense of the world' (p.3) in order to see what we could learn about literacies in a digital and globalized future context. In identifying meaning making as multimodal, and these processes as taking place in complex and meaningful ways long before children can read or write, Kress's theory of multimodal literacies opened up the possibilities for thinking about young children's literacy practices beyond their observation of and participation in the literacy practices of adults.

Kress (1997) describes young children navigating a complex, fast-moving, digital (and thoroughly human-dominated) world, arguing that human motivation/design/intent is required in order for children to navigate, thrive and understand. This, he proposes, is achieved by semiotic meaning making as motivated, intentional design, conveying messages to other humans '*as transparent as is possible*' (p.14, emphasis added). In making a case for young children's multimodal sign making as a serious field of study, Kress's (1997) argument relies on understanding young children as making active choices about materials and actions, in order to create motivated signs, reflecting their criterial interests in a given topic. Describing young children's interactions with pillows arranged as cars, or a cardboard box used as a pirate ship, Kress argues that these activities should be considered communication rather than 'expression' (p.9) or 'play' (p.13), for the explicit reason that, as communication, they could be valued more highly in school classrooms and taken more seriously as objects of research. In other words, Kress elevates multimodal meaning making of young children before they can read or write, to the level of language (understood in a Western ontological context as the special preserve of the human species). Through multimodal meaning making, Kress argues, young children can achieve the same kinds of mastery, rational ordering and control that older children and adults do through written and spoken language.

Notions of literacy that rely on humans intentionally acting on and making use of a (presumed inanimate) world fall back onto a conceptualization of literacy competencies as capable of being separated from and transcending place, even whilst simultaneously arguing that literacy is social and situated. Notions of the child as intentional and masterful designer of pre-conceived and carefully composed signs work as another move to separate human from more-than-human and position agency and intentionality solely within the human. However, semiotics, that is, systems of sign making, advocated by Kress as an alternative to linguistics in this field of study (1997, p.6), has always been thoroughly more-than-human (Favareau and Gare, 2017; Kohn, 2013), in that it is not only humans who make and interpret semiotic signs. This offers an opening for rethinking process of young children's literacies as more-than-human.

Biosemiotics, for example, a field that bridges biology and semiotics to consider more-than-human sign making, has interrogated the implications of understanding living beings as inherently semiotic (Favareau and Gare, 2017). For example, rather than a wholly conscious, cognitive process, a biosemiotics view of intentionality would view it as a broader term describing biological processes 'that occur "in order to" or "for the sake of" something else' (Favareau and Gare, 2017, p.418), without that purpose or end-goal needing to be explicitly defined. Extant scholarship bridging posthumanism with literacy studies has also begun to unpick the issue of intentionality in literacy practices[1] (Hackett and Somerville, 2017; Kuby, 2017; Wargo, 2018). In a similar vein, work around post-developmental approaches to children's art has argued for the need to view children's art making more expansively, beyond what it intends to represent, to encompass 'how matter matters in ways that are not immediately perceptible' (Osgood, 2019, p.113). For example, de Rijke (2019) celebrates the 'riddle' of the scribble (p.153) as a mode of communication through a productively less transparent code (see also Schulte, 2019; Trafi-Prats, 2019b).

Kuby et al. (2015), grappling with the unpredictable and seemingly in-the-moment way in which they observed children's literacy practices unfolding in classroom spaces, have proposed the notion of literacy desiring, rather than designing, to better describe the in-the-moment becoming that seems to sit at the core of many of children's multimodal literacy practices.

> Literacy desiring emphasizes the fluid, sometimes unintentional, unbounded, and rhizomatic ways multimodal artifacts come into being through intra-actions with humans and nonhumans such as time, space, materials, and the environment.
>
> Kuby and Gutshall Rucker, 2016, p.ix

Whilst Kress's 'design' emphasizes pre-planning and human intentionality, Kuby and colleagues' notion of 'desire' draws on Deleuze and Guattari's work in order to re-conceptualize literacies as posthuman, that is, as occurring beyond human intentionality and control. I, too, turn now to desire in order to develop and play with the notion that young children's literacies are always more-than-human and shaped by affective flows and movements across bodies and places. How might this enable a clearer articulation of the multimodal literacies of the youngest children? What shifts are required in the field of early childhood literacies in order to understand literacies as always, inescapably, more-than-human? In particular, working with Tuck's (2010) writing on Deleuze and desire, I will demonstrate the centrality of uncertainty, contradictions and 'break downs' (rather than purpose, transparency and progress) for young children's literacy and language practices.

Desire, Uncertainty and Unpredictable Outcomes

D, 1 year old, crawls up the hill, his body getting closer and closer to the grass as the incline gets steeper. The grass brushes his stomach, and he smiles and gurgles, lies fully down on the grass to bring his body closer. Slowly D moves down the hill, on this stomach, stopping frequently to flatten himself against the grass and earth, press his cheek against it and declare 'arrhhh!'. She sits at the bottom of the hill,

watching him. At the bottom of the hill, he rolls and twists one way and the other,
resting his cheeks on the grass and then on her knee.

The Deleuze-Guattarian notion of desire refers to a creative force, reaching
towards something with intensity, but without a predefined goal or rational
purpose. The outcome of this production or creativity is the forming of
connections, or the construction of assemblages (Parr, 2010). Deleuze writes:

> Desire does not comprise any lack … … it is affect, as opposed to feeling … … it is
> event, as opposed to thing or person. And above all it implies the constitution of
> a field of immanence …..which is only defined by zones of intensity, thresholds,
> gradients, flux.
>
> Deleuze, 1997, no page number

Kuby et al. (2015) employ the notion 'literacy desiring' to consider the force or
intensity with which multimodal artefacts can become, rhizomatically. Whilst
Kuby et al's (2015) interest in desire is primarily as a way to describe the in-
the-moment and unpredictable nature of what happens between children and
materials, I turn to another important aspect of Deleuzian desire, as highlighted
by Tuck (2010).

> That desiring-machines 'work' by malfunction that they produce through
> unintended outcomes of incomplete production-cycles is one of the most
> overlooked yet profound epistemological shifts offered by Deleuze and Guattari.
>
> Tuck, 2010, p.641.

> Desire is an unstable element – it works by breaking down. Desire is radioactive.
>
> Tuck, 2010, p.641.

Desire, writes Tuck (2010), is radioactive. Here Tuck is drawing attention to a
key aspect of Deleuze and Guattari's concept of desiring machines, that they
necessarily 'fail' and that these malfunctions allow the machine to open up to
new events. That desiring machines are only productive via malfunction has
particularly significant consequences for early childhood literacy. The contrast
between technical and desiring machines provides an interesting parallel to
alternative ways of thinking about the purpose and drivers behind young
children's multimodal literacies. Technical machines produce what they intended
to produce, what was expected, or they are out of order, and produce nothing.
A crayon machine only produces crayons (Tuck, 2010). In contrast, unlike
technical machines, desiring machines depend on that which is unresolved, and
incompatible, for their continued productivity, their continued striving towards

an unspecified goal. Operating through and beyond bodies at different scales, 'fueled by experiences' (Tuck, 2010, p.640), as 'bits and pieces accumulate over a lifetime' (p.640) desiring machines are growing assemblages, in a constant state of becoming. Desire is a process of ongoing production, its energy taking it in multiple directions, yet at the same time is 'unpredictable, loyal to no one, can interrupt that which seems already determined, and set in stone' (p.642).

Tuck's interest is in the way in which desire helps to explain the unfolding of events in unexpected and paradoxical ways. This not only applies to the way in which events are outside human control, but also to the nature of human action, as something frequently contradictory or difficult to explain. 'How is it that human beings act in ways that do not match their intentions? Even betray themselves?' (Tuck, 2010, p.639). Tuck's emphasis on desire as paradoxical, as it moves through both human and non-human actants, problematizes the figure of human as rational and objective. It dismantles the image of the developing child as 'individual, bounded, abstracted from their communities, separated from the more-than-human, free of emotion, performing various competencies such as stacking bricks or crawling, in their preoccupation with moving competently through their milestones' (this volume, Chapter 1). *Desiring machines describe a process that is about as far away from the Enlightenment figure of rational, intentional and literate Man, as it is possible to get.* Whilst the literature on multimodality and early childhood tends to describe young children as having a yearning to constantly make sense of their worlds, as striving to identify and pin down fixed and understandable meanings, a process of desire would depend on almost the exact opposite; on holding a continuous space that includes contradictions, uncertainties and multiple meanings.

The malfunctions and incomplete circuits of the desiring machine are not merely accommodated within young children's literacy and language practices, they are what drives continual production and experimentation. Olsson's (2009, 2012) research with young children and language similarly discusses what we might mean when we talk about young children's production of knowledge. Often within the scholarship on multimodality and childhood, what is described as competent, creative or productive could also be described, in Olsson's words as 'imitat[ing] "stable" knowledge' (2012, p.89). In an alternative proposition, Olsson describes young children's propensity to engage with 'intense, undomesticated, and vital experimentation' (p.89). In other words, the unstable, multiple and wild aspects of the world are essential routes for young children to genuinely produce something new.

Desire Swallows Its Own Fist[2]

Desire is complex and complicated. It is constantly reformulating, and does so by extinguishing itself, breaking apart, reconfiguring, recasting. Desire licks its own fingers, bites its own nails, swallows its own fist.

Tuck and Ree, 2013, p.648

What might the notion of desire offer to accounts of young children's literacies in communities? Prior intentionality, with a rational logic, are key underlying assumptions of a 'fix, reduce and separate' conceptualization of children's literacies (Chapter 3, this volume). Tuck's (re-) conceptualization of Deleuze's notion of desire (Tuck, 2010; Tuck and Ree, 2013) accumulates generational wisdom, and is political in its rejection of notions of rationality, progress and functionality. Applied to the field of early childhood language and literacy practices, desire rejects design and human intentionality in the process of doing literacy and language, but it also rejects literacy and language practices as a sign of human exceptionality, or as *an instantiation of the objective, masterful, bounded individual decision maker.* For these reasons, rejecting functionality, with regard to what we recognize as young children's literacy practices, seems urgent. How might aesthetic-affective openness, or a force of intensity without a rational purpose, work to offer a counter to a politics of mastery-through-naming?

When I write or speak about desire, I am trying to get out from underneath the ways that my communities and I are always depicted. I insist on telling stories of desire, of complexity, of variegation, of promising myself one thing at night, and doing another in the morning.

Tuck and Ree, 2013, p.648

For Tuck and Ree (2013), speaking of desire is an 'antidote' (p.647) to narratives of lack, damage and pathologization. As I outlined in the preceding chapters, the pathologization of children and families in the majority of communities that are not WEIRD (Blum, 2016) frequently references a seeming refusal to use literacy and language practices as a 'pedagogy of order words' (MacLure, 2016), in order to name, categorize and commentate on their worlds in abstract and explicated ways (Ivinson, 2018). At the same time, there seems a sense of bewilderment from policy makers at the way in which parents refuse to 'follow the instructions, take the medicine' (this volume, Chapter 1). In the face of international Western anxieties about young children's lack of words, and intensification of government efforts to address perceived lack of parenting skills within certain communities, a rejection of functionality and rationality with regard to literacy practices, through a turn to desire, offers a response that extends beyond accommodating diverse families within existing logics of literacies (Truman, 2019a). Instead, desire demands a complete re-conceptualization of what early childhood literacy and language practices are, and what drives them. Perhaps, the incommensurability is the point (Tuck, 2010). As children move and are moved by the more-than-human world, the refusal of transparent meanings, the honouring of that which remains unsaid and the multiple, never fully realized possibilities are what jam the desiring machine, and in doing so, keep it productive.

What Can Emerge from a Desiring Machine?

She stands with H in the outside space next to a pop up tunnel. It is a warm day so the playgroup has moved outside. The ground here is sloped, and the play tunnels have been slowly rolling away down the little hill and needing to be fetched back all afternoon. H pushes the play tunnel and as it rolls back towards him, as says 'oh oh'. H and the tunnel repeat this several times, with mum and a staff member as an audience.

Writing with Margaret Somerville (Hackett and Somerville, 2017), I describe young children's multimodal literacies as emerging from more-than-human sound and movement; sound and movement that extend beyond human action and even human perception, but within which young children can become caught up and act.

> Human words and stories give way to sensory entanglement with mud and water. Movement and sound are the ways in which the mud and water pose these questions, and the children's answers, through gestures, full body movements, vocalisations, songs and words, are deeply entangled with these wider more-than-human movements, some of which result in sounds and words at the level of human perception.
>
> Hackett and Somerville, 2017, p.385

In the videos that Margaret and I work with in this book, of children playing by the edge of a river and in the corridor of a museum, gestures, words and sounds produced by the children and by the place are inseparable and difficult to transcribe. This however is not a methodological inconvenience, but an important insight into the more-than-human nature of literacy and language practices. Similarly, in many of the example vignettes of more-than-human multimodal meaning making in this chapter, the role of the human is deeply entangled with place and movement, and it is difficult to establish at what point this sound and movement became something meaningful, either to the child in the vignette, or to me as the researcher. Many of these examples of meaning making are tiny, debatable, easily overlooked. What if this is not an inconvenience of the data available, but a key point about what young children's literacy and language practices can look like?

In the example of H and the tunnel at the start of this section, as H happens to push the tunnel and it seems to roll back towards him, he exclaims at the indignity of the wind. In that moment, the tunnel somehow transforms into a cheeky, boundary-pushing character, teasing H in its defiance to stay where it is pushed. Mum, the staff member and I smile, almost laugh, attention of all three adults is focused on this dialogue between H, tunnel and wind, and everyone it seems, shares a sense of the humour in the narrative. In this way, a tiny multimodal story seems to emerge through the repetition of movement and reaction between H, the slope, the breeze, the tunnel, the audience.

> Language and story emerge *and disappear* simultaneously when we consider movement as a world-forming communicative practice.
>
>   Hackett and Somerville, 2017, p.386 (emphasis added)

Hackett and Somerville describe young children's literacies as entangled in more-than-human sound and movement. To add to this, desire, through its malfunction, jamming and ceaseless striving towards an undetermined goal, is a way of describing how human and non-human bodies become caught up in this sound and movement and invested in what might emerge, even without a fixed intention for what that might be. H and the tunnel is an example of the open-ended purpose, malfunction, and emergence of a shared idea from more-than-human sound and movement, which are all involved in young children's literacies. Understanding young children's multimodal meaning making as emerging from more-than-human sound and movement, through the force, intensity and jams of the desiring machine, offers a different way of thinking about human's role in literacy and language practices. It holds in tension the impossibility of humans authoring their own meaning making in a pre-intentional way, with the possibilities for human bodies to respond to what happens in different ways.

Attending to the way in which things can come together to be more than the sum of their parts is particularly relevant for those interested in understanding processes behind young children's language or literacies. As described in Chapter 4, children and families become caught up in, and respond to, affective flows and intensities. Although affect is pre-personal, it also sticks to, and is experienced by, different bodies differently (Ahmed, 2004). Ehret (2019) describes literacy activities as partly unconscious, the result of 'people doing things that they did not explicitly "decide" to do' in response to 'the very quiet internal "yes"'. Affect, then, might be personal yet not quite conscious. Reaching towards something without a fixed goal in mind. Re-reading the vignettes at the start of this chapter, as O places bugs in the seats of the merry go round, and J leans forward giggling with a strawberry over his eye, it is possible to imagine that small, internal, not quite conscious – 'yes'.

Not-Literacies

W walks to the plastic hoops that lie in the grass near the tunnel, looks at them, half steps on one with her foot, is unbalanced slightly. She picks up the hoop and places it over and above W's whole body, moving it down to the ground. W stands completely still when the hoop passes over her, as if to completely experience this sensation. W tries again to stand on the hoop, but legs catches and W falls over on the soft grass. W on her hands and knees, feet and hands sinking deep into the grass and clumps of slightly dry grass cuttings, as the wind whips up pink blossom petals from a nearby tree, so that they blow across the lawn. There is the sound of a man in the house just over the way drilling a window frame.

In the previous section, I described how the rolling tunnel became a story, an instance of multimodal literacy, albeit a tiny, easily overlooked one, which emerged between the tunnel, the wind, H, his surprise and his audience. W's manipulation of the plastic hoops in the vignette above (see Figure 5.2) could perhaps have tipped into a similar kind of story, or, perhaps, become a joke, like D and the strawberry at the start of the chapter. Yet somehow, this time, it did not. Burnett and Merchant (2018) draw on the Deleuzian notion of the event, in order to think about the multiple potentialities in any literacy event, including those that remain unrealized. I argue that these 'not literacies', the things that remain provisional, are not named, do not become a story, and do not tip into anything that can be read as a multimodal sign, need to remain closely involved in our analysis of young children's language and literacy practices.

Figure 5.2 W and the Plastic Hoops

As Burnett and Merchant (2017, p.3) write, 'Separating out literacy studies – in a kind of disciplinary silo – starts to feel ethically problematic.' Leander and Boldt (2013, p.41) similarly appeal for us to travel 'in the unbounded circles that literacy travels in'. Thus, there is a close connection between young children's literacy practices and not-literacy practices. That is, between things happening that seem to carry a shared meaning or idea about something not immediately present, and things happening that have a certain kind of intensity, a certain capacity 'to affect or be affected by human and non-human materialities' (Anderson and Harrison, 2010, p.16), but without becoming representational. Young children's multimodal more-than-human literacies can carry multiple possible shared representational meanings, which can emerge or come into view at different levels of certainty. Viruru makes a similar point, drawing on Glissant's notion of Relation to highlight

> the importance of the idea of opacity, or un-understandability, which functions as a defense against essentialization and reductionism, while maintaining the importance of ethical subjectivity.
>
> Viruru, 2001, p.37

In others words, the seeming randomness and unpredictability of young children's literacies, the way in which they seem constantly in likelihood of dissolving back into not-literacies, is important for their emergence. Like any emergent system, emergent literacies require 'a degree of randomness and autonomy, not control, to function' (Rautio, 2019, p.232).

N kneels on the grass, her jeaned knees pressing into mud. She holds her toy bunny tucked under her arm and three worms, wriggling in her palm. The wind blows, ruffling N's hair and blowing strands across her face. Two bigger girls bustle around N, making a home out of leaves and petals for the worms in an upturned tyre, and narrating everything they are doing.

> Older girl 1: *d'you wanna … … right … … do you want get three more of those*
>   *big leaves*
> Older girl 2: *find some of them big leaves*
> Older girl 1: *and er we need three more petals.*

N is silent in contrast; but the worms are hers and although the bigger girls want to make a house for them, they do not want to touch them. N runs her fingers very gently over each worm body in her hand, before picking one up between finger and thumb. Slowly, a long wiggly worm body emerges from her hand.

> N: *shall I put em in the four beds?*
> Older girl: *yeah. Is that your first one you wanta put? Which one do you wanna*
>   *put where?*

N continues to hold the worm, wrapping its stringy body around her finger, bringing it closer to her face to gaze at it. Gradually, she is coaxed to put the worms one by one in the tyre house.

In this vignette, the older girls draw on whatever 'medium that is to hand.' (Kress, 1997, p.8) to make a multimodal sign that is evocative of the examples Kress provides in *Before Writing*; everyday objects assembled together to represent something else, according to their semiotic potential. The worms are incorporated into domestic play with a hetero-normative family (the worms are named daddy, mummy and baby according to their size) who sleep in beds and sit on a sofa. The leaves are perfect as beds because they are flat and smooth. Three worms of different sizes serve to represent adults and children. What, then, are we to make of N, and her role in all of this? Is it not-literacy? As custodian of the worms, N overseas all that is happening. Her gaze and movements are orientated to the presence of the worms, through her cupped hand, her stroking finger, her lack of body movement (see Figure 5.3). N's attunement to the worms, and the materiality of their bodies, compared to the older girl's interest in their potential as abstract signifiers, might be another example of horizontal versus vertical relationships between children and animals (Duhn and Quinones, 2018),

Figure 5.3 N and the Worms

as described in Chapter 3 (this volume). Yet N's silence, her refusal to name, categorize or abstract, also holds open multiple possibilities. In comparison, the 'sophisticated' and tightly annotated multimodal sign of the older girls' worm house closes down all other possible interpretations at an early stage. As a multimodal sign, it is transparent (Kress, 1997, p.14). Writing specifically about language, Olsson (2012) contrasts the possibilities for language to comment, interpret and reflect on events, that is, lock them into place, on the one hand, with the possibilities of language and semiotics systems to operate as a form of experimentation. Similarly, when considering the emergence and constitution of meaning making across multiple different modes in early childhood, theories that recognize both locking into place and open spaces of ambiguity are required.

How can researchers and educators take more seriously children's not-literacies, that is, actions that cannot be easily categorized as representational meaning making? I am drawn again and again to the vignette of N and the worms, despite being told on several occasions by more established scholars in the field that this example is 'not about literacy'. As Viruru (2012) writes, 'A key feature of literacy is that it is often defined by its other: the illiterate.' Many years ago, my doctoral supervisor told me a story of presenting her data of a small child using prayer beads to make maps on his bedroom floor (Pahl, 2002) and being told by a colleague 'that's nothing'. Are we, as literacy scholars, to discard these moments of intensity, of not-literacy, without considering what we might learn from them? Perhaps young children's literacy and language practices depend on not-literacies and not-language for their emergence. Perhaps 'not-literacies' are important moments of jamming in the desiring machine (Tuck, 2010).

In Conclusion: Inhuman Dancing

Once all the worms are placed in their 'beds', the girls gaze at their creation (their multimodal sign?), when something unexpected and extraordinary happens:

> *Older girl 1: one's escaping!*
> *Older girl 2: oh one's wriggling. A LOT. What's he doing?*
> *Older girl 1: what is he doing?Laughter*
> *Older girl 1: IS HE DANCING??*
> *N: (scream of laughter and amazement) He is ah! Ah!*
> *Me: woah, he's so wriggly.*
> *N: is he dancing??!!*
> *Older girl: ahahaha he were going crazy for a minute there (reaches in to re-*
> *arrange the worm on the leaf).*

Laid as a representation of family members on leaves (representing beds), one worm unexpectedly begins to thrash about wildly. The worm dance is a timely reminder of more-than-human nature of multimodal literacy practices. Although the symbolic narrative sought to position the worms as objects within a certain kind of semiotic sign (worm-people living in a house), the worms themselves are animate beings. They had already shaped N's role in what was happening, her body held still and her tactile and haptic engagement with what unfolds. The worms 'dance' in their home, bringing a wild and unpredicted change to the girls' creation. This also produces a range of sounds from the girls' bodies; squeals of excitement, amazement and laughter. The sounds coming from the girls are difficult to transcribe at this point, because they are partly words and partly some deeply affective, intensive, non-linguistic sounds that burst from vocal chords (MacLure, 2013a). The worm's dance produces non-linguistic squeals from the vocal chords of the humans.

As I described in Chapter 3, Singh (2018) shows how 'human practices of mastery fold over onto themselves and collapse' (p.19) when they create a false illusion that the welfare and actions of the 'master' are able to operate separately from that which is 'mastered'. With regard to the multimodal literacy practices of young children, this chapter has presented an argument that models of multimodal meaning making that assume logic, human intent, mastery and pre-intentional design are misconceived, overlooking as they do the necessity of malfunction and jamming in the creative production of the desiring machine. The field of early childhood literacies itself risks folding in on itself and collapsing if we continue to 'see' intention and design in the actions of young children, viewed as bounded individuals, whilst simultaneously overlooking or disregarding that which does not seem to 'evidence' intent as 'not-literacy'. Instead, accounts of young children's literacy practices could stay in the messy and provisional area between 'literacy' and 'not literacy', between human action and inhuman action, between the vocalization that can be heard as a word, and the one which is a pure and a-representational squeal of surprise. The next three chapters will continue to explore and wonder about these 'wild literacies' by examining how they might be manifested across vocalizations and movements of human and non-human bodies.

6

Moving Bodies

She stands with H in the outside space next to a pop up tunnel. It is a warm day so the playgroup has moved outside. The ground here is sloped, and the play tunnels have been slowly rolling away down the little hill and needing to be fetched back all afternoon. H pushes the play tunnel up the small hill and as it rolls back towards him, he says 'oh oh'. H and the tunnel repeat this several times, as the adults look on.

H and the tunnel is a story we encountered in the previous chapter; a tiny, subtle multimodal story told through the movement between H and the tunnel and the breeze, combined with facial expressions and a tiny gasp of 'oh oh' (see Figure 6.1). What began as bodies moving together and sounding together in place – the feel of the tunnel, its lightness, and the way it traps air and so rolls away and back down the slope in a particularly satisfying way, a small vocalization that seemed to respond to those sensations – became something more. The way in which the tunnel rolling seemed to convey a narrative ('I try to roll away the tunnel, the tunnel has its own ideas and rolls back towards me, oh dear!') seems to have both a shared meaning within a group (H, his mum, the staff member, me) and some kind of affective pull that moves bodies to respond. Adults smile and exchange glances. H swells with pleasure and repeats a little more deliberately. In Chapter 4 (this volume), I described how atmospheres (Stewart, 2007) or vapours (MacLure, 2013b) can hang in the air, shaping what is possible and how an event seems to 'gather itself together in its singular just-so-ness' (MacLure, 2013b, no page number). These moments of just-so-ness seem to vibrate with intensity and significance when I am with families in community places, yet often when I come to write them down, the way in which meaning was expressed seems slippery, contingent, so easily challenged or dismissed. As I argued in Chapter 5 (this volume), the emergence and disappearance of meaning in these moments is not just an inconvenient hiccup in the examples of multimodal meaning making I have encountered during my research, but an integral facet of the nature of young children's wild, more-than-human literacies.

Figure 6.1 H and the Tunnel

Looking for Wild Literacies

Where, then, might we begin to cast our attention if we are to understand multimodal literacies that rely on an atmosphere (Stewart, 2007), or on malfunction (Tuck, 2010)? The purpose of the next three chapters is an in-depth interrogation of what exactly I might be referring to when I talk about (multimodal) literacies that begin at birth, and through what processes these literacies might become manifested through the sounds and movements of human and non-human bodies. In the previous chapter, I termed these 'wild literacies' messy, provisional and holding in tension multiple possibilities, meanings and affects, moving and slipping between the representational and non-representational, between 'literacy' and 'not-literacy'.

In the next three chapters, I take three different starting points for delineating and considering what literacies in very early childhood are and what comes into play when literacies emerge together with children and the more-than-human world. More-than-human sound and movement is always the starting point for multimodal meaning making (Hackett and Somerville, 2017). How this sound and movement begins to manifest itself as a shared understanding or a meaning that refers to something beyond what is immediately apparent, can take different (over-lapping) forms, and this is the focus of the next three chapters. Chapter 6 is concerned with the movement of young children's bodies, in and with place, and the kinds of meaning making that can emerge through, for example, a gesture or full bodied play. Meaning can emerge through the intensities, entanglements, through flows of affect or moving bodies, and how these things seem to make sense in the moment. At the same time, meanings expressed in this form can often seem multiple, provisional, and evade capture or easy explanation by adults; this, I argue, is a key aspect of why they so powerfully open up possibilities for being in the world, for young children. Chapter 7 focuses on the relationships that can emerge between material things and young children. Energies are often invested in relationships with objects and materials that exceed function or signification, and are instead concerned with the vibrancy of these things, and powerful affective pulls. Seeming to demand responses from children such as treasuring and secreting objects, sorting and arranging them, laying out patterns or experimenting with how things hang together, the literacies that can emerge between children and material things are political in their frequent refusal to foreground functionality or signification. Chapter 8 builds on Chapter 3 by offering a counter to the dominant assumption that words are intended to clearly transmit specific messages to pre-intended audiences. Instead, I argue for an expanded consideration of young children's words and vocalizations, including how these collective bodily responses sit in and respond to soundscapes and places, whilst experimenting with how bodies can participate with the more-than-human.

Throughout the accounts that follow, the ways in which intensities and energies can flow around places and move bodies (Stewart, 2007) remain central to my analysis of young children's meaning making. In addition, I will pick up and expand on three propositions for more-than-human literacies that I made in Chapter 1; firstly that literacy and language practices are bodily practices, usefully conceptualized as the result of human and non-human bodies moving and sounding in place. As I discuss below, both human and more-than-human bodies are understood to be porous and unbounded, affecting each other in unpredictable ways. Thus, I have suggested that the process of emergence of literacies is more-than-human (proposition 2, from Chapter 1), with randomness and provisionality being important aspects (Rautio, 2019). If literacies manifest when energies, desires, affective flows, or malfunctions shape bodies and set meanings or responses into motion, my third proposition is that these manifestations are collective rather than individual. A theory of wild literacies continues to honour and take seriously the intensity with which children move and sound 'in order to ... ' (Favareau and Gare, 2017), without this sentence being completed with an explicit pre-stated goal. All life has purpose, yet that purpose could be the continuation of the flow of what is unfolding (Schrader, 2012). Thus, a more-than-human understanding of intentionality in literacy practices (Hackett and Rautio, 2019) does not rely on pre-design of certain and fixed meanings, but on deliberate engagement with the generative and essential nature of jams and contradictions that keep the desiring machine productive.

Literacies and Moving Bodies; Spilling from Intensity and Possibility

In many of the examples of young children's literacy and language practices I have described already in this book, the movement of bodies in place is central. In Chapter 1, J vocalizes 'wawawawawa' as he walks through the water and little streams flow around his ankles, and T drops onto the grass and rolls down the hill over and over. In Chapter 5, O carries plastic bugs around the grassy space, looking for the perfect place to position them, and D grabs and wiggles a strawberry and turns it into a joke. As each of these examples show, sound and movement are closely related (Hackett and Somerville, 2017), and both are deeply entangled with place (Gallagher, 2016).

A focus on place foregrounds what unfolds in the moment with materials, rather than pinning action against trajectories of development (Hackett et al., 2015; Jones et al., 2016). The characteristics of places can have profound impacts on the lives of children and families (Kraftl et al., 2012) and, in a context where children's spaces are increasingly separated out from those of adults (Rasmussen, 2004), as Jones et al. (2016) write '"making space" for and with children ... is a political act' (p.1128). The impact of place on learning is well established (Daniels, 2019; Ellsworth, 2004; Mannion et al., 2012), and several classic studies have demonstrated the differences in children's talk and multimodal literacies in different locations (Flewitt, 2005; Heath, 1983; Tizard and Hughes, 1984). However, there are few recent studies examining the difference place can make to children's choice of modes for communication (the *how* as well as the *what*). Importantly, this conceptualization of body and place is not one of a bounded individualized human body, drawing in, processing and interpreting experiences of that which is 'outside' of it. From a posthuman perspective, place is not just something that can act on or influence children's bodies. Instead, bodies and place co-constitute each other in so many ways, that the boundaries are unclear. My colleague Riikka Hohti once said to me (pers. comm, July 2019) – it is not so much that bodies are *in* place, but rather bodies *are* place. Bodies are unbounded, leaky, vulnerable, deeply affected by place, not just in the immediate moment but in the sense that place/body memories (Somerville, 2007), histories, hauntings (Ivinson, 2018), political discourses and historical trajectories, are not so much held *within*, but rather *constitutive of*, bodies. For Alaimo (2016), a foregrounding of the body in place acts as a counter to human exceptionalism, grounded as it is in the Enlightenment separation of human from nature. Conceptualizing place in this way, we might ask: *What kinds of literacy and language practices seem possible, relevant, safe, comfortable, difficult or easy in any given time-space? How is this way of being in, moving in, answering the world, working?*

This chapter foregrounds, then, the relationship between young children's literacy and language practices and place, asking firstly what kinds of opportunities for moving and being caught up in affective flows different kinds of places might afford, and secondly how might we understand the relationship between these affordances and the kinds of multimodal literacies that occur. In terms of literacy practices, a focus on how places and affects move bodies, without 'leaping to interpret our observations of young children's behaviour' (Hackett and Somerville, 2017, p.377), could include attending first to what is unfolding and its intensities, and only attending second to whether this seems to be literacies. This involves honouring both literacies and not-literacies (as discussed in Chapter 5) as well as the close interrelation between the two.

Writing with Pauliina Rautio (Hackett and Rautio, 2019), we proposed Ingold's (2013) notion of correspondence as one way of understanding unfolding meaning between moving bodies in young children's literacy practices. Writing against mastery of the material world by humans, Ingold (2013) looks to the work of craftsmen [*sic*] to emphasize the importance of correspondence, or a deep attunement, learnt over time, between human and more-than-human materials or bodies. Drawing on examples such as flying a kite, playing a cello and throwing a pot, Ingold argues that, in a relationship of correspondence, the focus is not on how the world is represented, but rather that correspondence is a process requiring 'a lifetime of intimate gestural and sensory engagement' (Ingold, 2013, p.29). 'What does this notion of slowly growing experience in corresponding with the world, mean for young children as literacy practice-ers?' Pauliina and I wonder (Hackett and Rautio, 2019, p.1028). Writing against the notion of mastery of skills (such as language or writing) in order to fix meaning in place (MacLure, 2013a), we suggest 'an increasingly skilled craft in more-than-human literacies would require an ever deeper wrapping together of human and nonhuman processes of growth and dissolution, and ever expanding notion of what it might mean to make oneself present in the world' (Hackett and Rautio, 2019, p.1028). For this reason, the first chapter of this part looks to moving (human and non-human) bodies, how bodies respond to each other and processes of making oneself present in the world, as a starting point for tracing more-than-human literacies in early childhood.

Moving Bodies and the Spatialities of How Things Hold Together

She catches W's eye and makes a gesture where she does a shrug and a smile. W copies her, which makes her laugh. They continue exchanging the gesture, passing back and forth half a dozen times. W's mum notices and says 'she always copies gestures at home'. W's mum describes W copying a gesture where she crooks her fingers and beckons her to come. She says 'the other week W was running away from me so I made that gesture and instead of coming, W just imitated the gesture.' They both laugh.

Sitting on his chair, D leans forward slightly and presses his hands gently into the seat, between his legs. He tells her 'dig dig'. 'Dig?' she asks. His sister tells her – 'he is saying digger'. Oh is this your digger? she ask and D smiles, as if in affirmation. He gestures towards the space in front of his chair. She imagines the arm and bucket of the imaginary digger occupying this space.

Mum holds V in her arms, V stretches out her hand towards her and waves it in a kind of greeting. This gesture moves her across the carpet, stretching out her hand in a wave as she is drawn towards V. V repeats the same gesture several times, like a wave but also as though she wants to touch her hand. She allows V to touch her hand, and V buries her nails lightly into her palm. Then V puckers her lips, ever so subtly. She interprets this as blowing a kiss, and blows one back, using hand as well as mouth. V's mum laughs and joins in, both adults do 'blowing kisses', and in response V puckers her mouth again.

Many years of fieldwork in community settings has taught me that the best way of being alongside and together with young children is to approach slowly and join in with whatever they are playing with. The least successful thing to do is to look a child in the eye and ask them a direct question such as what their name is or what they are making. This almost always causes the child to fall silent, drop what they are doing or, frequently, run away. Each of the vignettes above attempts to describe how meaning unfolds slowly between bodies and how these bodies move and respond. Counter to a 'pedagogy of order words' (MacLure, 2016) approach to early childhood literacy, which advises the pinning down and elaboration of meanings as quickly and clearly as possible (e.g. see

Figure 1.2), moving, sounding, responding in ways that hold open the possibility for multiple meanings for as long as possible often seemed preferable. This aspect of fieldwork with young children is not something I have seen discussed much in the literature; perhaps this is because it exposes the researcher's errors and awkwardness in an uncomfortable way.[1] However, just as the difficult-to-transcribe nature of children's sound and movement is an essential characteristic of early childhood literacies, rather than an inconvenient aside (Hackett and Somerville, 2017), I argue that the willingness of the children in my research to engage through body movement more than through words has something to teach us.

Olsson (2012) advises 'listening to and taking seriously children's *production* of knowledge' (p.230) in order to understand representational logics children are inventing. In a similar vein, Kress's (1997) approach for his original theories of multimodality was to start with 'how children themselves seem to tackle the task of making sense of the world around them' (p.3). Inspired by Kress and by Olsson, by attending carefully to how children themselves navigate meaning making, it is possible to frequently notice the importance of the provisionality and multiplicity of the meanings that might (or might not) emerge. The role of gesture in young children's multimodal literacies has been well documented (e.g. Flewitt, 2005). I argue here for a deeper investigation of the nuances between, for example, gestures with culturally established shared meanings (those which Morris et al., [1979] would term 'symbolic gestures'), those that seem to carry a particular meaning in-the-moment, and those that deliberately seem to sit in a contingent and experimental position, playing with the possibilities of what a gesture might or might not activate. In my research, even when children perhaps knew some of the socio-cultural meaning attached to a gesture (such as a wave or blowing a kiss), they often continued to experiment with what the gesture could mean, with what bodies moving together could do in this particular place, with what and how meaning might emerge in such moments.

What young children can do with their bodies changes week by week. I remember M trying to crawl commando style (thighs still dragging on the floor) through the pop up tunnel at playgroup and getting tangled up in the polyester fabric. A couple of weeks later he was crawling on all fours (thighs off the ground) and the tangling up did not happen. When I first met W she had just begun to walk, and was wearing brand new shiny shoes. She walked back and forth over a mat on the floor, experimenting with the way in which the change in texture seemed to unbalance her in her new shoes. The constant becoming of a young child's body lends a particularly striking kind of serendipity or chaos to what a body might end up doing in a place² (see, for example, Løkken, 2000). These subtleties take on a new significance for young children's literacies when we notice how entangled the emergence of multimodal meanings are with how bodies move and affect each other. Seemingly unplanned and serendipitous movements between bodies and places (such as the tunnel rolling down the slope at the start of this chapter) can be the thing that sparks a new idea or shared meaning. The way bodies move in relation to each other, the ongoing search for a way for a body to be in a particular place, is a starting point for understanding the emergence of young children's meaning making through bodies moving in places.

How J Became a Cat

On a visit to a farm, the children are ushered through the main part of the farm, past some goats, and into the classroom. They are to wait here for their 'animal handling experience' to start. The atmosphere in the room is tense with expectation. As they wait, it feels increasingly difficulty to contain bodies on seats and keep still. The adults coax and encourage, aware both of the difficulty and the expectation to control bodies. To the children they say 'Come sit down, do you want to sit here, do you want to sit with me?' To each other they mutter 'Where are they, do you think?'

Several of the children run around the room, away from the circle of chairs the group have been allocated to sit in, and try to get out of the door, through which they can see goats in a pen. Time continues on, slowly whilst they wait. The chairs face an empty space, where the animals will be shown, and on the wall behind hangs a larger poster of trees in a forest. In desperation, J runs to the poster and tries to touch it, to pull it, to climb up the trees in the image. The poster is at risk of being damaged, so the adults remonstrate with him to stop.

The intensity of this period of waiting, and the worry about the children's difficulty to wait with still bodies, is something I remember clearly. Frustration, mixed with excitement, seemed to move the children's bodies, as they jiggled on seats or moved towards doors. A problem that cannot be solved, but for which we (parents and staff of the trip) will be held responsible for if something were to go wrong (such as the poster being damaged). Jones et al. (2016) describe the way in which both preconceived imagined childhoods around which spaces have been designed and socio-historical conditions and legacies can shape how spaces feel and move bodies. The arrangement of little chairs in a circle seemed to gesture towards schooled and placid children who would willingly sit on them. The visit to the farm itself fitted into an historical pattern of 'free trips' offered by Children's Centers as an incentive for parents to engage, and there was certainly a sense that such trips were rewards to be earned – only parents seen as regular attendees of the playgroup were offered a place on the trips. Thus, perhaps, the sense of the specialness of going on the trip was coupled with some unarticulated sense that we (the participants of the free trip) should be grateful and behave well.

> *Then J flings himself onto the floor in the middle of the circle of chairs, and*
> *lies there flat. He lifts himself onto all fours and crawls across the room to her,*
> *mewing. J is a cat.*
> *She plays along*
> *come here little cat have a cuddle … … … ….*
> *J crawls to her on all fours, nuzzles, mews, pretends to eat from her hand and*
> *curls up on her lap.*
> *"here's some food little cat … … … …*
> *go to sleep … … … …..*
> *wake up time".*
> *They play out this game, a whole day as a pet cat.*
> *Then J again flings himself on the floor, rises mewing, and they repeat the cycle.*

From frustration, excitement and a general sense that something could go wrong at any moment, something new and unexpected emerged; J became a cat (see Figure 6.2). In J's portrayal of a cat, body posture, movement and sounds came together to create a shared meaning that was recognized by everyone in the group. J-as-cat was an embodied multimodal sign. This embodied sign emerged from intensity, the difficulty of holding a body still on a chair, whilst politely, gratefully waiting, for the promised experience to handle and learn about the animals. In this sense, it is very specific not only to this place and moment in time, but to the particular histories, biographies, geographies, discursive constructions and affective flows that shaped experience and moved bodies in this time/space. Stewart writes:

> The body hums along, rages up, or deflates. It goes with the flow, meets resistance,
> gets attacked, or finds itself caught up in something it can't get out of.
>
> Stewart, 2007, p.75

Caught up in something he can't get out of, as affects bubble up and threaten to overwhelm, J flings his body onto the floor; trying to find a way to wait, a way for a body to be. And then, J's body rises, phoenix like, from its defeat on the

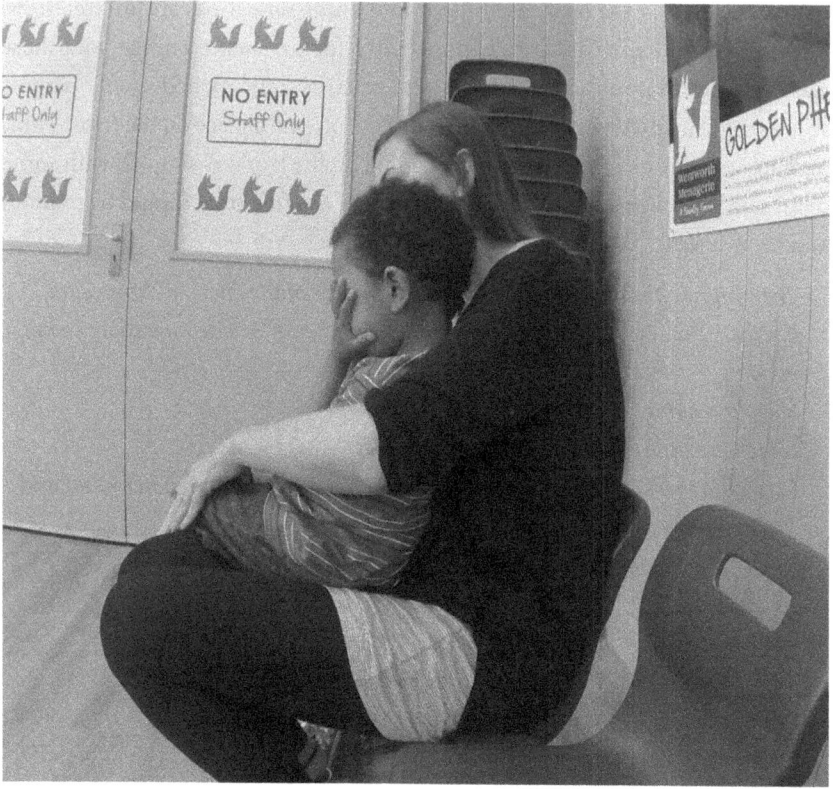

Figure 6.2 Go to Sleep Little Cat

floor. Muscles tense a little, holding the body on all fours. Some new thing is created. Being on all fours, somehow, the idea of a cat. An idea that could have flickered into existence and then disappeared in the same moment (Burnett and Merchant, 2018), instead seems to take hold. Being a cat is a way for a body to be *here* and *now*. The notion of an embodied sign carefully constructed by objective human-as-designer does not seem adequate to describe what takes place in this moment. This is not a sign that is capable of being abstracted from or transcending its material and affective environment, but rather meaning that is deeply entangled with and specific to time, place and affective flow.

Once it has arrived, what does this multimodal sign do? J-as-cat, on a simple level, represents something that is not there (a cat). However, more than that, J-as-cat carries multiple possible meanings, which emerge or come into view with different levels of certainty. It represents a cat, an animal common within the world of early childhood (e.g. in books, as toys, as pets). It represents an animal in a space where there are no animals, yet animals are desired (because we are waiting impatiently for the animal handling session). In its playing out of eat-sleep-wake-up-do-it-again, it comments on waiting and the passing of time (days go by, a metaphor perhaps for the time we wait). It represents a restless energy of the body (all our impatient bodies) finding a way to be uncontained without getting into trouble. It calls for kindness and to enter into play, rather than to reprimand and order back onto a chair. It creates a relationship between J and a member of staff (the one who joins in the game) that can include play, touch, cuddling and care.

Does J-as-cat consciously represent all the meanings listed above? To J? To anyone? In that moment? As a pre-intended design? J-as-cat emerged, rising from his prostrate position on the floor, in a moment of crisis, frustration, of seeking a way for a body to be. Because J-as-cat emerged from more-than-human intensities, the range of meanings described above is not fixed or clear. To ask which of these meanings are correct, which did J intend or truly mean, seem like the wrong questions to ask, because these questions assume human mastery or pre-design. The power of this multimodal sign came from its provisional nature, its multiplicity. It meant more than one thing at the same time. The way an embodied multimodal literacy can come to shift a mood, mean several things, affect other bodies is not evidence of an individual's social competency, but an example of the way in which meaning making spills from intensity and possibility, slowly comes into view, takes hold and gathers an energy of its own.

Taking a Risk on Shifting Ground

The water tray catches E's interest. E wants to get in. E negotiates this by touching it several times. Then E puts one foot in, looking at her, she protests mildly, 'no no, you're not getting in'. When E puts her foot in, she removes E's sandals so they don't get wet. E puts a full foot in three times, each time looking at her; each time she tells her 'no'. Then E gets in with both feet. 'Ohhhhhhh' all the adults exclaim 'she did get in! It was always going to happen!' E stamps with both feet, making splashes, and declaring 'g'in'! (get in).

As young children, bodies and places move together, the mundane politics described in Chapter 4 are always present. How is it possible for a body to be? In what ways does a moving body comply with or rub up in tension against the expectations, aspirations and hierarchical ordering of a place? How are those expectations shaped by community histories, biographies, embodied and inherited ways of knowing and making sense of the world (Ivinson, 2018)?

The water tray is provided for the children to play in, to have a sensory experience with. Perhaps certain forms of water play (pouring water in a not-too-splashy fashion with the cups provided) were envisaged over others (jumping in the water tray fully clothed). As I discussed in Chapter 4, these partially articulated rules for how resources should or should not be used seem to be something children tended to be aware of, and respond to, moving towards or against (such as the example in Chapter 4 of the boy and the tray of lentils). However, because these rules tended to be unspoken, they were also provisional and subject to change. Not getting into trouble can be a complex endeavour (MacLure et al., 2011). Certainly, some children are likely to be more quickly perceived as breaking the rules than other children (Dyson, 2015; Gillies, 2007). Jones and colleagues write:

> We are also aware of how these children's bodies are often perceived by community outsiders and likely even some educators. Where we see intellect, creativity, and ingenuity, others might see rowdiness, destructiveness, rudeness, and even reason to pursue diagnoses that will label children and youth as socially, psychologically, and/or academically abnormal.
>
> Jones et al., 2016, p.1152

From their own subject positions, children navigate these complexities. In the vignette above, E navigates breaking the (unwritten) rules and getting into the water (see Figure 6.3); the gesture enables her to negotiate in a different way to words, keeping the meaning open, the action unspecified in order to establish how 'naughty' this action was going to be whilst it was still a speculative possibility.

> *D is eating toast at the snack table. She kneels down next to him to chat. He eats and chats with his chair half a metre from the table. He leans and wobbles on it, falling off it twice. D chats to her for a long time with one leg straight and foot on the floor, one leg bent and knee on the chair, leaning on the chair with one hand and rocking back and forth. She says, 'shall I take a photo of you with your toast?' and snaps a quick shot. When she looks later, she realizes D sat down fully with his bottom on the chair, four chair feet on the floor, for the split second of the photo.*

How a body is arranged, such as the way a body moves, or rocks on a chair leg, or stays still on a chair, can be political. Moving bodies can enact a minor politics, a gesture of refusal. As described above, gestures and vocalizations rather than words can help with this by keeping meaning provisional. As well

Figure 6.3 G'in the Water Tray

as navigating the constantly shifting goals posts of what it takes to be 'good', 'developmentally appropriate' or 'respectable' in any given time/place, how and when young children use literacy and language practices must be deeply entwined in my own practices of engaging and recording during the research. As J places his chair legs back on the floor and bottom firmly on the chair seat, he shows me what is and is not open for examination and capture by a researcher (Tuck and Yang, 2014).

Individual children, parents and communities are frequently pathologized for how children's bodies do or do not move in places, and children themselves are well aware of what is at stake. Skeggs (1997) writes extensively about respectability and working-class families, and the way in which women's caring and child-rearing roles have historically been closely scrutinized for evidence of respectability or moral disrepute. These discursive constructs shape the way in which bodies feel in places, how bodies can move and experiment with place. My doctoral research involved visiting a local museum with families from this community, and I well remember the way in which the families paused outside of the large doors, waiting for me to lead the way and enter first. New children arriving at playgroup during my research would tend to enter gradually and uncertainly, and opt first for toys and activities that seemed the most self-explanatory and familiar. When the nursery I worked with as part of this study introduced a new outdoors pedagogy, the children were visibly cowed, unsure how to act when first brought outdoors and distressed by getting muddy hands for which they thought they might be reprimanded (see also Hackett et al., 2020b). Whilst discourses of naughtiness, respectability, pathology and judgement are never fully articulated, they can still seem to hang in the air as atmospheres that children sense and can constrain bodies, at least at first.

Why should it matter for early childhood literacies if bodies feel constrained in places? Many of the examples of literacies I have described in this book rely on the kind of experimentation that involves 'opening up and letting go – of tongues, vocal chords, arms or bodies perhaps, in order to play one's part in bringing the world into relation with itself' (Hackett and Rautio, 2019, p.1027). When bodies shrink, curl and freeze in uncertainty, when words stick in the throat (Hackett et al., 2020b), when children are unsure whether they can run across the space or cross the threshold or climb into the water tray, the possibilities for 'answering the world' (Hackett and Rautio, 2019; Ingold, 2013) can become less numerous. As Daniels (2019) writes, 'Children's ongoing movements create possibilities for "doing" and "being" that flow across and between children.' Experimentation with meaning making, to explore what makes sense, what a thing can do or what can emerge in the moment, is only possible when bodies can move in places in ways that feel safe and comfortable. Describing her own work with young children and literacies, Olsson (2013) appeals for opportunities for movement and creation that are 'irresistible', with 'expanding of bodily potential and for joyful passions' (p.250). Similarly, Daniels (2016) finds the most productive moments of children's expanding repertoires for meaning making were the novel or the unexpected. In my own research, it is possible to trace both the familiar scenarios and navigation of something new and mysterious as essential components for children to develop a wide and experimental range of meaning making (see, for example, Hackett et al., 2018). Sometimes places and objects are important for young children's literacies because of their familiarity, their repetition, the well-worn routes a child walks every week, the places in a favourite toy where the texture has changed from too many months of holding, rubbing, loving. At other times, it is the out-of-the-ordinary nature of a place or a thing that drives the intensity, the desire, the flows of affect, behind process of emergence. The habitual, the surprising, the expected and the serendipitous that can run through the everyday lives of children and families all offer different opportunities for experimentation with what a body can do in a place. Bodies become caught up in material-discursive intensities, and shared ideas come into view, like ripples settling on the surface of still water.

Movement, Affect and Literacies

Starting with tracing affective flows (Stewart, 2007), how bodies feel and move in places, and how these flows and movements can establish a 'just-so-ness' (MacLure, 2013b) that seems to be more than the sum of its parts, offers a different starting point for noticing what is involved when literacy practices unfold between bodies. How a body feels in a place, what the possibilities seem to be for a body to move through space and how affective flows shape what feels right or seems to fit are all important aspects unfolding literacies. Young children's movement in places can be read as a certain kind of solution to a certain kind of intensity.

A common theme throughout much of the (not)literacies I describe in this book is the juxtaposition between the vibratory intensity with which something seems to move my body into action, shape my sense-making in the encounter and stick afterwards in my memory, and yet seem so slippery and provisional when I come to describe it in words here. Kathleen Stewart writes:

> Affects are not so much forms of signification, or units of knowledge, as they are expressions of ideas or problems performed as a kind of involuntary and powerful learning and participation.
>
> Stewart, 2007, p.40

Through movement, young children's multimodal literacies might arrive, either provisionally or more firmly, in the space, and take on a life of their own. A new thing, such as an embodied J-as-cat sign, or a story about a rolling tunnel, has an oblique relationship with the milieu already jumbled into the room (animals, bodies in need of control, a breeze, a circle of chairs, a muddy slope, imaginative play) as well as with the biographies, community histories and discursive constructs that already circulate. For Stewart (2007), inchoate meanings are not contained within semiotic messages, rather they 'move through bodies, dreams, dramas and social worldings' (p.3), gathering intensities, textures and potential as they go. Drawing on Barthes notion of 'third meaning' Stewart describes how impersonal forces can call something to mind or set something in motion before meanings themselves come clearly into view or fix themselves into place. 'The question they beg,' writes Stewart (2007), 'is not what they might mean ... but where they might go' (p.3).

Concluding Thoughts

How do places, objects, materials, bodies and ideas move together to shape young children's literacy and language practices? A more-than-human theory of young children's literacies does not view places, bodies or gestures as resources that children can perceive, survey and choose to draw upon as appropriate in order to convey their 'already thought' ideas about the world. Instead, an interplay between places and children makes certain ways of being and moving in the world possible or impossible. More-than-human understandings of purpose, intentionality and emergence (Hackett and Rautio, 2019) are necessary to fully notice and appreciate processes of literacy emergence through movement in place, and point to alternative kinds of considerations with regard to supporting children and families to experiment with potentialities and possibilities of multimodal literacy practices. For example, the feel of a place, its atmosphere, how bodies move and sound, where familiarity and unfamiliarity lie in a landscape offer a starting point for the emergence of new kinds of multimodal literacy practices through movement and experimentation.

When bodies move in places, meaning can emerge suddenly and clearly, such as the example of J-as-a-cat, or gradually over time, such as the building up of repeated rituals in a particular place (Hackett, 2016; Hackett and Rautio, 2019). It can hold itself in a state of possibility and uncertainty, such as V and blowing kisses described above (did she ever intend to blow me a kiss?) or firmly grasp a position and state it more definitely, such as D's creation of an imaginary digger. Often, in my research, the provisional nature of the meanings, and their multiple possibilities, seemed to be particularly attractive and generative from the point of view of young children. I have suggested this is because children are constantly navigating the complexities and politics of how they are placed in the world, and thus how their movements are interpreted and the consequences this might have.

Thus, across all of this work with bodies, movement and place, children's sense of entitlement and awareness of the circulating of mundane politics, has an important impact. When children and families are constantly positioned as wrong, out of place, or with a sense they should be grateful for what has been provided for them, creative literacy possibilities may be more tightly constrained. Attending to atmospheres, affects and the materiality of the places children encounter, then, becomes a political endeavour for researchers, teachers and families, closely related to an understanding of (not) literacies as dependent on how bodies can feel, sound and move in place.

Thing-ness and Literacies

L peers slowly at her from behind mum's legs. Thrusting out her hand, L reveals; a squishy orange unicorn. It has accumulated quite a lot of fluff and dust. L squeezes her hand to demonstrate its squishy-ness. 'Oh wow, so nice, what's he called?' she begins to enthuse, but L has already walked away.

A key aim of the research with which this book is concerned was a better understanding of the role of objects in young children's language and literacy practices. There are significant and pervasive ways in which objects, children and families co-exist together and affect each other. As Rautio asks, 'To witness something seemingly pointless, yet inherently rewarding for those who engage with it, is an occasion to ask: what is it that takes place in the moment?' (Rautio, 2013, p.399). Tiny toys, found objects or pieces of rubbish are stuffed in pockets or hidden in shoes and on shelves (see Figure 7.1). Objects that seemed somehow in that moment to belong together are placed deliberately in a line, or slotted inside each other. Small curated piles of plastic figures, or stickers, or stones, or hairclips inhabit tables or corners of the room and parents trip over them or move around them each day. Hovering on the cusp of mess (Pahl, 2002) seeming to serve no purpose and signify nothing clearly, yet still shimmering with some kind of intensity or weight, adults must frequently make decisions about whether and how these strangely alien objects are to be allowed to continue on in the worlds of young children.

In her book *Vibrant Matter*, Bennett (2010) affirms the recalcitrance of objects (i.e. the way in which the material can offer a resistant force to human-led cultural reform) as a productive power in its own right. She describes this phenomenon as 'thing power'; the capacity material objects have to make things happen, and to exist in excess of their human meaning and allocated purpose. Material things can come together in a 'contingent tableau' (p.5) with unpredictable consequences.[1]

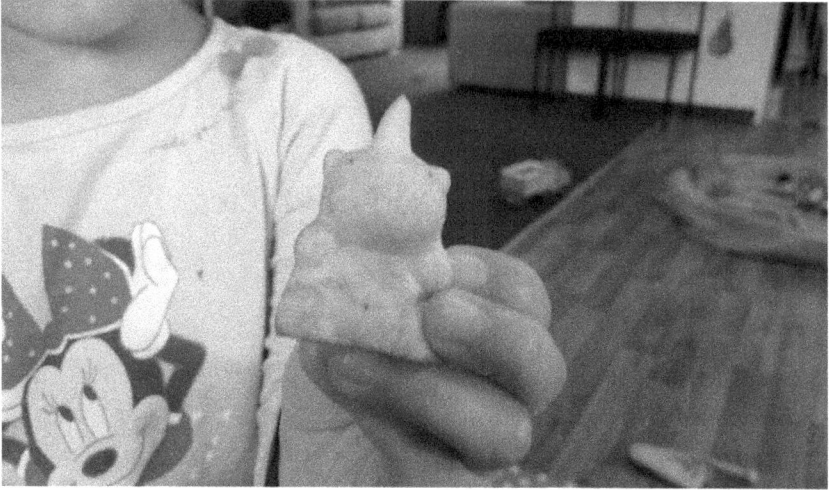

Figure 7.1 L and Her Unicorn Squishy

In her important paper 'Children who carry stones in their pockets', Rautio (2013) draws on Bennett's notion of thing-power to pay attention to the intra actions between children and things that seem to serve no rational purpose; picking up stones and putting them into pockets, or arranging coloured pins on a pincushion. For Rautio, these kinds of actions are not only beautiful to observe, they are political to notice and value. She writes:

> In a world of increasing mobility and pressure to be more productive, practices that bear no economic or otherwise measurable significance are political statements. Stones worked with in quarries, in mining, as property, as gravel on streets, blocking entrances or dividing nations as walls, are political material entities. For children, intra-action with stones provides a political niche: a virtually irrelevant material (unless used to break windows or causing washing machines to break down) lends itself to be carried, collected, moved, exchanged, valued and worked with through means that children possess, on their own without adult help, supervision or acceptance.
>
> Rautio, 2013, p.405

Taking my cue from Bennett (2010) and from Rautio (2013), I propose that an understanding of the relationship between objects/things and early childhood literacy requires hesitating before jumping straight to the representational purpose of the object or its intended role in the cognitive-design of the child-as-meaning-maker. Instead, an account of the role of material things in more-than-human literacies involves starting with the affects generated when children and things 'slip-slide into each other' (Bennett, 2010, p.4) coupled with an interrogation of the intensities, pulls and flows that occur between children and things. It is from these intensities, this slipping and sliding, that various kinds of literacies might emerge. I have described (in Chapter 5, this volume) multimodal literacies as 'wild', more-than-human, always exceeding and surprising human attempts to design, predict or control (and that this wildness is actually essential for productive carrying-on of young children's meaning making). Children's entanglement with objects is one example of this, depending, as they do, on what Bennett describes as 'an efficacy of objects in excess of the human meanings, designs or purposes they express or serve' (2010, p.20). In other words, affective bodies (Bennett, 2010), both human and non-human, drive, move and shape each other and meanings emerge (and transform and disappear) as a result of this 'thing-power'.

Objects and Early Childhood Education

Whilst the role of objects and the material are not overlooked in extant scholarship about early childhood education and pedagogy, they are most frequently understood as an instrument for human use. Often when objects are offered to young children, there is a hope they will stimulate children, create new neural connections, build vocabulary, or just generally inspire the children's literacy practices in new ways. As Hargreaves writes:

> The nonhuman in these early years settings is deployed only as a means to develop increased accuracy in children's attribution of meaning to signs and symbols as an early literacy skill.
>
> Hargraves, 2019, p.187

MacRae (2012) writes of 'a long educational tradition where objects are harnessed in terms of their ability to instruct. With the object rendered docile in the service of "learning" from it' (p.123). Bomer (2003) for example, describes how material objects in a literacy classroom were regarded as 'tools', taking their sanctioned uses from 'motives tied to the classroom structure' (p.241). An object in a classroom, then, can carry a human-ascribed message, it can have something explicit to teach or signify. The notion of early years classroom as 'third teacher' carries some of this legacy; a teacher might be assumed to be rational and intentional, facilitating movement and engagement in pre-intended ways that result in clear messages or outcomes. *What does it mean to think about a classroom space or object solely or mostly as an intentional teacher producing intended learning outcomes?*

In a similar way, objects made for young children in home and community spaces carry a biography of their design and conception, reflecting the intentions and investments of the adults who made them and provided them for children (Lange, 2018; Yamada-Rice, 2018). Objects dedicated to children's learning and development in early childhood, in classrooms and increasingly in homes, frequently carry an adult-inscribed notion of what children need or are like, and the (usually functional) role this particular object should play in what unfolds between children and objects. Commenting on the representation of children in museum collections, Brookshaw (2009) points out that most museum objects related to children are designed and made by adults for children. Objects found, appropriated or made by children for themselves are much rarer in the curatorial record. Whilst children also frequently appropriate, make or repurpose objects for themselves (as this chapter will foreground) these actions are often overlooked, unrecorded, corrected or treated as unfortunate glitches in the design of the 'classroom as teacher'.

This instrumental view of objects and places not only renders matter as dull, inanimate, only present in the world 'for us' (Bennett, 2010) but overlooks the way in which affect moves and flows, and things can come together in unexpected ways, to somehow become more than the sum of their parts (Chapter 4; MacLure, 2013b). An over focus on the role of human adults in socializing young children, and the propensity for human adults to ascribe meaning to objects and put them to use for intended purposes, overlooks the intensity and focus young children tend to give to objects in early childhood spaces (see, for example, Martin, 2019; Myers, 2019; Yamada-Rice, 2018). In community playgroup and other locations of my research, adults were frequently on the sidelines, whilst the children interacted intensively with material things. This chapter will begin by outlining some of the most striking and pervasive occurrences between children and objects in my research. Only after considering what these kinds of intra actions seemed to produce, will I go on to consider what this might tell us about things, children and literacy practices.

Treasuring

As she arrives at day care, Y and his mum are stood at the door waiting for it to open. Y greets her by holding out a brown autumn leaf in each hand, then he holds them to his nose to smell. Y then reveals to her a tiny clear plastic wheel he has nestled in the palm of his hand. 'What's that?' she asks and his mum says 'it's a wheel of a car that he's had a bath with, slept with ….'. It is off a Paw Patrol vehicle. 'Oh wow,' she enthuses, 'let's have a look', but Y points at his coat which has Paw Patrol characters on it, and says 'paw'. Y wanders off holding his leaves. The wheel is hidden back safely in the pocket of his special Paw Patrol coat.

She keeps noticing where the unicorn squishy is all through the playgroup session; sometimes in L's hand, sometimes by her side. One time forgotten and abandoned in the pasta tray whilst L eats snack. She feels concerned for it, and places it on L's pushchair.

Frequently in my research, children clung to or treasured a particular object, often something they had brought from elsewhere into playgroup with them. Often the choice was surprising, something that might be considered rubbish, or with seemingly little aesthetic appeal. Sometimes the children would show me their treasure, other times it would be tucked away in a pocket or a sleeve. Objects within the playgroup could also acquire a particular kind of desirability, exerting a pull over several children at one time, who all competed for control of the object (see also MacRae, 2012). A plastic doll with a particularly grumpy face, a toy vacuum cleaner close to breaking. Suddenly one of the toys would acquire an irresistibility that could draw children together in cooperation or send them spinning across the room in conflict. A third frequent feature of this enchantment of objects was that it could end abruptly. One moment an object could be the most carefully guarded thing in the room, the next moment it might be found abandoned, seemingly no longer needed or remembered (Figure 7.2).

I want to dwell for a moment with these pervasive features of treasured objects; their frequently tactile or aesthetic nature, often coupled with no fixed signifying purpose, the desiring pull they can exert, and the way in which these objects can be both treasured and then forgotten in the space of a few moments. For Bennett (2010), 'things', as opposed to objects, are less tied to stable meanings, fixed words and common-sense ideas. 'Things' might provoke curiosity or intense responses, without a firm sense of why and what is causing a pull, a reaction, an affinity perhaps. Pulls and intensities are lodged neither in an individual child nor in the material object itself, but are created in a particular place and moment, gathering a momentum or petering out (MacRae, 2012).

MacLure (2013c) describes 'the wonder of objects' as 'the intimate and clandestine bonds that objects are capable of contracting with children (and with adults)' (p.230).

Figure 7.2 Abandoned Doll at Playgroup

Choosing and chosen by an object, a child forms a bond that is not amenable to adult intervention. Moreover, the engagements that objects invite and receive are multisensory, and touch is often especially important. The intimate contact that this involves between objects and children's bodies amounts to a kind of *secrecy* from the viewpoint of ideology and surveillance.

MacLure, 2013c, p.230

The recalcitrance of things (Bennett, 2010) has a productive power. Holmes et al. (2020) describe this as a certain 'wildness', an always-present possibility for objects to 'rearrange thoughts and perceptions'.

A does not want to sit at the mark making table. Instead he holds a glue stick in one hand, and a pink felt tip in the other. He walks from the mark making table in a circle line around the whole playgroup, she follows him one step behind – that glue stick and felt tip constitute a risk to the playgroup in so many ways! He walks in the same circle route three times in a row. Third time, she rolls her eyes as she walks past – "oh my goodness!" Four times he walks the same route, before a staff member spots the felt tip and tries to remove it from his hand.

J was holding a tiny ball of white clay, which he had been carrying around for some time. He put the ball of clay down, then asked where it was and, relocating it, continued to hold it. He also held a metal boat, which he really seemed to like. Then he dropped the clay accidentally in the boat! Whilst the grown-ups peered into the boat to see where the clay had gone, J ran over to the craft table to get a fresh tiny ball of clay to hold.

MacRae et al., 2018, p.509

Children's desire to move through space with a particular object, and seemingly no fixed intention or purpose, was a frequent occurrence in my research. Perhaps a piece of duplo was carried around the museum, placed experimentally and momentarily on different surfaces and in different spaces, or a child did not put down a plastic animal for the whole playgroup session. Rather than viewing objects for their purpose or affordances (e.g. Bomer, 2003), understanding what happens between children and objects might be more productively served by an emphasis on their wildness, their potential secretiveness or subversiveness (MacLure, 2013c), their ambivalence, the possibilities they open up or close down for something new to happen. Moving with objects that have an open-ended purpose, in particular, is one way to open up even greater possibility for the not-yet-known to unfold.

Patterning

Z comes into the gazebo, observes that the others are drawing on brown paper with egg-shaped chalks. Z fetches wooden egg cups from play kitchen. Places them in a neat line on the brown paper. Places a chalk egg in each one. The egg cups stay now in the gazebo, and from time to time someone places the chalk eggs back in them.

There is a little jug lying on the floor. H picks this up and put it on the table. He looks for a moment, picks up a pine cone and places it in the lid of the jug. It is a little big and cannot be pushed inside. Discarding the pine cone he picks up a feather – this fits inside well. He pushes more and more feathers into the jug, until it is full with a few poking out the top.

S brings the Paw Patrol toys to show her, and she crouches to receive them, placing each one in the deep, dandelion scattered grass. S brings another and another, placing each vehicle next to the one before, facing the same way, as a particular angle so they all point in towards each other. Each figure is placed on the appropriate colour matching vehicle. S comments whilst doing this, 'dat' 'dere', she thinks S might be saying the names of the characters to herself, but it is hard to discern her words. She casually places one of the figures in a different coloured vehicle, and S reproves her 'that doesn't go there' and moves it to the correct colour match vehicle.

In my research I encountered multiple and constant examples of children sorting, arranging, grouping and curating things (see Figure 7.3). Mini flowerpots were placed in a line with a pine cone in each one (Figure 7.4). Wooden egg

Figure 7.3 S Arranges the Paw Patrol Figures

cups were carried from the other side of the playgroup in order to join the egg-shaped chalks. Duplo was up-ended to provide a series of perfectly sized holes for crayons to be slotted in to. Plastic beetles and bugs were placed into the seats of the plastic merry-go-round (Figure 5.1). Often there seemed to be a sense of being driven to place the 'just right' object in the 'just right' location (Thiel, 2020). Picking up the arguments from Chapter 5, a foregrounding of multimodal meaning making as communication would lead us to try to attribute purpose, intended meaning and human intentionality to these creations: Why did the child connect the egg cups with the chalks? What might this indicate about the criterial features of the egg cups and chalks from the child's point of view? What message is intended to be conveyed 'as transparent[ly] as is possible' (Kress, 1997, p.14) by these actions? Rautio critiques this over-concern with rational purpose with regards to young children and objects, commenting:

> Were we to ask why children carry stones we could proceed in trying to find out a clear rationale … Explanations would surely surface and lend themselves to be neatly categorized. However … we would do well to let go of insistence on causality, linearity and 'neatness' in our conceptualizations.
>
> Rautio, 2013, p.395

Perhaps we are asking the wrong questions.

In response to the pathologizing discourses around 'good parenting' and their grounding in human exceptionalism, Trafi-Prats (2019) draws on the work of Puig de la Bellacasa, amongst others, to propose modes of attuning to and caring

Figure 7.4 Arranging Pine Cones and Flower Pots

for the world. Writing about her own experiences with her daughter, Trafi-Prats describes collecting empty snail shells, and arranging cucumber slices for a 'cucumber party' to attract more snails, small examples of what this kind of attunement to the world might look like. Searching for a way to sustain place and self, Crinall (2017) describes attending to her everyday life artfully, by mindfully looking for beauty in the ordinary rhythmic everyday practices that sustain life in a circular way. As Trafi-Prats points out, these kinds of practices do not have an instrumental purpose, with regard to 'child development' or 'proper parenting', and thus risk being erased or under-valued in the stories we tell about young children. These modes of being in and with the world, are absent from policy documents or parenting advice. They find no explanation in discourses of 'proper' child development, and can be ascribed no rational purpose. For parents who are already subject to particularly harsh pathologization, monitoring and judgement, whose children were already judged as being 'at risk' before they even began (Chapter 1, this volume), making practical and conceptual space for these ordinary modes of tuning in to the world might be doubly hard. Foregrounding the relationship between young children and objects beyond the instrumental, beyond the affordance of the objects for human appropriation, how might we notice, describe, value and encourage what happens between children and things? And what, then, might be the implications for our understandings of literacy practices that involve these things?

Making Literacies

Inside the gazebo, the blue acetate keeps slipping from the ceiling pole and onto the floor. F tries to pull it up and indicates to her that she should help to replace it. Then

F indicates to her to add other pieces of paper to the ceiling pole in turn; another piece of orange acetate, a piece of silver shiny paper, and three pieces of green and brown tissue paper. Once every piece of paper is slung up, the display is complete and F does a pose in front of it with outstretched arms at a diagonal, as if to say 'ta-da!'. F tells her 'It's my rainbow' and gestures an arc like a rainbow in the air with her arms.

In the second phase of the fieldwork, I collaborated with artist Steve Pool, who brought open-ended materials to playgroup to see what might happen between the children and the things.[2] For several of these sessions, we set up a pop-up gazebo, and filled it with provocative things; large sheets of brown paper, coloured acetate, crayons and chalks, a light box table, feathers, tissue paper, pine cones. At each visit, the children were initially reluctant to enter or approach the gazebo. Steve and I made sense of this as being something to do with the activities being unfamiliar or open ended. In the playgroup space, every other activity station was familiar, present in a slightly different guise every week (mark making, sensory, role play, small world, baby toys), and with clearly understood shared rules about how to use it. In contrast, the gazebo was deliberately ambiguous. Ironically, given the extensive way in which I have argued for children's preference for the provisional and ambiguous in meaning making, the gazebo, with its ambiguity seemingly created by adults rather than children, seemed to be suspiciously regarded as a potential trap, too easy to get it wrong. As somehow, altogether too much.

Gradually, over the course of each session, children would approach the gazebo, first one child, encouraging a few more. Perhaps the first child would observe and move away a couple of times, before picking up a crayon and leaning in to colour on the brown paper lining the floor of the little tent, but with feet firmly outside of the gazebo, before eventually entering. By the end of every session, the gazebo would be filled with most of the children from the playgroup, frenetically making, moving, experimenting together. Thus, the gazebo became a space for interesting making and experimenting with materials (Figures 7.5 and 7.6).

The gazebo is also perhaps an interesting space to think about both children's early literacy practices and their art making beyond representation and function. I particularly offer the vignette of F's 'ta-da' moment because these moments when an external audience seemed to be invited into the making were rare and fleeting. There was no 'ta-da' moment, for example, as L tucked his plastic wheel into his coat pocket, or Z placed a chalk egg into each egg cup, or as S lovingly

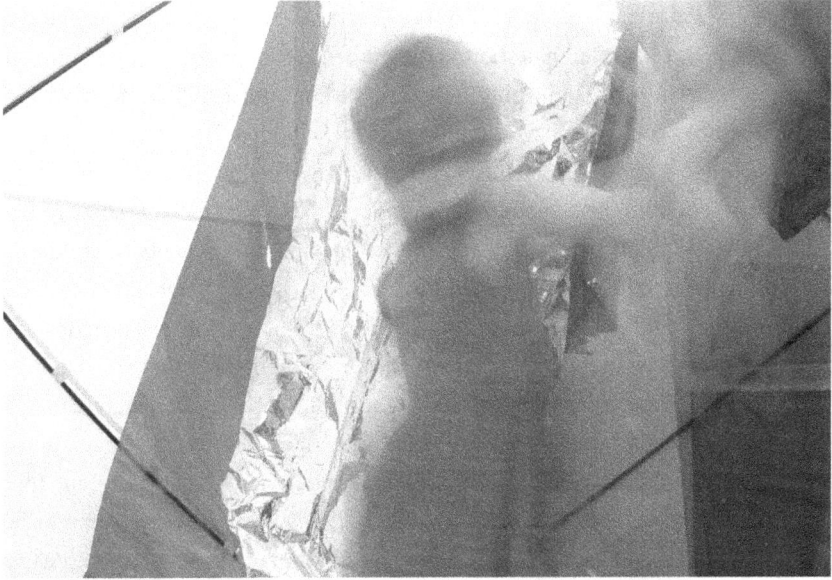

Figure 7.5 F Makes a Rainbow in the Gazebo. Photo credit: Steve Pool

Figure 7.6 Experimenting in the Gazebo. Photo credit: Steve Pool

laid the Paw Patrol figures out in a line (all described above). By this I mean there was no moment when an invitation for an audience to view, admire or comment seemed the most important thing. L had tucked her unicorn squishy away and run off before I could begin to compliment or ask about it. Even when F seemed to present her 'rainbow' to an audience gaze, this was only momentary, before she and other children stepped in to dismantle, change and recreate some more.

As Schulte (2019) points out, certain aspects and components of children's art making tend to be precedence over others. As well as an emphasis on human actants' agency and design in accounts of children's making, there also tends to be a particular interest in finished products, 'ta-da' moments, and that which adults can most easily interpret or understand.[3] Noting similarly in her own research, a disinterest from many children in adult attention or audience for their creations, Thiel (2020) argues that children's motivations and hierarchies are different, that they do not prescribe to 'the narratives that tell us we must always strive to be bigger, stronger, greater, faster' (p.83). Whilst dominant accounts of both early childhood literacy and young children's art making emphasize intent, function and representational purpose, increasingly, studies of what unfolds when children interact with materials (whether we call this multimodal literacy, art or something else) demonstrate the need to think beyond design and function (Kuby et al., 2015; MacRae, 2011; Pacini-Ketchabaw et al., 2016; Sakr and Osgood, 2019; Somerville, 2015; Trafi-Prats, 2019). Critiquing adults' tendency to limit and pin meaning onto what is involved in children's art making, Schulte (2019, p.94) asks 'How do we work against the feeling that we ought to know and that we can know a child's drawing?'

One conceptual tool that might help to disrupt our tendency to try to 'know', or to pin functional meaning to what children make, is Deleuze and Guattari's (2013) notion of territorialization. Territory marking, a key aspect of human and more-than-human life, they argue, depends on the expressive rather than the functional (p.366). Whilst colours in fish or birds, animal scent marking, or the way in which the stagemaker bird arranges leaves, can be functional, all of these acts also transcend function and become primarily expressive. The making of territory, that is, making a mark on the world in a way that is expressive and transcends function, and the assembling of disparate elements to make something new, depends on desire (Colebrook, 2002; Parr, 2010).[4] As I discussed in Chapter 5, desire as a productive force of life, relies on its malfunctions (Tuck, 2010). Similarly, assemblages 'function despite the persistent presence of energies that cofound them from within' (Bennett, 2010, cited in Schulte, 2019, p.98).

Malfunction, confounding energies, expression beyond function.

Understanding what children do with things and materials (whether we call this multimodal meaning making, art or something else) as territorialization, as the construction of assemblages through desire, helps to shed further light on the question of individual interest and how this might drive young children's literacy practices (or not). According to Deleuzian theory, we do not come into the world with specific interests or desires, rather 'interests are produced from chaotic flows of desire' (Colebrook, 2002, p.93) and these flows of desire require 'the concrete and specific connection of bodies' (Colebrook, 2002, p.92). F did not set out that day in the gazebo interested in rainbows, or even in the materials provided in the gazebo. The 'ta-da' moment of inviting an audience to view the rainbow was not the manifestation of her pre-existing interests. Rather, through the 'concrete and specific connection' (Colebrook, 2002) with the material world, driven by flows of desire, new interests, in their singularity and specificity, were produced momentarily (Trafi-Prats, 2019). This has deep implications for our interpretation of young children's literacies, both in how we understand the relationship between interest, meaning and what unfolds, and the importance of randomness, of confounding (Bennett, 2010) or jamming (Tuck, 2010) energies in the assemblage.

What happens between living beings and material things in these cases, has a materiality and a spatiality about it; they are expressive compositional acts (Rousell and Cutter-Mackenzie, 2019), working like a signature, making a mark in the world. There is also a liveliness, a vitality, a refusal or a wildness at the heart of what is unfolding that confounds function and rationality. 'Take anything and make it a matter of expression' urge Deleuze and Guattari (2013, p.368).

Stories and Things

Gradually, more and more objects are gathered from around the playgroup and brought into the gazebo; dried pasta pieces, a plastic dinosaur, some leaves, a plastic baby in a bathtub. Steve props the dinosaur up next to the baby bathtub to say hello to the baby. The plastic dinosaur head rests at an angle against the baby doll. Someone says "they are eating the baby."

Dinosaurs are eating the baby.
No, no dinosaurs eat leaves, don't they?
Dinosaurs eat baby snot.

Sometimes, material things became entangled with surreal and unusual stories during my research, such as the dinosaurs-eat-baby-snot story above.

Whilst it is possible to tell a story without words (such as H and the rolling tunnel story in Chapter 6) (Phillips and Bunda, 2018), words are frequently required in order for the story to develop and become noticeable to others. Words and their emergence in the more-than-human milieus of community early childhood spaces are the subject of the following chapter. However, for now, I want to offer the example of the dinosaur-baby-snot story as an example of how the wildness of material objects can be the spark for a new story or idea. Essential to the dinosaur-baby-snot story was not only the gathering together of heterogeneous and out of place objects from around the playgroup space inside the gazebo, but also the angle of the dinosaurs head and neck, which unexpectedly resulted in its mouth leaning against the baby's head (Figure 7.7). As discussed at the start of the chapter, there is a tendency for objects in early childhood classrooms to be understood in terms of their sanctioned uses or what they are intended to teach children (Bomer, 2003). The dinosaur-baby-snot story illustrates the kinds of opportunities that may be missed when the ways in which objects and children should entangle together is too tightly prescribed and too little room is left for thing-power instability (Bennett, 2010) and the potential for objects to rearrange possibilities (Holmes et al., 2020).

Olsson (2013) writes about the importance of invention in young children's language practices and the rarity of truly original ideas. In her work in early years settings, offering objects in an open-ended way led to a 'production of new realities' (p.236). Olsson uses words such as 'irresistible' and 'aliveness' to describe the feeling of collectively producing new realities. Similar to Olsson, my research was peppered with moments that felt intensively productive, in which new ideas or realities seemed to become possible. These moments rely on that which cannot be pre-planned or predicted. It is hard enough to think of an original idea (Deleuze in Olsson, 2013). Objects with fixed meanings and intended uses are hardly going to help. For this reason, an account of young children's meaning making with objects needs to encompass

- Autotelic practices and the desire and intensity that often drives them
- Actions and attachments to objects that do not have a rational explanation
- Aesthetic actions of patterning and unpatterning, of creating and destroying
- An attention to moments of 'ta-da' when the movement and production pauses, but also an honouring of the constant undoing, the seemingly unproductive, and the frequent times when a child refuses to answer the question 'what is it?'.

Figure 7.7 Gathering Heterogeneous Objects Together in the Gazebo

Concluding Thoughts

When Rautio (2013) describes the political importance of children picking up or arranging objects they encounter, she emphasizes the 'aesthetic-affective openness' (Bennett, 2010, cited in Rautio, 2013, p.395) that characterizes these acts, in contrast to the propensity for early childhood education to look for purpose, what can be learnt and how children's actions can be rationally explained. Similarly, in starting with the thing-ness of objects, and what can unfold between children and objects that exceeds both adult intended purpose and children's pre-design, this chapter seeks a different starting point for understanding the material in early childhood literacies. Treasuring, moving with, sorting and patterning with objects are not a precursor to faster, more direct meaning making, but an enduring component of literacies and meaning making of all kinds, essential to sustaining thinking and creating with and in the world.

Whilst an appeal to make space for the creativeness of young children in how they play and what they make is not new, what is at stake here is an understanding of what comes into play during young children's literacies. MacLure (2016) writes against the pinning of meaning to the world, and I have argued throughout this book that children tend to favour forms of meaning making that remain ambiguous, that offer multiple possibilities for interpretation, that might dissolve back into 'not literacy' (Chapter 5, this volume) at any time. Literacy practices can emerge from and rely on attunement, wildness, affective flows of desire (MacRae, 2012) and the movement between literacies and not-literacies (Chapter 5, this volume). Following Rautio's (2019) insistence on the necessity of randomness as a criteria for emergence, I theorize the malfunctions of the desiring machine (Tuck, 2010) as a way to understand young children's literacy practices. The fluff-coated unicorn squishy, the plastic dinosaur that falls over, the pine cone that does not fit into the toy jug. If we are to understand the close relationship between literacies and not-literacies (Chapter 5, this volume) we need to attend to the role of that which jams the production of the (desiring) machine, that which does not make sense, that to which there is no answer to give, in relation to how objects and young children produce literacies.

8

Vocalizations as More-Than-Human

J seems to move with the wind. He wanders the outdoors space outside of playgroup. He picks up a particularly round white stone and says 'looook', then he glances at the trees blowing around in the wind and says 'awwwwww'. He runs inside with his stone, runs back out and throws it in an arc into the air and onto the paving, saying 'yeaaahhhhh'.

Children's language during my research was characterized by playfulness with words, sounds and vocalizations that seemed to respond to and merge into the surrounding soundscape (such as J saying 'awwwww' into the wind). Often there did not seem to be a human audience for the vocalizations, which were made into the air (as in the vignette above) or towards the horizon. Children murmured under their breath, or wandered around a space vocalizing as they went. In vignettes throughout this book, words children say and vocalizations they make are mingled in with moving bodies, place, play and emerging meanings. They were frequently incomprehensible to adults, onomatopoeic, not directed at humans, not for the purpose of conveying information, difficult to record or to replicate.

This way of thinking about language, as both bodily and of-the-world sits in contrast to dominant conceptualizations of young children's talk, in the UK at least, that tend to emphasize the deliberate, the clear, the intentional and the functional. As I discussed in Chapter 3 (this volume), this approach to language as an intentional clear declaration of static meanings and positions, can be understood as a 'pedagogy of order words' (see MacLure, 2016), teaching young children that their role is to categorize and order the world, to pin meaning to it. In prevailing models of language informing early childhood pedagogy and policy there seems to be an imaginary of young children's talk, in which they look an adult in the eye, speak clearly and declare their opinion to the world (Figure 1.2). These imaginaries are grounded in particular conceptualizations of language that tend to assume the primary purpose of language is to convey information or to signal meaning (Ahrenkiel and Holm, 2020, p.41-57; Finnegan, 2002; Hackett et al., 2020b). In this chapter, I focus specifically on young children's vocalizations and talk as bodily and expressive and of-the-world, considering how these bodily utterances might be conceptualized within a wider more-than-human milieu of movement, affective flows, desire and (not) literacies.

Playing with Sound and Wrapping Lips around Words

B sits with an apple. She holds is against her open mouth and goes 'lululululululu' with her vibrating tongue against it.

T is painting at the easel with red paint on a brush, jabbing the brush quite violently against the paper on the easel. The paint brush hits the paper with a thud, bristles bent back, in time with the thuds T chants 'Daba. Daby. Dabdabdab' There is a specificity to the three versions of dab – each one said separately with a pause between each.

A great deal of humming, non-linguistic sounding, rhythmic gesture and onomatopoeia (Laing, 2019; MacLure, 2016) was folded into young children's talk and vocalizations during the research. In addition, for very young children, sounds emerging from mouths were inter-mingled with things being put into mouths (sometimes simultaneously, such as M's cheesey, dribble-y vocalizations in Chapter 1, this volume). Objects might be held against lips whilst vocal chords simultaneously sounded, or children might vocalize while mouthing a dummy (pacifier), sucking clothing or teething on a toy. In her research in a bilingual early years classroom, Martín Bylund (2018a) describes a slowly growing familiarity with a new language as a creative and experimental time when language is 'juicy', when 'words are present and delicious as food' (p.24).

> [Encountering language for the first time] I threw myself over the new language like a starving dog on a juicy piece of meat. I ate up Swedish. I filled my mouth with words, chewed them, and swallowed them. [...] I took some words in my mouth like chocolates.
>
> Kallifatides, 2001, cited in Martín Bylund, 2018a, p.23

In a parallel to Martín Bylund's insights, the children in my study, whether monolingual or multilingual, were all encountering language as something constantly new and unfolding. What counted as a word, what words were supposed to be for, and the functionality and rationality that WEIRD research

(Blum, 2016) tends to assume is at the heart of speech, were not taken-for-granted truths for babies and young children in the study. The children's starting point, instead, seemed to be an experimentation with how vocalizations feel in the mouth, manifest in the soundscape, and what they activate socially, aesthetically, politically and materially. For all of these reasons, language in the early years of life could be seen to have a particular quality, one that finds generative parallels with Martín Bylund's description of bilingualism as material, juicy and playful.

To make unfamiliar words and sounds (whether that is to pronounce words for the first time, to learn a new language, or imitate a new non-linguistic noise) is to give them a materiality; attention is drawn to the work of the body (lungs, breath, throat, lips, tongue) in a more conscious way (LaBelle, 2014). Words and language are not the same thing (MacLure, 2013a), and perhaps there is much to be gained when language remains juicy, like food (Martín Bylund, 2018a), something to wrap lips around before considering the abstracted meaning of the words.

Whilst it is helpful to think of language as a bodily and experimental act, it is also important to bear in mind that bodies are not bounded and separate from place, but unbounded, leaky (Alaimo, 2016), constantly shaping and shaped by more-than-human bodies and place (Chapter 6, this volume). In his account of language as 'vocal gesticulation', Abram (1996, p.74) describes learning language as a bodily act which begins with experimental vocal sounding joining in with a surrounding soundscape. Thus, language is primarily expressive rather than symbolic (argues Abram, drawing on Merleau-Ponty) and the 'complexity of the interchange that we call "language" is rooted in the non-verbal exchange always already going on between our own flesh and the flesh of the world' (p.90). In the vignette above, vocal utterances 'daba, daby, dabdabdab' are movements of mouth, lips and vocal chords, existing alongside jabbing arm movements, fingers gripping a paint brush and a fairly still torso that remains near to the paint easel, awkwardly clad in a stiff, slightly too big, waterproof overall. 'Daba, daby, dabdabdab' also exists alongside the spreading dampness of the red paint, the bristles of the paintbrush bending back and splaying out, and the vertical sheet of paper precariously pinned to the easel. T's 'daba daby'-ing resonates with de Rijke's (2019) account of watching a five-year-old boy scribbling across a chalk board, whilst babbling and jiggling dance steps; here sound and body movements are tightly bound up with each other, and the sensation of movement and what is might activate is foregrounded. Drawing on Gardner, de Rijke (2019) describes impersonal developmental forces (perhaps akin to Favareau and Gare's 'in order to … … ' [2017, p.418]), rather than a child's internalized pre-design, driving what unfolds. From Abram's perspective, 'daba, daby, dabdabdab' are not (only) slightly incorrect versions of the signifier 'to dab [the paint]', but also vocal gesticulations that gather their sense, energy and expression from more-than-human bodies and movement.

Abram (1996) traces the development of Western conceptualizations of language as primarily symbolic (rather than bodily and expressive) to Descartes's separation of human mind from bodily nature, arguing this emphasis on symbolism and abstraction was the only way for human language to be distinguished from the complex and expressive bodily languages of other animals. Rethinking language as a bodily and situated practice, rather than abstract and mainly cognitive, recognizes the kinds of intensities, responses, meanings and relations that vocalizations and words and young children activate more expansively. Vocalizations do so much more than communicate needs or preferences. They do so much more than label familiar objects. They do so much more than transmit information to adult humans. In doing so much more, vocalizations gather their power and potential to activate something in the world from wider human and non-human gesticulating movements that surround and leak into them.

Just as I argued that there is a close relationship between literacies and not-literacies (Chapter 5, this volume), it may be generative for those interested in children's talk to consider an expanded notion of children's vocalizations, including easily recognized (by adults) words, not-words and everything in between. Recognizing the materiality and more-than-human nature of vocalizations and talk enables a consideration of young children's language practices beyond human exceptionalism, beyond the familiar trope that language (together with, for example, tool use) is what sets the human species apart from the rest of the natural world (Finnegan, 2002). Perhaps the assumption that vocalizations need to be pinned down and shifted towards recognizable (to adults) words as efficiently as possible is an assumption that needs to be reconsidered. What would it mean to look for and foreground the juicy, creative and experimental in children's vocalizations, rather than to search for and promote the recognizable and symbolic?

What Does It Take for Words to Be Recognized as Words?

She sits with Y. He has a basket of diggers and other vehicles, touches and picks up each one in turn, saying the same sound. She hears it as is either 'car' or 'what's that'. He points to the basket of cars just out of his reach, indicating she should pass

him each vehicle at a time. Then he holds each one, and says the (possible) word;
'Car/what's that?'

The children frequently look up at the sky. R looks up at a line of cloud and traces
it with his whole arm several times, whilst saying woooooow. R points repeatedly
at the sky where some kind of bird of prey is cruising and circling. He says 'baebae'.
It is not clear what the word is. If anything, it sounds more like baby than bird. R
repeats the word several times.

Two weeks later, she is outside again with R. R points up at the same part of the
sky, where the house roofs reach up past the perimeter fence of the day care, and
again says 'bae bae'. It is exactly the same word, she still does not understand what
it means. She gazes up at the roofs, at the telephone aerials, searches the sky for a
bird or a plane. There is nothing.

Frequently during the study, children made vocalizations that seemed to exist
in a grey area between words and not-words. These were vocalizations presented
as words, that sounded like they *might* be a word; and adults worked hard to
try to hear them as words and incorporate them into a conversation. Unclear
(to adults) pronunciation is common when young children talk, and is usually
assumed to be evidence of a need for improved speaking skills in order for the
child's words to be more easily understood. However, there sometimes seemed to
be a strong sense of specificity to the vocalizations the children made; for example,
in the second of the vignettes above, 'baebae' was repeated several times. When
I returned to the site two weeks later, R again pointed at the same part of the sky
and said the same word again 'baebae'. In the first vignette, 'car/what's that' really
did sound very convincingly like both those words, and either of those words
would have worked in that context. However, the two possibilities would have
cast the interaction in slightly different lights; was Y confidently informing me
what the toys are, or asking my opinion? Perhaps young children are not always
aiming to shape their vocalizations into words as quickly and clearly as possible.

MacLure (2009) advocates attending to non-linguistic aspects of language,
such as laughs and coughs, because of the way in which they can allow people
to mean more than one thing at once, to avoid complete transparency and
readability. As a very young child in a new context (both the examples above are
drawn from the first couple of months the two years olds have been attending
day care), speaking to unfamiliar adults clearly, firmly, decisively involves a
certain kind of putting oneself out into the world (LaBelle, 2014). Words that
hold onto ambivalence, that could mean several different things or nothing at

all, work to keep meanings contingent and unfixed, and also hold something back, keeping something out of bounds from the adults. In a similar vein, Martín Bylund (2018a) describes playful compound words preschool children invent during conversations in a bilingual preschool as 'atypical expression that deterritorializes language' (p.34) by revealing the limits and variations of language. I am not suggesting that the children in the vignettes above deliberately mispronounced words, or invented words that could fit one of two different meanings, as a firm interpretation of what the children consciously intended to enact during these exchanges. Rather these possibilities are offered as a way of disrupting the kinds of ontologies of language that sit behind the 'pedagogy of order words', in particular the assumption that word meanings should be fixed, clear, familiar and easily translatable, and that all speakers and listeners share this aspiration.

Z plays in the water, carefully wrapped in a waterproof overall, splashing gently and picking up the various plastic pourers. Z looks at her intently and say a word – too softly for her to hear the sounds, she can just hear the rhythm of it. Z's mum tells her 'she said water in our language.' 'What language?' 'Punjabi – water is "pani"'. 'Her talking's coming on now' Z's mum says – before her operation she could only say 'mum, dad, brother, sister', now it's been a month since the operation she has started talking again, and saying more things. She says things in English and Punjabi. When she climbs the stairs at home I get her to count them, she counts them in English. But she says mummy in our language.

J brings a book to show her, shows her the front cover and says the same word, urgently, over again 'di-saur'. Playgroup is noisy, and she struggles to tell what he is saying. Instead she murmurs 'oh it's a nice book, he has claws, yes claws and sharp teeth', J keep repeating the same word, seemingly waiting for her to hear it right and repeat it back to him. When she finally does – 'dinosaur!' J responds with a 'raaaaar', as if in affirmation. J throws the book into the air with another 'raaaar', and it lands upside-down. Oohhhhh he says, noticing the picture on the back and pointing 'di-saur'!

One of the two playgroups involved in my research (Northwood) was particularly multilingual, with more than half the parents speaking more than one language. The story of Z and her water tray (see Figure 8.1) warns of the ease with which words in children's home languages can be overlooked by monolingual staff and researchers (like me). These issues are particularly heightened for very young children, who are still playing with pronunciation, babbling, vocalization, experimenting, and at the same time, are frequently

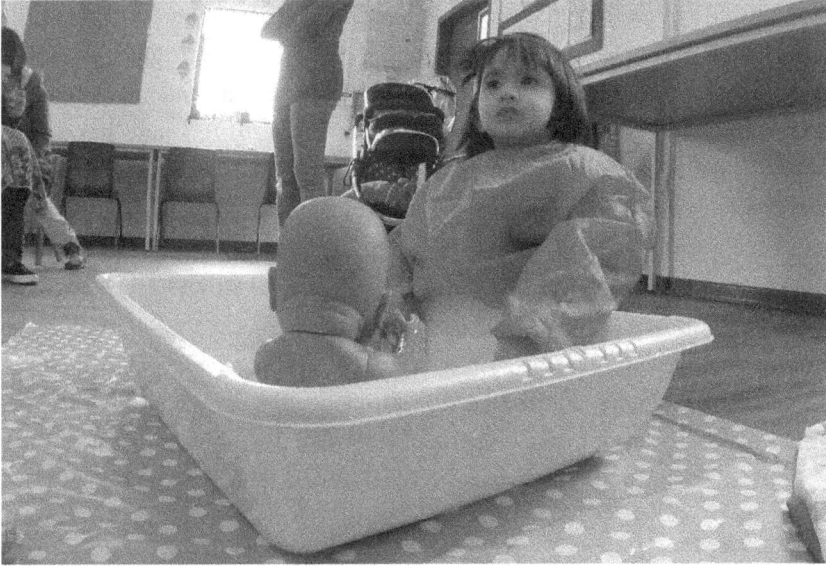

Figure 8.1 Z Plays with the Water Tray

assumed (by adults) to have few words. The two vignettes above, of J and the dinosaur book and Z and the water tray, might prompt us to reflect on how much sustained attention, confidence and trust it takes for the word to be recognized as a specific thing ('I said dinosaur, I did not say claws!')? What are the implications of this, when you are two years old? What does it mean and what is involved for us as adults to genuinely listen to children beyond our own values, priorities and investments (Davies, 2014; Yoon and Templeton, 2019)?

As Viruru (2001) points out, 'Dominant Western discourses about language are almost overwhelmingly unilingual' (p.41), and children's practices of translanguaging, that is, the fluid movement and invention across different languages, are frequently overlooked, marginalized or misunderstood in formal education spaces (Axelrod and Cole, 2018; Zhao and Flewitt, 2019). Assumptions accompanying monolingualism, for example that young children's talk should be as easily understood as possible for (largely English monolingual) staff and professionals, and should involve the acquisition of as much vocabulary in the dominant language as quickly as possible, all also work to uphold existing colonial hierarchies (Burman, 2008; Saavedra and Esquierdo, 2020; Viruru, 2001).

Just as dominant language models assume the speaker bears sole responsibility for the words and their meaning (Hackett et al., 2020b), there is also an assumption that young children bear sole responsibility for their words to be recognized as words and understood by the adults in any given situation. A child's word might be recognized as such in one moment, and not in another. Sonic environments can shape identities (Brownell, 2019); sound has effects beyond what is intended by humans. The story of Z and the water tray, above, demonstrates the practical challenges of recognizing when young children are using symbolic words with well-established meanings in their talk. Whilst earlier I questioned the assumption that children themselves are always deeply invested in their words being understood by adults and attached to a single symbolic meaning, conversely, the story of J and the dinosaur book above illustrates the potential work young children need to do if they *are* committed to ensuring adults really hear what they are saying.

From a starting point of language as 'vocal gesticulation' (p.74), Abram (1996) suggests:

> In order to learn a community's language, suggests Merleau-Ponty, it is necessary simply to begin speaking, to enter the language within one's body, to begin to move with it.
>
> Abram, 1996, p.83

An imaginery of language as primarily symbolic, bounded and for the purpose of conveying meaning, overlooking the bodily, expressive and experimental nature of language, and the power of just 'enter[ing] the language within one's body, to begin to move with it' (Abram, 1996, p.83), has particular implications, then, for any child for whom the notion of language as symbolic and bounded is particularly alien. This includes children growing up in bilingual families or communities, whose daily experience of languages might be particularly fluid and unmoored (Badwan, 2020). On the other hand, a conceptualization of language that foregrounds the expressive and bodily, rather than symbolism, mastery and efficiently conveying meaning, might disrupt problematic assumptions that languages should be bounded, fixed, either correct or incorrect, and something that must first be learnt before it is applied.

Abram (1996), as I described above, traces the over-emphasis on symbolic aspects of language (rather than expressive), to a rhetoric of the special status of humanity. Gurney and Demuro (2019) describe how twentieth-century linguistics developed out of a colonial interest in making languages countable, measurable and connected to nationhood. This Enlightenment invention of language as a series of separate bounded symbolic code systems has had real and material consequences, particularly for marginalized communities, for many years. In *How to Tame a Wild Tongue*, Anzaldua (1999) describes the close connection between identity and the way people speak, and the damage 'closing linguistic borders' (p.33) can do to those who live in borderland communities, who speak and mix multiple languages. In many communities, memories of being banned from speaking home languages in public spaces, or being belittled for translanguaging practices, are recent and current (Anzaldua, 1999; Crago et al., 1993; Saavedra and Equierdo, 2020). Martín Bylund (2018b) writes that silence in early childhood is a contradiction; we long for children to speak, but also children need to learn when to speak and when to be silent.

> Do not speak with your mouth full. Do not speak at the same time as others. Do not speak inappropriate language. Do not speak too loud. Listen. Keep quite. Don't interrupt. But answer the question, please.
>
> Martín Bylund, 2018b, p.349

Ahmed (2017) draws on *How to Tame a Wild Tongue* (Anzaldua, 1999) to discuss the notion of willful tongues that run away with words before one's brain has consented to their appearance. Ahmed's description of willful tongues and 'a desire to speak in ways other than you have been commanded to speak' (p.191) is perhaps a fruitful way to consider the kinds of runway vocalizations that emerge more as expression than as symbolism, from the bodies, mouths, tongues and vocal chords of young children (and others). Spraying spittle and half-chewed biscuit, running away into the wind, mixing in with the water and the sand tray, muttered, murmured, animalistic vocalizations in which tongues and lips and out-of-breath pants mix and leak from human bodies and mingle with non-human bodies and places.

Sensation, Purpose, Audience: Not Speaking Surrounded by Four Walls

> The soundscape is altered: human noise mingles with animate and inanimate sounds that are largely excluded in the classroom, while other kinds of sound are absent or diminished in the open air – the scrape of chairs, the toppling of bricks, the distinctive pitch and tone of adult voices monitoring and directing children. Speech issues from bodies on the move, connects speakers across distances that expand and contract, and is carried on air that registers differently on the skin.
>
> Hackett et al., 2020b

At the day care I worked with as part of this research, a new outdoors-orientated pedagogy was introduced near the start of my fieldwork. As I trace elsewhere (Hackett et al., 2020b), the children's talk in the day care was markedly different after the introduction of periods of time spent unstructured and out of doors to each day care session. This outdoors approach in day care was considered so successful that the attached Children's Centre then ran a series of outdoor playgroup sessions, for parents and children to attend together (Figure 8.2). The usual church hall playgroup was temporarily relocated to a grassed area, where traditional playgroup things such as role play figures and the pop-up tunnel mingled with grass, caterpillars, the wind, the barking of a neighbouring dog (Figure 8.3). Messy play (such as moon sand and playdoh) was easier outdoors than in the church hall, and other activities were offered for the first time, such as painting with mud, trays filled with natural materials and squirting water pistols.

Whilst not wishing to offer outdoors pedagogy as a universal panacea to anxieties around children's (lack of) talk, I have written with Maggie MacLure and Sarah McMahon about what this example of shifting language and literacy practices might demonstrate about the material and relational nature of young children's talk. In our work together, Sarah McMahon, day care manager, put it thus; when outside 'you are not speaking surrounded by four walls.' Why does it matter to talk *not* surrounded by four walls? Or what might this mattering have to teach us about young children's vocalizations? Drawing on examples from the

Figure 8.2 Outdoors Playgroup

Figure 8.3 Finding a Caterpillar at Outdoor Playgroup

outdoors playgroup, together with other examples of children's vocalizations from other kinds of spaces during the research, in this section, I will reconsider three commonly taken-for-granted aspects of young children's talk. Firstly, I want to think in more detail about the sensation of vocalizing (as both a bodily and placed act) because bodily sensation is often overlooked in accounts of children's talk, in favour of a focus on the words uttered and the meanings these conveyed. Secondly, I will reconsider purpose, and thirdly audience; this is because dominant advice offered to parents in the UK (including frequently offered to parents at my research site) is that children require a purpose to talk (i.e. talk has a rational function) and a human audience who is willing to listen, interpret, respond to and extend the child's talk.

1. Sensation

R looks up at an aeroplane line of cloud and traces it with his whole arm several times, whilst saying 'wooooooow'.

C and her friend sit completely in the tray of 'snow' (moon sand). The grains of white moon sand cover their trousers, t shirts, small smears are on their faces and hair. One corner of the tray is a little extra sticky, where another child has poured a watering can of water into it earlier on. White petals from the nearby tree blow down over them, adding to the snow like effect. They scoop up the snow in their hands. C holds a lump of the snow in flat palm of one hand, patting it rhythmically with the other, whilst saying 'patpatpatpatpat'.

Drawing on Lecercle, MacLure (2013a) warns us to avoid 'boring, bloodless, angels' (p.665), that is, to resist the tendency of research to separate words from the bodies and material entanglements from which they emerge. In the vignettes above, the relations between place, bodily sensation and vocalizations seem particularly pertinent. Sometimes place and affect can sweep us up, and words run away with us (such a J's movement with the wind, the blowing trees and the trajectory of the stone he throws, which opened this chapter). Sometimes there is a deep absorption, in which we focus intently in one direction (such as C's careful moon sand patting). In these cases, words seem to exist in and reference a more-than-human milieu.

Sarah's description of 'not talking surrounded by four walls' has parallels with Feld's (2012) description of the 'song texts' of the Bosavi in Papua New Guinea, in which the interweaving of singing, speech and the sounds of the rainforest was an essential aspect. Abram (1996) describes language beginning as bodies expressing and responding to a changing environment, pointing out that in many Indigenous communities, language is understood as something possessed by animals, living beings and places as much as of humans. He writes:

> By actively making sounds – by crying in pain or laughing in joy, by squealing and babbling and playfully mimicking the surrounding soundscape, gradually entering through such mimicry into the specific melodies of the local language, our resonant bodies slowly coming to echo the inflections and accents common to our locale and community.
>
> Abram, 1996, p.75

This is a more-than-human understanding of vocalization, in which we might consider 'language, the human and the material as completely imbricated' (Somerville, 2016, p.1161). Bodily sensation, place and soundscape do not just influence the selection of words and sounds, but play a part in how they emerge and are constituted moment by moment. Changes in young children's talk and multimodal communication in different contexts have been documented in extant literature (Flewitt, 2005; Richardson and Murray, 2017; Tizzard and Hughes), although there is still much work to be done in this direction. In addition, there are accounts of children speaking unexpectedly or for the first time in different contexts (Arculus and MacRae, 2020; Davenport, 2019; Hackett et al., 2020b). Despite this, dominant models of children's language acquisition and measurement tools for assessing young children's language competence continue to assume language is a stable and steadily accumulated resource. Within a model in which language is an accumulating resource within the brain; the more-than-human world might inspire or influence the topic of communication ('look, a green tree!'), but it would never have a more significant role than this.

> Neither linguistic nor non-linguistic elements can be treated as resources that are used in order to accomplish certain communicative goals. Rather, the collectiveness of the assemblage makes it possible to pull into the same line of variation both linguistic and non-linguistic elements, both bodies and statements.
>
> Martín Bylund, 2018a, p.27

Western models of children's language acquisition often involve the isolation of word sounds from their wider soundscape, and word meanings from their complex relations with matter, sensation and affect (MacLure, 2013a). When curriculum documents in the UK refer to children's listening skills, for example, this is often underpinning by an assumed narrow Western conceptualization of listening, in which human words or instructions need to be foregrounded and other sounds that do not convey pedagogic priorities or specific symbolic meanings are meant to be filtered out (Gallagher et al., 2017; Gershon, 2011). In other words, this is a version of 'listening skills' that involves encouraging young children to attend to and tune in to human words in particular, blocking out or disregarding other sounds. Thus, this is an approach to listening (and speaking) in early childhood education that separates human from more-than-human, symbolic from non-symbolic, language from body and communication from place.

2. Purpose

She sits on a child-sized chair, watching P play nearby on the floor with the toy kitchen and food. As P plays, she vocalises things she needs her to fetch 'dut dut, oh, oh'. Each sound P makes instructs her to get up off the little chair and fetch a knife, fetch a spoon. She fetches P a knife, and P 'cuts' the Velcro wooden vegetables up. P rolls with a rolling pin, before declaring 'Cha-Pa-Ti.' She searches around the play kitchen and finds a piece of grey felt to bring. P finds a pan, and slaps her grey felt chapatti down into the pan. P uses her knife to flip the chapatti in the pan, saying a couple more times, in a very specific way 'Cha-Pa-Ti'.

Z and F play around on the rocks; there are seeds scattered across the rocks and over the ground. She guesses they are off the trees overhead. 'What are they, stones?' Z and F ask her. 'No, they look like seeds' she replies. Then Z and F begin shouting 'argh the seagulls are going to get us!' They run up and down around the rocks and back and forth to the trees. 'The seagulls! The seagulls!'

Inside day care, she and B play with the rice and containers, using spoons to put the rice into bottles. It is trickier than it looks! B plays happily and calmly, and then murmurs, out of the blue and under her breath, 'mummy's coming back'.

The vignettes above all have a different relationship with the notion of purpose, meaning and conveying of information through language. Sometimes young children's talk is intended to convey a need, give instructions or make a key point. However, in the examples throughout this chapter, there are also playful experimentations with how vocalizations can accompany other noises in the soundscape (such as the dabbing of a brush) and how seemingly unrelated words can sound similar (such as seeds and seagulls) and spark unexpected directions for play (see also Martín Bylund, 2018a; Laften, 2019). Words can reference children's deepest hopes and fears (such as mummy coming back), yet at the same time, Viruru (2001) reminds us that often that which is most important is left unsaid.

The notion that young children require a purpose and an audience in order to talk is threaded throughout early childhood policy and advice given to practitioners and parents in the West. In a conceptualization of children's language unique to the West (Avineri et al., 2015; Blum, 2016; Burman, 2008), it is assumed that children will not vocalize/talk unless adults make a particular effort to model or perform certain kinds of talk and demonstrate its functionality. When young children use a new word, or speak a word particularly clearly, adults are encouraged to praise them and direct attention towards the act. As Blum (in Avineri et al., 2015) points out, when Western middle-class adults address young children as conversational partners and are encouraged to reward them with attention and more words, 'these linguistic exchanges have no communicative function except to reward children with parents' approval for passing the test' (p.75). The notion of vocalizations being solely for the purpose of directing recognizable words at one or more other humans, for the purpose of conveying a fixed and specific piece of information, becomes its own self-fulfilling logic.

3. Audience

W sits on the grass playing playdoh. She can hear W sing song babbling under her breath as she plays.

P likes it very much in the sandpit. She uses the plastic spades to fill a bucket, before tipping it over like a sandcastle. However, the sand is very dry and fine, and does not keep its shape. After sand play, P sits on the table of a wooden bench and table set, whilst she brushes off her feet and puts her sandals on. Gazing at her feet, and the hands that brush away the sand, P vocalises 'mamamamamamamomomomomo ditiditiditiditiditi.'

Closely related to the question of the extent to which the purpose of language is always to convey information, is the question of audience. Perhaps the biggest shift needed in order to re-conceptualize early childhood language is that we, as adults, need to give up the conceit that young children's words are always for us, that we are always the intended audience. Secondly, even if we are part or all of the intended audience (see Figure 8.4), the purpose may not be to render interests, investments, hopes and desires to adults as clearly and transparently as possible.

The question 'are we the intended audience when young children talk?' does not have to involve a yes or no answer. Perhaps we are partially the intended audience. Perhaps we are welcome to be part of what is unfolding as long as

Figure 8.4 P in the Sandpit

we do not try to impose our own agenda. For Zembylas (2019), hospitality involves '*produc[ing]* a space in which the affective and material practice of *my* crossing is made possible'. What would it mean to think about becoming an invited audience for children's vocalizations as a hospitable act, one that creates vulnerabilities (Barad, 2019) as well as connections, rather than assuming that being the intended audience is a privilege to which we (adults) are automatically entitled?

In his distinction between interaction and correspondence, Ingold (2013, p.105–8) describes a process of moving along together, walking abreast with eyes of the horizon, rather than face to face 'in walking along together, companions share virtually the same visual field, whereas in face-to-face interaction ... stopped in their tracks, each blocking the other's path, they appear locked in a contest in which views are no longer shared but batted back and forth' (Ingold, 2013, p.106). This kind of consideration of gaze invites us to ask what kind of audience we might be invited to be. It encourages a nuanced interrogation of what is included and what is disregarded within children's talk. Are we interested in symbolic words being 'batted back and forth' or might we also consider the way in which human and more-than-human sounds entangle together, as we move along, walk abreast and gaze over to the horizon, now that we are not surrounded by four walls?

Conclusion

> Often, studies of child language tend to focus on how children's speech develops (in other words becomes more like adult language), rather than recognizing the complexities and integrity of the language and other forms of communication that children do use.
>
> Viruru, 2001, p.39

This chapter has begun to ask some speculative questions about frequently taken-for-granted assumptions around the nature and purpose of children's vocalizations and the (un)intended audiences for these contributions to the soundscape. A consideration of affective sensations involved in sounding with lips, throat and tongue, and what these sounds might activate (intentionally or unintentionally) in their widest sense, pushes an analysis of young children's talk and vocalizations beyond the transmission of information, or even the exchange of meaning. Rethinking young children's talk and vocalizations as something primarily bodily, rather than cognitive, may be a route to attending equally and non-hierarchically to the different kinds of vocalizations/talk young children make. By a non-hierarchical reading of young children's vocalizations, I mean establishing a lens through which non-linguistic vocalizations are not considered merely as a precursor to 'real' words. A hierarchy in which vocalizations that are clearly symbolic/recognizable/functional/in a familiar language are preferred or seen as the end goal, not only panders to the trope of human exceptionalism, but also continues to perpetuate a Cartesian body–mind split, by privileging reason and cognition over sensation and embodiment (Finnegan, 2002). As I have argued with colleagues elsewhere, models of literacy and language that do not disrupt mind–body splits '*always* end up by producing intense divisions and social inequalities' (Hackett et al., 2020a, p.5).

Approaches to language that emphasizes all words as intentional, meaningful, significant and the sole responsibility of the speaker can sometimes serve to curtail children's talk, particularly if young children are taught that the speaker 'alone bears the burden of her own speech' (Hackett et al., 2020b). Being asked to 'own' speech in this way, for adults and children alike, can cause anxiety, and often registers in the body, as stomachs churn and words seem to stick in the throat (Jones, 2013; Thiel, 2015b). Conversely, in my research, situations where children could use their voices collectively, playfully, and with little emphasis on intended recipient and correct message, often seemed to encourage more vocalizations. If human voices, and human meanings, are enabled by the vibrational, affective turbulence of sound (Gallagher et al., 2017), perhaps immersion in a rich sonic milieu is the most likely situation from which children may feel able to join in, to 'move with' language (Abram, 1996, p.83), to have their voices carried along and mingled with the sound and movement of the more-than-human world.

Part Three

Where Did We Get to?

Beyond Progress? What Is Lost and What Is Gained

E's mum becomes animated. "Yes!! Before kids have words, they use all these little gestures. And then, when they have the words, they stop using the gestures. And then you forget them, don't you." says E's mum

Towards the end of the fieldwork, I returned to playgroup on a beautiful sunny afternoon. I sat with Jo, a mum and a friend whose older children are the same age as mine; they were participants in my doctoral research and that is how we met, nine years before. Jo has K now, who is almost one year old, and they have been coming back to the playgroup. We sit with our feet in the sandpit (Figure 9.1). K sits in the sand between his mum's legs, and tries to stand up, pushing his weight through his legs but relying on Jo's arms for his balance. 'Do you remember the photo of [my daughter] in the sand?' Jo asks. I say it is my favourite. I remember that Jo, as co-researcher on a past project, took that photo of her middle daughter on a trip to the beach. It shows her staring out to sea, but it does not show the way in which her hands are buried in and moving through the sand. I have written about it (Hackett, 2017) and presented it so many times, it appears instantly in my mind's eye. K stands with feet flat on the ground and leans forward, looking intently at close range at what is below him; the sand, his shadow, his feet. He leans his face closer and closer as if to get a better look. Jo holds him strongly, otherwise he would face-plant into the sand. I remember when Jo and I (with others) wrote together about another sandpit (not far from where we are now), about sitting together with feet buried in sand, sharing snack and watching our children play (Hackett et al., 2018). We wrote about a sense that all of this was so important, so significant, even though we struggled to put into words why it is so crucial to tell about this (Somerville, 2013). I chat to Jo and make a video of K wriggling his toes in the sand, and lifting it between his fingers. He shoves some sand in his mouth, and looks unconcerned, as Jo and I try to pull it back out and brush the particles off his chin and cheek.

Figure 9.1 Sitting in the Sandpit

> Little experiences of shock, recognition, confusion and déjà vu pepper the most
> ordinary practices and moves. Sometimes you have to pause to catch up with
> where you already are.
>
> Stewart, 2007, p.63

Seeking to understand young children's language and literacy practices from a
starting point of place, community and everyday life, this book has described
a mundane politics playing out in community spaces of early childhood
(Chapter 4, this volume). I have noted the pervasiveness of literacy practices
that seem to resist the separation of the human from the more-than-human,
and children's preference for gestures and vocalizations that avoid fixing of
meanings, but instead hold open meaning as provisional or multiple. In my
discussion, I return again and again to that which is difficult to articulate, to
the glimmers and glimpses of a version of early childhood that seems to defy
the rational, subvert the functional, dwelling instead in moments of absorption,
body/place memory and affective flows. An account of early childhood language
and literacies capable of reckoning with all of this, an account of wild literacies,
requires paying attention in a different way. It would involve attending to what
happens between children, bodies and places when events are easy to explain
in words and have a clear purpose, together with those that seem to defy such

a rational account, as well as paying close attention to the interconnectedness between these things.

By dwelling in the intensities of everyday life with young children in community spaces, shaped by their own logics and affective flows, indivisible from body-place knowing (Chapter 1, this volume), this book challenges three key assumptions underpinning early childhood literacies;

1.   That young children's acquisition of *more* literacy practices *earlier*, is an unproblematic and apolitical goal.
2.   That nothing is lost, or risked, or given up when young children acquire literacies.
3.   That humans (particularly adults) are central to what it takes for young children to be(come) literate.

I suggest we (researchers, practitioners, teachers, parents) consider the possibility that there are place-based, bodily, community ways of knowing young children's literacy practices that fully embrace the complexities, gains and losses of changing language and body practices in the first few years of life, in a way that mainstream accounts of children's literacies, cannot. There is an excessiveness and a creativity to this messy process and particularly in the generative spaces that open up for adults and children when they attune to each other and to more-than-human place through bodies, gestures, movement and vocalizations, as much as through analysis, logic and carefully articulated words.

What Is Lost?

As Viruru pointed out nearly two decades ago:

> Acquiring language is often perceived as a crucial tool in the growth of young children; however, the question is rarely asked, what is lost when language is gained.
>
> Viruru, 2001, p.31

E's mum, in the vignette opening this chapter, reflects on what is lost as she watches her two-year-old's practices change. 'When E doesn't want to do something, she tells me, she just says "no" now, but she used to cling onto my leg in a particular way.' 'Oh yes' joins in G's mum, E's auntie, 'G puts his hands over his ears in a certain way, and it means he is worried about something.' The meanings of gestures might be secret, an intimate knowledge known only between family members. They might be frequently repeated (such as E's gestures for saying no), or they might happen unexpectedly (such as J-as-cat in Chapter 6). They might have a specificity, only used in certain contexts or with certain people. They might not have a clear representational meaning, but rather be an experiment with what a certain vocalization or movement might activate in the world (Chapter 6, this volume).

Over twenty years ago, Kress wrote:

> In learning to read and write, children come as thoroughly experienced makers of meaning, as experienced makers of signs in any medium that is to hand.
>
> Kress, 1997, p.8.

Kress's book *Before Writing* emphasized the risk that an increased or too early emphasis on reading and writing would come at the cost of children's proficiency in other modes, such as making, drawing and movement. In the intervening years, the field of early childhood literacy has unpicked certain assumptions underpinning this work, such as the assumption that children's meaning making usually involves intentional pre-design (Kuby et al., 2015), or that multimodal meaning making is the sole preserve of human actants (Hackett and Rautio, 2019). However, the point remains that when young children are not talking, or reading or writing, they are not doing 'nothing', but rather their movements, energies and playful experimentations are invested elsewhere.

The question of what is lost when language and literacies are gained is an essential if inconvenient question, if we are to conceptualize wild, more-than-human literacies. Answering it may require paying attention in a different way (Tsing, 2015). By beginning this chapter by drawing attention to what is lost, I intend to highlight early childhood literacies as a messy, complex, contradictory and experimental process of young children's sounding and movement in places and with things. Thus, it is not merely of process of iterative gain or accumulation of, for example, words, or skills, or multimodal proficiencies. As Viruru (2001) argues above, one way of being in the world always supplants other concrete or virtual possibilities (Burnett and Merchant, 2018). These choices are always political rather than neutral, involving a moving towards or away from what is proposed (Millei and Kallio, 2018). When young children seem to reject the agenda of individualized linear development carefully laid out for them (in, for example, curriculum and policy documents), perhaps they know what sometimes we adults run the risk of forgetting; *the emergence of early childhood literacies is not merely a progress narrative.* This chapter, therefore, explores what it might mean to conceptualize early childhood literacies beyond a linear, unidirectional progress narrative (Tsing, 2015). It begins this work by urging the reader to consider seriously, what is lost as well as what is gained when young children's language and literacy practices change over time. When, for example, words begin to more frequently replace, accompany or adapt gestures, glances, a reach, a point, a groan or a tug, as literacy practices. Dwelling in those moments of being under thirty-six months when words are not central – can we take the following question seriously; *what is lost, what is gained and what is risked as literacy and language practices change during early childhood?*

More Words? Earlier?

> If being a child or a stranger is a fugitive stage of life with specific opportunities, one might ask what specific knowledge or skill it is that a person loses in the processes of growing up or learning a language/conquering estrangement.
>
> Martín Bylund, 2018a, p.2

In the quote above, Martín Bylund (2018a) emphasizes that encountering a language for the first time and knowing it intimately are two modes of being, each with their own possibilities, rather than a fixed hierarchy in which familiarity is superior to unfamiliarity. Viruru's (2001) original ethnographic research in early years classrooms in India raised the question of whether the acquisition of language in young children was really the apolitical and linear process it is often assumed to be. Thus, it is important to disrupt the imaginary of early childhood literacies as a straight line, upward-trajectory-accumulation of an increasing number of useful 'tools'. Chapter 3 (this volume) traced some of wider scholarship highlighting the possibilities that lie in silences (Ivinson, 2018; Viruru, 2001), modes of expression not intended to transmit information (Ingold, 2013; MacLure, 2016) and language gaps (Vladimirova, 2018), all of which help to question and unpick the dogma that more words, as quickly as possible, is unquestionably better.

Expressing oneself verbally always 'exists within traditions and hegemony' (Viruru, 2001, p.32), in which dominant forms of speaking and dominant languages command the most power. At the same time, the investment in speech as the premier or only way to express what matters in the world is an explicitly Western cultural position (Avineri et al., 2015). Writing about the relationship between global languages, colonialism, power and capital, Phipps (2019) describes moments during her research when she was in too much pain to speak as creating a deep connection that disrupted power relationships between her and her colleagues. Colonial languages, dominant ways of structuring speech and even what is explicated and what is left unsaid, create and reproduce hierarchies of power (Phipps, 2019; Viruru, 2001; Walkerdine and Lucey, 1989). Across different scales and in different contexts, language and literacies can work to solidify or fix the order of the world (MacLure, 2016). This fixing can play into existing power structures, silence the experiences of some, or make too raw, public or explicit the experiences of others. 'Imposing speech in a situation where it did not belong' (Viruru, 2001, p.34) might reframe pain or expose trauma anew (Ivinson, 2018; Viruru, 2001). Particular kinds of power positions can be occupied or validated (Phipps, 2019); relationships (human and more-than-human) more tightly explicated in ways that can narrow possibilities or close down connections (MacLure, 2016).

Scholars have also traced the creation, reproduction and fixing of hierarchies of knowledge in early childhood classrooms, where, for example, certain kinds of talk, or talk in particular kinds of contexts, can create or affirm power relations between adults and children (Arculus and Macrae, 2020). Stripping back words in early childhood classrooms can sometimes create more inclusive spaces, in which children feel more comfortable to participate through both movement and talk, and in which adult practitioners felt less pressure to constantly perform and interact (Hackett et al., 2020b; Holmes et al., 2019; Martín Bylund, 2018a; Olsson, 2012; Pitt and Arculus, 2018).

Thinking back over the vignettes that pepper this book, all of which I have selected because of a certain kind of intensity, significance or affective flow that seemed to shimmer from these moments, we might ask: Where are words and where is silence? What is happening to power relations and how fixed/reduced/ordered are the meanings being exchanged between human and more-than-human bodies? In Chapter 1, M mutters 'mmmmmmmm' to himself whilst eating cheese, and then wordlessly tips milk splatters over the floor and begins to play with them. In Chapter 3, R traces a line of clouds with his whole arm, and vocalizes 'wooooooooow'. In Chapter 4, T silently rolls playdoh into 'wiggly worms' and in Chapter 5, D presses his cheek lovingly against the wet grass of the small hill. What kinds of relations, with both other humans and the more-than-human world, are opened up, closed down, reframed and fixed into place, in these instances? Vocalizations, words that clearly describe or name, silent attunements, gestures or movement can all activate different things in any given time/place. A careful attending to what these different modes of world-making

(Hackett and Somerville, 2017) do, will enable different questions to be asked about how to care, attend to and nurture what happens in the moment.

For Abram (1996), habitual ways of talking about or being silent in and with the natural world, shaped possibilities for noticing animacy and hearing non-human languages. Joks et al. (2020) make a similar argument in their discussion of the problematics of translating between Sami and Norwegian words; languages that are grounded in different ontologies and thus 'enacts different versions of what it is to know'. *How we communicate with and about the world changes our relationship with it.* In other words, how individuals choose to name the world (Somerville and Powell, 2018), answer the world (Hackett and Rautio, 2019; Ingold, 2013), the extent to which silence is filled with words, the modes chosen for communication, and what they do in terms of fixing meaning and relations into place has profound consequences. Words are powerful; this is not a call to reject words, but to treat them with respect and carefully interrogate what effect their presence or absence might be having in community spaces of early childhood, rather than greedily and anxiously gathering as many of them as possible as quickly as we can.

Thinking Early Childhood Literacies beyond Progress

The equation of 'time on task' and efficient use of time with increased and faster learning has a long history (Compton-Lilly, 2016, Pacini-Ketchabaw, 2012). As Jones and colleagues point out, narratives of time as linear and progressive are evoked in notions such as 'developmentalism, organizing education by age and for specific periods of time, emphases on "time on task" and "progress," predicting students' potential based on past performances, etc.' (Jones et al., 2016, p.1129).

Just as the notion of 'language' is deeply entangled with powerful rhetoric of the special nature of human species (Finnegan, 2002), time as 'progress' is tightly plaited into the notion of human life as special, as distinct from other life (Springgay and Truman, 2019; Tsing, 2015). Calling for different configurations of time in order to break habitual ways of thinking about learning, Springgay and Truman (2019) point out that whiteness, heteronormativity and colonialism all rely on progressive or chronological time. Tsing (2015) describes how terms such as 'intent', 'agency' and 'consciousness' (note the centrality of all of these terms to mainstream accounts of young children's literacy practices, that we have been interrogating throughout the book) are drawn upon to create a narrative in which, 'humans are different from the rest of the living world because we look forward – while other species, which live day to day, are thus dependent on us' (Tsing, 2015, p.21).

Progress, as defined by Tsing (2015), is a unified coordination of time. As I described in Chapter 1, child development is often understood as a generalizable and linear line of progress, however:

> In order to compare, to chart a generalized line of progress, it is essential to discard that which is not deemed relevant to the comparison … The ordinary experiences of those who spend time with children, particularly women, particularly women in powerless positions, must often therefore be disregarded, in order to maintain the truth and power of the line.
>
> (Chapter 1, this volume).

I argued earlier in this book that this erasure gives an incomplete picture, missing aspects of life with young children and families that are actually deeply significant to the lived experiences of those involved. In addition, I have shown how this is a political position; separating parenting from its material conditions (Trafi-Prats, 2019) makes it possible to blame and marginalize parents and practitioners for 'failing' to produce children who stick to and follow neatly along those linear trajectories. However, more than this, by disrupting and smudging the neat line of progress (Tsing, 2015), early childhood research might disrupt a much larger project, about the special nature of humanity, together with its assumed mastery and autonomy from the rest of the more-than-human world, enacted through tropes of agency, intentionality and being forward looking.

For Tsing (2015), breaking habitual ways of thinking about time involves noticing the narratives that exist beyond 'promise and ruin' (p.18). Giving the example of the progress of the railroad across Northern America, Tsing describes the progress narrative of the advancing railroad bringing improvement and civilization (promise). The counter narrative would be one of the consequent destruction of the forest, what the railroad has destroyed. This is the 'ruin' narrative, which Tsing argues is not enough because 'what it shares with the first, however, is the assumption that the trope of progress is sufficient to know the world, both in success and failure. The story of decline offers no leftovers, no excess, nothing that escapes progress. Progress still controls us even in tales of ruination' (Tsing, 2015, p.21).

Reading Tsing's narrative about the forest and the matsutake mushroom, thriving unexpectedly in former North American timber plantations as an example of 'life in this ruin' (p.6), my mind returns to the carpeted floor of the playgroup during singing time at the start of Chapter 1, to my feet buried in the sandpit at the start of this chapter. Living up to the intensity, complexity and vibrancy of these moments in community spaces of early childhood requires more than neat linear narratives of child development, but equally it requires more than resistance. In other words, how to think beyond *promise and ruin*?

Urging us to pay attention to 'unruly edges' and 'unpredictable encounters' which dominant forces 'refuse to acknowledge' (Tsing, 2015, p.22), Tsing advises 'look[ing] around rather than ahead' (p.22). Thus, imagining early childhood literacies beyond a progress narrative could involve starting with lived everyday experiences, and what unfolds between children, families and more-than-human worlds. The smear of saliva, the sand between the toes, represent the excess, the leftovers, that which escapes and precedes and denies the hegemony of the truth of the narrow linear line of child development (Chapter 1, this volume), of progress. Tsing (2015) calls attending to these excessive and escaping aspects of life 'arts of noticing' (p.37).

> How do gatherings sometimes become 'happenings', that is, greater than the sum of their parts?
>
> Tsing, 2015, p.23

Offering the notion of the assemblage to help us to look around, to notice how things are connected and what has been overlooked, Tsing describes the study of assemblages as the study of things 'coming together' (p.23), becoming more than the sum of their parts. Tsing calls these 'happenings'. In some ways, the noticing of things becoming more than the sum of their parts, in any given moment, parallels Stewart's (2007) interest in the way in which things 'pick up densities and textures' (p.3) until 'something throws itself together in the moment' (p.1). Drawing on Tsing's (2015) work to reimagine place literacies in her own fieldwork, Thiel (2020) describes Manuel, a little boy who draws effusively with a red pen:

> Manuel's drawings are much like the matsutake, emerging despite a hyper capitalist mesh of pedagogy, policy, and practice that produce Manuel as a body to be commodified, one that must be made "college and career ready" through early learning initiatives.
>
> Thiel, 2020, p.71

As Thiel (2020) demonstrates, a particular challenge for researchers and practitioners working with young children is to notice what unfolds in the moment beyond binaries of literacy/not literacy, meaning making/not meaning making, relevant to the research/not relevant. These binaries feed into narratives of 'promise and ruin' (Tsing, 2015) in early childhood, and disrupting them always involves 'looking around not forward', that is, thinking beyond progress. Inspired by Tsing (2015) and by Thiel (2020), I turn now to a vignette from my own research, in order to 'look around' and try to describe literacies that fall outside narratives of promise and ruin.

Noticing Unruly Edges

H arrives at playgroup a little late, she doesn't see him to say hello until he is sat on the little chair at the little table for snack, which has been dragged outside into the sunshine this week. Children have eaten their fruit slices and waffles pieces ('what did they think of the waffles?' 'No, not keen ….'). Now snack is finished and just H is left sitting there. H looks intensely up at the blue sky several times. She notices, looks up too, tries to figure out what he is looking at. H notices her following his gaze.

H looks again, gestures towards the sky, perhaps he traces a line with his arm. Suddenly H stands up from his seat, and chants backwards from ten to one. She says 'blast off' because H has got to zero, and this seems to make them both look up to the sky, imagining the rocket.

H looks upwards again, he says 'ahhhhhh' and looks at the sky. She still does not see, she looks up, feels bashful, she does not see.

Finally she notices the aeroplane tracks in the sky. Oh 'is it the aeroplane, they are blast off, wow!' words gabble out of her mouth. Then she falls silent and they pause together; perhaps there is a moment, not so much of agreeing and fixing a meaning, but of not being quite so lost and apart from each other in terms of what they are attuning too.

Blue chalks lie on the floor. The same intense sort of blue as the sky, though she does not notice this until later. H gestures towards the chalk, she picks one up and tries to draw an aeroplane with chunky blue chalk on the uneven concrete. It does not look like an aeroplane. But it has a sense of the intensity of the blue chalk and of multiple lines going in the same direction as each other.

H also picks up and draws with the blue chalk, thick blue lines, all in the same direction, one next to the other to form a thick band of blue.

'They go zoom' she says and adds lines of movement from the front of her 'plane' forward, and the same on H's picture. H stares at the blue, he gestures upwards and gazes at the sky.

Figure 9.2 Aeroplane Tracks in the Blue Sky

The vignette of H and the aeroplane tracks offers a chance to notice narratives of 'promise and ruin', and then to try to think beyond them, to 'look around' at the unruly edges (see Figure 9.2). Reading the vignette as literacy scholars, we might want to ask – is this an example of multimodal meaning making or not? Did H intend to communicate something about his interests, or what he noticed in the sky? And if so, can we describe that communication as sophisticated, competent, surprising, frequently overlooked by other research lenses, a possibly generative future direction for pedagogy, and so on and so forth? The narrative of promise. Or we can describe what unfolded as frustrating, a missed opportunity. Such a shame he did not vocalize, or that she was not more pedagogically effective. A vignette that offers no clear enough evidence of multimodal competency, it is really 'nothing' (Chapter 5, this volume). A familiar narrative from the ruins of growing up in a post-industrial northern town.

By the end of the above vignette, H and I had been making marks, gesturing and (I have been) using words for several minutes, yet the meaning of the words, the gestures, the blue chalk lines, still did not seem to be fixed or agreed (see Figure 9.3). They felt productively *unfixed*. H and I seemed closely attuned to each other, and to a sense of a something, a certain kind of intensity. H still had not confirmed whether this intensity, for him, had anything to do with aeroplanes, or rockets, or even with the track lines across the blue sky. Perhaps all of that was conjecture, or a rush to fixing meaning,

Figure 9.3 Drawing with the Blue Chalks

on my part. Yet I felt as though we both shared a sense of the blue-ness, and of some kind of line of movement forward and across. A movement forward and across could be traced through the gaze to the sky, the gesturing arm, the long declaration of 'ahhhhhh', the mutual sweeps of the blue chalk. Phipps (2019) describes something similar when she talks about gathering the 'gist' in conversations with those she did not share a common language. Instead of clear meanings, there is something of an atmosphere, a sense of connection that can still powerfully keep things in motion. Stewart's description of a net is perhaps a productive way to describe how meaning emerged, in little pieces and provisionally, as possibilities with trajectories, during my encounter with H and the aeroplane lines. She writes:

> It's as if a net has grown around a mutating gelatinous substance. It's also as if the net is full of holes, so that little pieces or whole blobs of things are always falling out of it and starting up some new thing in their own. It harbors fantasies and fears. It spawns trajectories.
>
> Stewart, 2007, p.88

In order to understand young children's multimodal literacies as productively unfixed, as a net full of holes and spawning trajectories, new ways of thinking about time, cause and effect are required, and how human intentionality can(not) operate within conceptualizations of wild literacies.

Scalability, Alienation and Attending to Unruly Edges

In common with many of the examples in this book, meaning in the above vignette seems to be stubbornly, productively unfixed, seeming to shimmer in and out of view, or, to draw on Stewart's analogy, as small pieces of signification falling through a net and seeming to spawn something greater than the sum of their parts. One way in which contingently agreed meanings might be productive is because they are not scalable; that is, they do not translate to other contexts, or to being reproduced at other times, or even to being described in confident or persuasive terms by a researcher after the event (such as I am attempting to do here). For Tsing (2015), scalability is a central tenet of the progress narrative, closely associated with capitalism, as well as being a required feature of knowledge if it is to be regarded as scientific. Tsing points out that 'scalability is not an ordinary feature of nature' (p.38), but rather must be created; it takes a lot of work to generate 'self-contained, interchangeable project elements' (p.39). Drawing on an example of Portuguese sugar cane plantations in Brazil, Tsing points out that scalability is achieved by alienation, that is, the isolation of both the sugar cane plants (clones with few interspecies relations locally) and the labour working on the plantations (enslaved Africans without local social relations).[1] In contrast, the matsutake mushroom cannot be cultivated or transplanted, although it relies on the ruins of scalable production (in the timber plantations) to flourish. As meaning, however provisionally constituted, emerges between me, H, aeroplane tracks, blue sky and blue chalks in the vignette above, it is inseparable from the more-than-human milieu. It makes no sense when extracted from its material context. It makes more sense when I try to explain it at the playgroup, than when I try to explain to you here on these pages. It is a form of knowing that resists being extracted from place (Watts, 2013, also see Chapter 1, this volume). Literacies that are difficult to evidence, to confirm, to codify, then, disrupt the project of education as the production of future economic citizens (Thiel, 2020) and narratives of child development as a predictable and controllable linear process (Chapter 1, this volume).

Thus, looking for non-scalability and non-alienation may be a starting point for a description of young children's literacies that disrupts the progress narrative (Tsing, 2015). While careful to point out that it is important not to assume that the scalable is always bad and the non-scalable always good, Tsing does argue that 'the nonscalable becomes an impediment' to progress, and therefore can be 'incitements to theory' (p.38). In Chapter 1 (this volume), I asked what we might learn about young children's literacy practices by starting with the ordinary in communities. Many of the vignettes that have emerged throughout this book, in response to this question, seem to act as 'incitements to theory' in the sense that they demonstrate pervasive and dominant features of the experience of being and being with young children in communities, that seem to be overlooked or insufficiently accounted for in dominant narratives of early childhood literacy. In other words, they demand new theories. Examples might include, when young children's literacy practices do not seem to involve an adult audience, when meanings and interpretations seem to shimmer into and out of view, when energies are invested in movements with bodies or things that do not carry a functional purpose, or when vocalizations and gestures are almost impossible to transcribe, describe or reproduce. Many of these overlooked characteristics of young children's literacies in communities resist scalability (because they are difficult to describe in words or attribute a logic too) and alienation (because they make more sense in that place or time than they do anywhere else). Perhaps Tsing (2015) might call these the 'unruly edges' of literacies.

Parenting Entangled with the World

Whilst I was writing this book, the Department for Education in the UK launched a new initiative off the back of a survey finding that many parents were not teaching their children the alphabet, numbers, how to read words or poems and nursery rhymes at home before the age of five years (Nursery World, 2019). The media headline for this initiative was 'thousands of children not learning at home'. The new initiative was launched with a video of Natasha Kaplinsky and Emma Kenny modelling 'how to chat, play and read' to your child at home.

She plays the video on her laptop. Dressed in a white shirt, blow dry and perfect make up, Natasha brandishes a sieve and a wooden spoon whilst vigorously agreeing with Emma that, despite being mothers with busy lives, there are strategies to make home learning really simple. 'You can point out the colour of the birds, you can talk about the different trees, you can go on a nature trail .....'

As I described in Chapter 1 (this volume), dominant conceptualizations of what it is like to parent young children often bear little relation to reality. At the same time, measures of academic achievement for young children frequently operate by 'papering over a long history of socio-economic marginalization of communities' (Nxamalo, 2020, p.166). As Burman (2008) points out, 'the child-centred approach ... sets up further means for the regulation of women', exhorting them to 'convert household labour into educational opportunities' (p.210). Notions of parents as responsible for the 'proper' socialization of their children, and for teaching as much as possible, as early as possible, play into a progress narrative (Tsing, 2015), via the route of meritocracy (Littler, 2018); families and children who put in enough effort, this narrative (false)promises, can accelerate faster along the linear trajectory of progress.

This is a seductive dream; yet in her book *Cruel Optimism*, Berlant (2011) warns of the potential damage when 'something you desire is actually an obstacle to your flourishing' (p.1). Writing, similarly, about notions of 'the good life', Stewart writes:

> Sometimes the scene of a finished life appears like a beautiful figure on the horizon. For a minute, it's like a snapshot hangs suspended in the air while we watch, wide-eyed. But a little detail out of place can be a telltale sign of something terrible wrong. Or just funny, quirky, a boink in the perfect scene. We're drawn simultaneously to the amazing bubble image and to all the ordinary affects that animate it and pull it apart.
>
> Stewart, 2007, p.77

The scene of 'finished life like a beautiful figure on the horizon' and the damage it can do puts me in mind of the Dick and Jane extracts that run through the novel *The Bluest Eye* (Morrison, 1994) like a haunting refrain. 'Here is the family. Mother, Father, Dick and Jane live in the green-and-white house. They are very happy' (Morrison, 1994, n.p.); in the shadow of the Dick and Jane family, key protagonists in *The Bluest Eye* struggle with trauma, poverty, dis-function, alcoholism and abuse, until the heroine Percola is driven mad by her desire for blue eyes (and the privileged life with which they are associated). The polished vision of the 'good life' (Berlant, 2011; Stewart, 2007), the perfect children with the bluest eyes who live in the beautiful house, or the false promise that children's school readiness relies mostly on a parent with a perfect blow dry brandishing a wooden spoon. These things can serve to erase structural inequalities (Dyson, 2015; Gillies, 2007), and the whiteness of the educational project (Nxamalo and Brown, 2020; Patel, 2014; Tarc, 2015), together with the differential investments, dreams and traumas that materialize in the daily lives of families and communities. As Littler (2018) points out, meritocracy is deeply problematic in the way in which it retains a commitment to the notion of hierarchy, whilst assuming a model of individuality and competition.[2] 'The American dream comes into a sharp-edged focus. There are only winners and losers now' (Stewart, 2007, p.93).

She is having a tough day today, too close to Christmas, it's emotional. She tries to wrap presents, can't fit the wrapping paper back in the drawer where the wrapping paper is supposed to be stored. So, she begins pulling items out of the drawer, spilling them over the floor. Why is there so much random crap in this drawer?

Her little girl, N, approaches.
'What are you doing?
Can I help?
Can I have these headphones?
But can I?
Can I just try them?'
She asks her to stop nagging, but N persists, until she cracks, snaps, start crying, N starts crying too. She stomps upstairs, slams about then shuts herself in her room, trying to steady her breath, feeling a panic attack threatening. It's too close to Christmas, when her friend died just over a month ago. Downstairs N sobs and dad steps in to help. Even in the midst of her grief she lives out her privilege – caring, capable partner makes up for her own weakness, her momentary slip.

The weeks after my close friend (and collaborator) Lisa Procter died, I never felt more human, more deeply entangled with the fabric of my emotions, my life, with others. I had never experienced a bereavement like that before. I began fieldwork for this project two months later. Exhausted, anxious, over-emotional, conscious of how tenuously and provisionally things were holding together in my life, how far I was from the vision of the 'ideal mother'. I had never been further. An 'ideal mother' would not have a friend who died. An 'ideal mother' certainly would not let this impinge on magical Christmas preparations, or allow her small child to see her crack and snap and break.

> *'Remember, you are your babies' first teacher .....Whenever you have playtime or spare time, just think about reading a book'. Emma Kenny and Natasha Kaplinsky tell us.*

How many other parents, right now, are snapping, cracking, not through their weakness, but through their strength, through their deep entanglement with, and care for their world and the people and places in it (Mayes et al., 2019; Walkerdine, 2017)? In continuing to perpetuate the myth of the progress narrative of early childhood development, together with its relationship to meritocracy, what dream, what vision, what strangely emotion-free, un-invested, un-affected version of what it means to be in the world are we offering children as a model? In a context of the global rise of the far right and the precarious environmental future children are inheriting, continuing to invest in the individual cognitive development of individual children, in order to give them a headstart navigating an increasingly unrealistic and competitive education system,[3] seem inadequate, immoral and dangerous. The need to dismantle the myth of 'ideal parent/child/ teacher', and the accompanying justification of racing to socialize children into the literacy and language practices that carry the most educational capital as quickly as possible, has never felt more urgent. I contend that these damaging and pathologizing myths are reliant on a progress narrative of early childhood.

All of this gives a particular significance to moments when a straightforward, meritocratic, un-conflicted model of being and being with young children seems real, or at least feasible. And all the moments when it doesn't work, and the perfect scene strains at the seams; perhaps we try to dismiss it with humour, or as a mistake, a glitch in the system (Chapter 4, this volume). 'We will try again tomorrow' we tell ourselves, 'perhaps tomorrow we can *get it just right*'. When asking 'what can we learn about young children's literacy practices by starting with the everyday in communities?' (Chapter 1, this volume) perhaps part of the answer is an insight into 'the ordinary affects that animate [a perfect scene] and pull it apart' (Stewart, 2007, p.77). These moments when the glitches in the perfect scene are exposed may be painful, or create vulnerabilities, yet perhaps they operate *as* the 'unruly edges' (Tsing, 2015), offering an opportunity to rupture the progress narrative. Perhaps those ruptures might be the route to reclaiming aspects of being and being with young children that have been erased in dominant narratives of early childhood, erased in order to maintain the 'truth' of linear, predictable development (Chapter 1, this volume).

The contradictions and compromises of everyday lives of families and young children are mirrored in the false starts, uncertainties, moments of connection and disconnect and jams in the desiring machine (Chapter 5, this volume) involved in early childhood literacies, as I have attempted to describe them in this book. Thus, these 'unruly edges' of what unfolds between children, places and things are not only necessary in order to understand the experiences of families without pathologizing them or holding them to unrealistic idealized standards (Chapter 1, this volume) but are essential for tracing the nature of the generative and ongoing emergence of literacy practices in young children's lives.

Conclusion

This chapter has offered a counter to some of the assumptions underpinning dominant accounts of early childhood literacies, namely that the acquisition of more literacies early is an unproblematic and apolitical goal which involves only gains and not losses. Instead, I argued for a more careful attending to the presence or absence of spoken words, to the greater or lesser degrees to which meanings can solidify or slip-slide out of view again. Countering the greedy and anxious gathering of as many words as quickly as possible, then, enables a noticing of the plaiting together of time, progress and intentionality in narratives of learning. Looking beyond the trope of progress (Tsing, 2015) for what persists in the lives of young children and families *in spite of* progress narratives could, I suggest, take the form of foregrounding everyday moments and intensities that are non-scalable and resist extraction from place. For parents and professionals who work with young children, the question is not so much how to accelerate children's literacies as quickly as possible along a linear trajectory, but to ask ourselves what mode of being-in-the-world we wish to convey to young children and involve them in. The assumption that human adults are central to what it takes for young children to become literate not only overlooks children's deep entanglement with places, things, objects and atmospheres, it also assumes a particular kind of sanitized adult, capable themselves of being extracted from place, community, pain, stress, trauma and affective flows.

Throughout this book, I have tried to understand the emergence of literacy differently, as something that relies on randomness (Rautio, 2019), its entanglement with the more-than-human (Hackett and Somerville, 2017), and on not-literacies and false starts (Chapter 5, this volume). I opened this book with an insistence on beginning with the ordinary and the everyday, on the importance of refusing to separate any consideration of early childhood literacies from the lived material conditions of parenting and living in communities. This final part of the book is concerned with the stories we tell about early childhood and literacies, asking how we can imagine young children's literacies beyond narratives of individual development, competence and accumulation.

Literacies Yet-to-Come

Then the next thing we read – the next word, the next sentence, the next article – crumbles the stability, deterritorializing that space, what we thought we might know, might someday be able to know. Caught again in the stream, the current grows faster.

Bridges-Rhoads and Van Cleave, 2017, p.307

Bridges-Rhoads and Van Cleave (2017) write about a felt sense that something is missing and must shift, in the midst of an increasingly standardized, narrow early childhood literacy curricula, backed up by the powerful certainty of dominant accounts of early childhood literacies. 'There are gated communities,' write Jones et al. (2014), 'walled gardens, and, worryingly, mighty fortresses protected by walls of certainty. They are well connected by roads, drawing straight lines of causality from A to B' (p.65). It can be hard to resist the flow as 'the current grows faster' (Bridges-Rhoads and Van Cleave, 2017, p.307). At the same time, Tsing (2015) reminds us that progress has stopped making sense; for children growing up into a future not defined by progress, finding ways to notice the alternatives, seems urgent:

> All this only raises the stakes for asking what else is going on – not in some protected enclave, but rather everywhere.
>
> Tsing, 2015, p.61

The title of this chapter is 'literacies yet-to-come' – which I mean in several senses. Firstly, young children are frequently seen as practice-ers of emergent literacies, as filled with yet-to-be-fulfilled potential. Research has looked for children's nearly-there literacies in their practices of ordering and labelling the world, in examples of design of multimodal signs as a parallel to the process of writing (Kress, 1997) and in young children's attunement to the already-here literacy practices of adult humans (Gillen and Hall, 2013).

Throughout this book, I have expanded on three propositions I made in Chapter 1. The literacy and language practices of young children are best traced by paying attention to how bodies move and sound in place (proposition 1). Within the affective flows and intensities of moving sounding bodies, collective, provisional, situated and inchoate meanings (proposition 3) might glimmer into and out of view within more-than-human assemblages (proposition 2). Whilst there is a strong critique against seeing children merely as pre-literate (Flewitt, 2013), young children's literacy practices *are* different between twelve and thirty-six months (compared to older or younger humans) and tend to change fast (Chapter 5, this volume). As I pointed out in Chapter 5, more fleshed out accounts of exactly what is and is not encompassed by the term 'emergent literacies' would enable a better interrogation of how inclusions and exclusions from the category of 'literacy' might play into or disrupt notions of young children as more or less 'adult like' or 'animalistic'. Thus, my first activation of 'literacies yet-to-come' is to ask a question about what does and does not tend to happen with young children's literacy practices, viewing this as a messy and complicated process of both gain and loss (Chapter 9, this volume) shaped by spatio-temporal, more-than-human flows.

A second reading of 'literacies yet-to-come', in the context of increasingly globalized world, accompanied by the rise of the far right and environmental instability and crisis, is to ask about the future of early childhood literacies. We can only speculate on the kinds of world young children will live in and with when they are adults. Young children's futures, then, may well involve or require different kinds of literacy practices compared to present-day adults. Writing twenty-five years ago, Kress (1997) wondered what kinds of future literacy practices would be useful in a digital globalized world. Mirroring this argument in our current context, I wonder what kinds of practices, skills, habits and ways of being might be most relevant in the precarious future the planet faces (Chapter 3). Early childhood literacy practices could/can, for example, emphasize or erase humanities' inter-connectedness with and dependency on the more-than-human world (MacLure, 2016), reproduce or disrupt racialized hierarchical categories of human life (Truman, 2019a), or offer (trans)language as a fluid experimentation rather than a bounded object closely connected to nationhood (Gurney and Demuro, 2019). I invite the reader to wonder, with me, which is these possibilities are desirable, generative, which might enable children of an 'Earth to Come' (Rousell et al., 2017) to exist and perhaps even to thrive in 'pockets of more-than-human livability' (Tsing, 2015).

Thirdly, I have tried in this book to explore literacies as productively unfixed, as both potential and actualized, setting into motion meanings that can be multiple, provisional or dependant on how they seem to work in the moment. Gestures, body movements, arrangements of objects or vocalizations can convey multimodal meanings, but at the same time, can be productively viewed as (not)literacies. By this I mean, understood as unfolding meanings that often instantiate in the moment, or temporarily, or with a greater or lesser degree of confidence (Chapter 5, this volume). This might be about negotiating permission or position (Chapter 6), or exploring what a word or movement might or might not activate in the world (Chapter 8). Paying attention more widely to entanglements and intensities between children and the world, and how they do or do not tip into meaning or literacies in deliberate or unexpected ways, is one more starting point for thinking about literacies-yet-to-come.

In Chapter 7, I discussed the many examples of children's intense connection to things and the ways in which these connections exceeded functionality. For children living in the Western world, this kind of investment in the animacy of their special objects involves a simultaneous holding together of different truths (Horton, 2018). My youngest daughter has a special bear, Ivey (Figure 10.1), who is deeply loved and viewed (by my daughter) as having her own needs and perspectives, yet when an adult tries to treat Ivey as animate, they will be told reprovingly 'it's only a cuddly!'. It can be tempting to characterize this holding together of contradictory or multiple positions are childishness; yet this characterization relies on a false vision of adult humans as rational, detached, uncontradictory (Tuck, 2010). This colonial move to treat childhood as a metaphor for the irrational or incapable (Mills and LeFranscois, 2018) mirrors a more general tendency of social science research to draw unjustified distinctions between truth and myth, between knowledge and belief (Watts, 2013). Stengers writes of 'the "great divide" refrain – they believe, we know' (Stengers, 2008, p.42).

Scholars across the social sciences have explored speculative storytelling as a mode that allows us to 'suspend disbelief about change' (Stirling et al., 2019), and as a 'mode of resistance' (Nxamalo and Ross, 2020), a way of articulating alternative desires for children and childhoods. Whilst speculative storytelling is not neutral (Truman, 2019b), Nxumalo and Ross (2019) see it as offering 'creative possibilities for movement away from instrumentalist, already-known approaches to teaching and learning young children' (p.508). Throughout most of this book, I have relied on careful attending to and describing what unfolds between children, families, places and things in everyday scenarios as a way of

Figure 10.1 Ivey: Simultaneously Animate and 'Only a Cuddly'

drawing attention to that which is commonly overlooked or erased. In this final short chapter, I draw inspiration from speculative storytelling as an alternate way to trouble the taken-for-granted assumptions about being and being with young children in communities, and to gesture towards the multiple immanent possibilities for literacies yet-to-come.

Material Conditions for Nurture and Growth

In an imagined future in which climate crisis has acerbated racial tensions to the point that few black families find it safe to send their children to mainstream schools, Nxumalo and Ross (2019) offer a speculative story about early childhood education. At a cadre called 'Wild Seed', Nyawela teaches a small group of children about relations with the more-than-human world. At Wild Seed, education is explicitly politically engaged, rather than seeking to maintain an imagined neutrality. As I discussed in Chapter 4, this notion of the neutral and apolitical is closely connected to the maintenance of a particular white colonial conceptualization of childhood as inherently innocent and in need a protection (Nxumalo and Brown, 2020). Within Nxumalo and Ross's speculative story, different kinds of childhood, particularly black childhoods, are affirmed, in which children can be high spirited, playful and resistant. They can hold political opinions, get angry, respond, love, hate, desire and tease. Whilst some of this takes place through words, awareness of and remembering of facts, this is also a space where a deep connectivity between people, living beings, earth and water, including a sharing of energies and traumas, is attended to. This involves, for both Nyawela and her students, working productively across human and more-than-human language gaps (Vladimirova, 2018; Chapter 3) gathering up an important gist (Phipps, 2019; Chapter 8), and responding to meanings that are not fully articulated, but rather remain provisional or unspoken.

> She tried to understand – to make out words or feelings in what she was hearing but it felt just out of her reach. As soon as she thought she heard something specific it was gone, folded back into the endless buzz.
>
> Nxamalo and Ross, 2019, p.512

Nxamalo and Ross's (2020) choice to name Nyawela's cadre 'Wild Seed' speaks not only of a connection with the more-than-human world, but also of particular kinds of conditions for more-than-human flourishing. In Chapter 8, writing about young children's vocalizations, and in Chapter 6, writing about children's movements in and through places, I drew attention to the importance of the conditions for experimenting, making oneself present in a space, for feelings of comfort, safety and welcome. Metaphors of seeds and growth might encourage us to attend more carefully and more critically to the conditions for growth. In Chapter 9, I referred to Morrison's (1994) novel *The Bluest Eye* in my discussion of the potential damage caused by perfect, privileged or contextually specific family situations being presented as neutral, natural or universally desirable/ attainable. In *The Bluest Eye*, Morrison (1994) parallels the abuse and demise of the protagonist, Percola, with the marigold flowers that failed to flower that year. The children who plant the seeds that fail to grow spend most of the book seeking individual blame or cause and effect (perhaps we planted them too deep?) before concluding in the final pages:

> The soil is bad for certain kinds of flowers. Certain seeds it will not nurture, certain fruit it will not bear, and when the land kills of its own volition, we acquiesce and say the victim had no right to live.
>
> Morrison, 1994, p.204

In her analysis of *The Bluest Eye*, Werrlein (2005) contrasts the ahistorical and abstract-able family of the Dick and Jane books (which Morrison adopts as a haunting refrain throughout her chapter openers) with Morrison's attention to the inter-generational histories and traumas of different members of Percola's family. Morrison shows how these shape a snap decision or how something can unexpectedly unfold in any moment. These 'intimate extensions of long familial, socio-economic, and national histories' (Werrlein, 2005, p.54) are difficult to account for within early childhood education. They illustrate how the material conditions for flourishing, and thus the shaping of more-than-human literacies, cannot merely be improved by the modification of the physical and immediate material environment. Rather, slow and careful consideration of how the immediate rubs up against community biographies and situated ways of knowing from a past that individuals themselves may only even be partially aware of (Ivinson, 2018; Mayes et al., 2019), might reveal the uncontrollable, unpredictable and constantly confounding conditions for literacy emergence.

Paying attention to the nonlinear unfolding of (not)literacies in place-specific ways then requires a political sensibility for the material conditions for living, and the ways societal structures might make parenting, childhood and flourishing very different propositions for different kinds of families. Attending critically to the material conditions for parenting and family life, must be coupled with imaginaries of childhoods and literacies yet-to-come that offer expansive, inclusive, heterogeneous accounts of young children and families' literacy practices in communities. *When the material conditions for parenting, family life, or young children's literacies are overlooked or instrumentalized, what are the consequences for the conclusions that might be drawn about who has the right to flourish, to live?*

Standing in contrast to the metaphor of things unfolding in their own time and in response to the conditions within which they are part, the current trend in early childhood education is to intensify, accelerate and place tighter and tighter constraints on what counts as adequate/quality parenting/educational provision. At the same time, in the UK currently, a logic of earlier start, faster success rate seems to operate, in which policies endeavour to give children a 'head start' and put more 'time on task' in (Jones et al., 2016; Chapter 9 this volume), in the years before formal schooling starts. As I discussed in Chapter 9, this intensification, acceleration model seems to be grounded in notions of meritocracy and used as a way of holding (particularly marginalized or powerless) parents and educators to account for 'proper' or 'satisfactory' development of young children. *What kind of flourishing might be imagined as 'literacies yet to come', beyond the trope of a forward moving, linear upward trajectory arrow? And what would it mean to shift our focus, as educators and researchers, from individual-child-influenced-by-an-environment to an analysis of collective more-than-human conditions for flourishing?*

Escaping the 'Hero' Narrative

In *The Carrier Bag Theory of Fiction,* Le Guin (1989) tells a speculative tale of early human life, in which human's first tool was likely not the spear but 'the carrier bag, the sling, the shell or the gourd' (p.166); something to carry, share and distribute, rather than conquer and kill. Le Guin argues that whilst the 'hero narrative' of the hunter and spear, killing and trapping in a fight for survival and success, is a seductive and exciting story, it is also a deeply incomplete story, in which the everyday reality of how life carries on and what drives it forward, is obscured. The 'hero narrative' hides the full extent of humanity from us, or, as Le Guin puts it, 'it is the story that hid my humanity from me' (Le Guin, 1989, p.168).

In her analysis of Le Guin's work, Leddy (2019) points out that the carrier bag and the spear give us two different stories about humanity; the spear speaks of domination, of life as a series of challenges and wins. 'Man' must always enter into conflict, and must always triumph, before moving on to the next challenge. In contrast, a theory of life that starts with the receptacle is messy, conflicted, harder to tell.

> It's hard to tell a really gripping tale of how I wrested a wild-oat seed from its husk, and then another, and then another, and then another, and the another, and then I scratched my gnat bites.
>
> Le Guin, 1989, p.165

Leddy (2019) points out, 'We have come to embrace the idea that a succession of one thing defeating another literally is history.' This notion of human life as founded on mastery and conquest, on *winning*, is tied in with narratives of progress, colonialism, land ownership, meritocracy (Chapter 3; Chapter 9, this volume). Understandings of young children as developmental projects filled with potential for future success also relies on this narrative. When we assume that good development for young children involves taking up certain literacies as early as possible, we might be asking *'how can children master speech and writing as quickly as possible, in order to understand the world as clearly as possible, in order to use this mastery and knowledge as tools that will help them to win at life?'* A common trope is that children need words and other skills as 'tools' in order to learn/express themselves/develop/form relationships/understand the world/ thrive. What kind of 'tools' do we imagine language and literacies as being? Are they spears, to help each child 'win'; to reach the solution faster than her classmates, to shout the answer louder, to express her needs clearest and have them attended to quickest? What other kind of tools could literacies be imagined as? *What would a carrier bag account of young children's language and literacy practices look like?*

In addition, dominant assumptions about the role of adults in young children's development can also take up a 'hero narrative' in which, if adults do the right things, enough times and in a skilful enough way, they will 'win' at parenting by setting their child up for future educational success.[1] Practitioners and parents might be presented with neatly packaged 'solutions' from research; if you follow this programme or that one, your practice will be research-informed. Your parenting will be good enough. You will be beyond rebuke. However, there are also the messy, conflicted stories about how things unfold in the moment, and the other ways of being that survive *in spite of* progress (Tsing, 2017). These are hard to describe in words. They do not seem to have a clear purpose or a logic and they do not guarantee results. They leave us, as adults, as 'experts' or 'professionals', exposed, vulnerable, unsure how to respond, and with snot or squashed banana smeared down our sleeve. Thus, in terms of young children and families, the story of the spear plays into a narrative of meritocracy and progress, in which parents can help their child be a 'winner' not a 'loser' if they put enough effort into the task[2]; 'truths' that fit neatly into a narrative of promise and ruin (Tsing, 2015; Chapter 9 this volume). *What other stories could be told about the material conditions of everyday life with families and communities? About connection, place, compromise, trauma and carrying on?*

How Could Community Ways of Knowing Re-conceptualize Early Childhood Literacies?

I suggest that for co-produced research to have any chance of success, it is the community that must call the shots. I have been at pains to explore why this might be much more difficult than is usually presented.

Walkerdine, 2017, p.711

In her paper on affect and community research in working-class communities, Walkerdine (2017) describes a community, in the face of precarity and adversity, continuing to hold itself together. The descriptions of scholars of marginalized communities, such as Walkerdine (2017), Ivinson (2018), Skeggs (1997), Gillies (2007), Stewart (2007), all speak of different ways of living a life and carrying on that rely on collectivity, connection to place and community, body/place knowing, unspoken yet significant histories and traumas, and mundane politics of resistance. They speak of life at 'unruly edges' (Tsing, 2017) in ways that perhaps resonate through some of the themes in the speculative stories described in this chapter.

Big social shifts float by on distant, cloudy discourses and scandals. The conditions of life assemble themselves into something and then morph into something else. Sometimes extreme trajectories take root and then take off with a life of their own.

Stewart, 2007, pp.64–5

Affective forces and intensities that shape how people experience places, connect with each other, make sense of their worlds, and ultimately, how different kinds of literacies might emerge from bodies during all of this, are both actual and virtual. By this I mean, such forces cannot be listed or measured, because they cannot be described in words or even perhaps consciously known at an individual level; they are powerfully present whilst still un-thought in the lives of young children in communities.

The research that informed this book is not coproduced in the sense that research participants shaped the research agenda or gave their perspectives on how early childhood literacies should be re-conceptualized. This would rely on the kind of knowledge that can be articulated in words (Ingold, 2013), and more importantly, on participants with time and interest to do that kind of labour. Instead, this research involved tuning into place/body knowing (Somerville, 2013) within one particular community, in a particular place, time and moment. It involved trying to think with the flows and logics of this place, in order to experiment with how these might reshape or reimagine young children's literacies in communities. Perhaps this is akin to de Freitas's (2013) account of speculative fiction as a way of interrogating concepts and offering 'an alternative model for how they might be reassembled' (p.120).

Working with community ways of knowing requires not only being prepared for community knowledges to disrupt or dissolve other theories and ways of making sense of the world (even the ones the researcher herself is heavily invested in), it also involves being prepared to finish without all the answers. Somerville (2007) describes working with awarenesses and images that might 'freeze .... die and lose their alive mobility' (p.231) if she tries to fix them into place and similarly de Freitas (2013) describes tracing flows and patterns where 'the actualization of any stable environment makes these rumblings imperceptible' (p.117). Drawing on Glissant, Viruru (2001) writes about the importance of opacity in encountering other's difference. Often such difference is not transparent, not available to be fully known (Tuck and Yang, 2014). Perhaps not everything is capable of being articulated in words. Perhaps it is, but it is not for you. Perhaps, because people are naturally contrary and conflicted, the way the thing made sense yesterday no longer holds today. The way in which literacies are not-yet or perhaps yet-to-come must include a consideration of these issues of access to knowledge and the kinds of forms that knowledge might take.

Attending to Not-yet Literacies

Seeking alternative accounts of childhood, Osgood and Robinson (2019) write of 'the persistent need to stay concerned by the small stuff that unfolds in the lives of women and children' (p.15). In this chapter, I have tried to build on my interest in the unfolding of 'small stuff', affective flows (Stewart, 2007), shifts and movements in everyday lives of families and young children by turning my attention to the actual/virtual/immanent/yet-to-come nature of these moments. Arguing that accounts of young children that 'dwell in the cuteness/competency/progress/learning of the child are no longer enough. They were never enough' (Chapter 1, this volume), I have tried to show the need to constantly interrogate whether frameworks challenge or validate existing unjust hierarchies of knowledge and human-ness (*even if* they seem simultaneously to be celebrating the overlooked competencies of individual children). I have also tried to demonstrate the risks inherent in focusing only or mostly on meanings that are fixed, clear, identifiable or fully emerged. Playing with the notion of literacies yet-to-come is one way to keep this kind of inquiry lively and in-motion, whilst avoiding an incremental accumulation of increasingly confident and definite accounts of what young children's literacies might involve.

I asked above what a carrier bag theory of young children's literacies might look like, and this book has not answered that question, but has hopefully begun or contributed to a conversation. These conversations are also yet-to-come, speculative stories that must still be grappled with, (dis)articulated, told or gestured towards. These might be stories of meanings that were possibly shared or understood, of moments of intensity that did not seem to have a logical cause, or flows of energy that made so much sense at *that* time, in *that* place, even if an account given after the event seems to falter and stutter. They might be stories of repeatedly gathering oats in a carrier bag (Le Guin, 1989). Thus, I leave the reader with Le Guin's invitation to keep thinking, walking, moving and telling stories:

> I said it was hard to make a gripping tale of how we wrestled the wild oats from their husks. I didn't say it was impossible.
>
> Le Guin, 1989, p.169

Notes

Chapter 1

1   My use of 'she' in vignettes throughout mirrors Stewart (2007) who chooses 'she' rather than 'I' in order to differentiate her writerly identity, and Blaise (2016) who writes as 'she' in order to de-emphasize personal experience. I use 'she' to refer to myself or any other adult (practitioners, parents) in the vignettes, and in doing so, find the pronoun also diffuses the sense of the watching, judging, pathologizing eye that often rests on adults working with and caring for young children. Often 'she' does not know how to respond, or tries and fails to resolve a particular situation ('she tried to dissuade him from eating the playdoh … '). Writing 'she' seems to disrupt the accusatory finger, and make clearer that these inabilities to respond or provide solutions do not stem from an individual's lack or poor decision making, but from unreasonable expectations, the assumed predictability of young children, and the singularity with which any event can and does unfold.

2   The more-than-human offers a critique of the Cartesian mind–body split that has guided so much Western social science theory and methodology in relation to children's learning (Braidotti, 2013; Osgood and Robinson, 2019). This split produces inequalities through the continuing erasure of bodies and affect in literacy research and policy (Hackett et al., 2020a; Kuby et al., 2019).

3   See Macrae (2020) for a tracing of the role of early film in visually shaping child development as linear progress.

4   In advocating for literacies beyond narratives of function and progress, I am not seeking to set up a dichotomy between home and school literacies. As I will go on to illustrate in the following chapters, place does shape literacy practices but in much more complex ways. In Chapter 2, I discuss what I mean by 'community' and why I think the notion, which I connect with place specificity, is so important for early childhood literacies.

Chapter 2

1   The community I chose to work in is one where I also carried out my doctoral research, starting 2010. Since that time, I had maintained relationships with the

community through small-scale and unfunded pieces of work, some carried out
in my own time, whilst completing my doctorate and working on precarious
contracts. I include this detail to highlight the challenges for early career
researchers to build up and maintain the kinds of long-term and ethically engaged
relationships with communities that I advocate should underpin this kind of
research.

2   I took less photos during phase 2 fieldwork in Northwood because I was
collaborating with visual artist Steve Pool who took many still photos and videos
during the sessions as part of his practice.

3   I was a community outreach worker for several years before becoming a researcher.

4   You will notice I have chosen initials rather than full names to act as pseudonyms
for the children. Some of my reviewers asked about this, commenting that it felt
like a move away from specificity, a bit impersonal, or something that makes
it more difficult to feel connected to the children. I know that it is common in
ethnographies to introduce the participants, the different families and their
backgrounds, and to encourage the reader to follow the experiences of each
participant as they move through the book. I have decided to stick with initials
for now. In some ways, it is a deliberate move to make it less likely the reader will
follow each participant as an individual they (feel they) come to know increasingly
thoroughly as they read on. When I was writing my doctorate, I adored a
(wonderful and influential) paper by Rosie Flewitt (2005) that described the
meaning making of Tallulah. I adored Tallulah. I had an image of her in my mind's
eye, I related to her, I remembered her by her name, I discussed with my supervisor,
how much we both *loved* Tallulah. However, perhaps this memory of a feeling of
knowing and relating to Tallulah is part of the reason I am providing only initials
to you now. Flewitt's (2005) point about meaning making over multiple modes
was an important one for me to hear. But I did not (or should not have needed to)
know Tallulah herself, even a pseudonym version of her; it was not my place. It
is not the job of pseudonym-children to delight, entertain, explain or make us, as
academics and educators, feel validated, comforted, vindicated or inspired. I want
to tell you a story in this book, but it should probably be a story about ideas and
moments and events, rather than characters who you follow and feel invested in.
Similarly to the use of 'she' I discussed in Chapter 1, initials are intended to disrupt
a sense of knowing and judging (and possibly even *loving*) the characters involved,
by de-emphasizing personal experience, and by gesturing towards the complex
unpredictability of how individual identities and experiences, place biographies and
the singularity of any given event intertwine.

5   MacLure et al. (2011) describe a different variation of working with data that glows,
which did involve several different fieldworkers, together with researchers who
were not familiar with the fieldsite, in dialogue together.

Chapter 3

1   Throughout my work in this community, opportunities for children to encounter animals were highly valued by adults, and when I offered to fund visits or events for the children as part of my research, encounters with animals were often requested by both staff and families.

Chapter 4

1   Playgroups were generally run weekly, or at some other regular interval, for ninety minutes. Parents and children could attend together, for free, to play, chat and eat a snack.

2   Currently in the UK, families on a low income are offered a free place at day care for the children from two years old onwards.

3   This chapter focuses on early years classroom and playgroup spaces, where these moments of insynchronicity seemed particularly stark. Outdoor spaces, such as the park, or the outside space at one of the day care centres in the study, had a different kind of feeling. Staff explicitly described how they and the children seemed to feel more comfortable in the outside spaces, and it was much less likely the children would get in trouble or need to be continually told off, because there were less rules to break outside.

4   Truman Burbank is the protagonist in a film called *The Truman Show*, in which he unknowingly lives in a fabricated world created as part of a television show.

5   The appropriation of the word 'tepee' by non-indigenous people has rightly been criticized, particularly in relation to children, where 'tepee' rather than 'tent' seems to signal something whimsical, historical or wild (Keene, 2011). I have chosen to retain 'tepee' in this chapter because it is the term by which staff and children constantly referred to the structure as.

6   Bold text indicates singing.

7   Beard's analysis shows the representation of women who speak publically in ancient Greek literature is enduringly of individuals who are sub-human, turned non-human as punishment or silenced in other ways. Beard give the example of Io, turned into a cow by Zeus so she could not speak of their affair, only moo.

Chapter 5

1   Kress (1997) hints at the issue of unintended, unfolding meanings in his chapter 'My Gawd, I made it like Australia', in which a child cuts shapes of paper before declaring in surprise that the shape looks like a map of Australia. He writes this

incident 'show[s] deliberation, planning, design, as quite a normal, expected, and unexceptional state of mind: even if, as here, the result was perhaps accidental more than deliberate' (p.34). However, he is unable to expand on this point because it undermines his key argument about design and intent as criteria for recognizing such actions as communication rather than expression or play.

2   This sub-heading is drawn directly from Tuck and Ree (2013) as illustrated in the quote below it.

Chapter 6

1   I also suspect that when researching in schools, young children are more likely to respond to an adult's questions, complete requested tasks or at least stay in the same space as the adult rather than run off; perhaps children have learnt these are the required rules of how to engage with adults in school settings.

2   The clearest example of this might be watching a very young child run across a space. As legs flay either side and it seems like the child might trip and fall at any moment, the direction of travel across the room and where she ends up certainly seems to be something that unfolds in the moment, rather than a route and destination pre-planned in advance.

Chapter 7

1   Significantly, this orientation towards matter as inseparable from animate life, rather than a binary opposite of it, unseats notions of human uniqueness, or the assumed ability of humans to stand outside of the material world. Instead 'human power is itself a kind of thing-power' (Bennett, 2010, p.10), in that human bodies and brains themselves are made up of lively and self organizing materials. The implications of this for research methodology are a dismantling of 'a masculinist disembodied subject' capable of understanding the material world from the point of view of 'a detached, rational mind' (Alaimo, 2016, p.181).

2   In the role of 'artist in residence' in the study, Steve Pool attended Northwood playgroup (see Chapter 2) 8 times during phase 2 of the fieldwork. Each time he brought open-ended materials as a provocation, including tissue paper, large sheets of brown paper, coloured acetate and natural materials. He also brought a pop up gazebo several times, as described above.

3   As Sakr and Osgood (2019) point out, what tends to be given precedence is also closely related to the dominance of unfolding linear developmental stages in how young children's art making is conceptualized within developmental psychology.

4   For Colebrook (2002), desires and assemblages constitute each other. 'The rationality, the efficiency of an assemblage, does not exist without the passions the assemblage brings into play, without the desires that constitute it as much as it constitutes them' (2002, p.465).

Chapter 9

1   As Thiel (2020) points out, stories of plantation economies and industrialization are not just powerful metaphors, as I am employing them in this chapter. They also literally impact 'lives of people whose sedimented histories are tied up in the plight of plantation agronomy and industrialization' including the children living in those communities today.

2   It is also possible to see a parallel between individual progress along a generalizable path and Tsing's (2015) notions of scalability and alienation as requirements for capitalist expansion.

3   Writing against meritocracy, Markovits (2019) points to an increasing acceleration of the skills and training individuals are required to gain, at increasingly earlier ages, in order to 'stay on top' of an increasingly competitive situation.

Chapter 10

1   As Markovits (2019) points out, meritocracy connects to acceleration, to an endless and limitless process in which parents are pressured to do more to help their children get ahead, earlier, to come out on top.

2   Such narratives are particularly satisfying and seductive for the many middle-class parents with children of their own who work in education. As middle-class children thrive in the school system (as they always historically have), this narrative tells middle-class families that they 'earned it', that the success of their children is the result of their own heroic actions.

References

Abram, D. (1996). *The Spell of the Sensuous*. New York: Vintage Books.

Ahrenkiel, A. and Holm, L. (2020). Documentation of Children's Language Development: A Critical Analysis and Discussion of the Conceptualization of Language in Widespread Language Assessments. In M. Alasuutari, H. Kelle and H. Knauf (eds.) *Documentation in Institutional Contexts of ECE: Normalisation, Power Relations, and Participation*. (p. 41–57) Wiesbaden: Springer.

Ahmed, S. (2004). *The Cultural Politics of Emotion*. Edinburgh: Edinburgh University Press.

Ahmed, S. (2014). Atmospheric Walls (online). Available at: https://feministkilljoys.com/2014/09/15/atmospheric-walls/ (accessed 10 June 2020).

Ahmed, S. (2017). *Living a Feminist Life*. Durham, NC: Duke University Press.

Anderson, B. and Harrison, P. (2010). The Promise of Non-representational Theories. In B. Anderson and P. Harrison (eds.) *Taking-Place: Non-representational Theories and Geography* (pp.1–36). Farnham: Ashgate.

Andersen, C. and Otterstad, A. M. (2014). Researching the Assemblage of Cultural Diversity in Norway: Challenging Simplistic Research Approaches. *International Review of Qualitative Research*, 7 (1): 93–110.

Alaimo, S. (2016). *Exposed. Environmental Politics and Pleasures in Posthuman Times*. Minneapolis: University of Minnesota Press.

Anzaldua, G. (1999). *Borderland/La Frontera: The New Mestiza*. San Francisco, CA: Aunt Lute.

Arculus, C. and MacRae, C. (2020). Complicité: Resisting the Tyranny of Talk in Early Childhood. *Global Education Review*, 7 (2): 43–57.

Avineri, N., Johnson, E., Heath, S., McCarty, T., Ochs, E., Kremer-Sadlik, T., Blum, S. et al. (2015). Invited Forum: Bridging the 'Language Gap'. *Journal of Linguistic Anthropology*, 25 (1): 66–86.

Axelrod, Y. and Col, M. (2018). 'The Pumpkins Are Coming … vienen las calabazas … That Sounds Funny': Translanguaging Practices of Young Emergent Bilinguals. *Journal of Early Childhood Literacy*, 18 (1): 129–53.

Badwan, K. (2020). Unmooring Language for Social Justice: Young People Talking about Language in/and Place in Manchester, UK. *Critical Inquiry in Language Studies*. Online first.

Barad, K. (2019). 'After the End of the World … ' – 2019-08-13. Available at: https://www.youtube.com/watch?v=68I0y1koakA&feature=youtu.be&fbclid=IwAR3PyLmh rkMyBDBJbmJ4y8j-xMI84BruG6-L3OmHo86A40V1lK1a2Kqvb7g.

Beard, M. (2017). *Women and Power. A Manifesto*. London: Profile Books.

Bennett, J. (2010). *Vibrant Matter. A Political Ecology of Things.* Durham, NC: Duke University Press.

Bentley, D. F. (2012). Making Messes and Taking Your Time: Art Making in Infancy. *Childhood Education*, 88 (1): 36–44.

Berlant, L. (2011). *Cruel Optimism.* Durham, NC: Duke University Press.

Birke, L., Bryld, M. and Lykke, N. (2004). Animal Performances. An Exploration of Intersections between Feminist Science Studies and Studies of Human/Animal Relationships. *Feminist Theory*, 5 (2): 167–83.

Blaise, M. (2016). Fabricated Childhoods: Uncanny Encounters with the More-than-human. *Discourse: Studies in the Cultural Politics of Education*, 37 (5): 617–26.

Blum, S. (2016). Unseen WEIRD Assumptions: The So-Called Language Gap Discourse and Ideologies of Language, Childhood, and Learning. *International Multilingual Research Journal*, 11 (1): 23–38.

Bomer, R. (2003). Things That Make Kids Smart: A Vygotskian Perspective on Concrete Tool Use in Primary Literacy Classrooms. *Journal of Early Childhood Literacy*, 3 (3): 223–47.

Born, P. (2018). Regarding Animals: A Perspective on the Importance of Animals in Early Childhood Environmental Education. *International Journal of Early Childhood Environmental Education*, 5 (2): 46–57.

Braidotti, R. (2013). *The Posthuman.* Cambridge: Polity Press.

Bridges-Rhoads, S. and Van Cleave, J. (2017). Writing Posthumanism, Qualitative Enquiry and Early Literacy. *Journal of Early Childhood Literacy*, 17 (3): 297–314.

Bright, G. (2012). 'Sticking together!' Policy Activism from within a UK Coal-mining Community. *Journal of Educational Administration and History*, 44 (3): 221–36.

Brookshaw, S. (2009). The Material Culture of Children and Childhood. *Journal of Material Culture*, 14 (3): 365–83.

Brownell, C. J. (2019). Sound the Alarm!: Disrupting Sonic Resonances of an Elementary English Language Arts Classroom. *Curriculum Inquiry*, 49 (5): 551–72.

Burman, E. (2008). *Deconstructing Developmental Psychology.* Hove: Routledge.

Burnett, C. and Merchant, G. (2017). The Case of the iPad. In C. Burnett, G. Merchant, A. Simpson and M. Walsh (eds.) *The Case of the iPad Mobile Literacies in Education* (pp.1–14). Dordrecht, Netherlands: Springer.

Burnett, C. and Merchant, G. (2018). Literacy-as-event: Accounting for Relationality in Literacy Research. *Discourse: Studies in the Cultural Politics of Education*, 41 (1): 45–56.

Campbell, E., Pahl, K., Pente, E. and Rasool, Z. (2018). *Reimagining Contested Communities. Connecting Rotherham through Research.* Bristol: Policy Press.

Canella, G. S. and Viruru, R. (2012). *Childhood and Postcolonization. Power, Education and Contemporary Practice.* London: Routledge.

Carlyle, D. (2019). Walking in Rhythm with Deleuze and a Dog inside the Classroom: Being and Becoming Well and Happy Together. *Medical Humanities*, 45 (2): 199–210.

Caton, L. (2019). Video Data Sensing: Working Post Qualitatively in Classroom Based Video Inquiry. *Video Journal of Education and Pedagogy*, 4 (1): 23–45.

Cocks A. (2006). The Ethical Maze: Finding an Inclusive Path towards Gaining Children's Agreement to Research Participation. *Childhood*, 13: 247–66.

Colebrook, C. (2002). *Gilles Deleuze*. London: Routledge.

Common Worlds Research Collective (2020). *Learning to Become with the World: Education for Future Survival*. Paper commissioned for the UNESCO Futures of Education report.

Compton-Lilly, C. (2016). Time in Education: Intertwined Dimensions and Theoretical Possibilities. *Time & Society*, 25 (3): 575–93.

Crago, M. Annahatak, B. and Ningiurvik, L. (1993). Changing Patterns of Language Socialization in Inuit Homes. *Anthropology & Education Quarterly*, 24 (3): 205–23.

Crinnall, S. (2017). *Blogging Art and Sustenance. Artful Everyday Life (Making) with Water*. Unpublished thesis.

Daniels, K. (2016). Exploring Enabling Literacy Environments: Young Children's Spatial and Material Encounters in Early Years Classrooms. *English in Education*, 50 (1): 12–34.

Daniels, K. (2019). Notions of Agency in Early Literacy Classrooms: Assemblages and Productive Intersections. *Journal of Early Childhood Literacy*. Available at: https://doi.org/10.1177/1468798419866489.

Davenport, H. (2019). A Voice in the Forest. In M. Sackville-Ford and H. Davenport (eds.) *Critical Issues in Forest Schools*. London: Sage.

Davies, B. (2014). *Listening to Children: Being and Becoming*. London: Routledge.

Deleuze, G. (1997). Desire and Pleasure. Trans. M. McMahon. *Magazine Littéraire*, 325. Available at: http://www.artdes.monash.edu.au/globe/delfou.html (accessed 6 April 2010).

Deleuze, G. and Guattari, F. (1987). *A Thousand Plateaus*. (Trans. B. Massumi). London, England: Continuum.

Deleuze, G. and Guattari, F. (2013). *A Thousand Plateaus. Capitalism and Schizophrenia*. London: Bloomsbury.

de Freitas, E. (2016). The Moving Image in Education Research: Reassembling the Body in Classroom Video Data. *International Journal of Qualitative Studies in Education*, 29 (4): 553–72.

de Freitas, E. (2017). Nonhuman Findings from the Laboratory of Speculative Sociology. *The Minnesota Review*, 88: 116–26.

De Rijke, V. (2019). 'It Might Get Messy, or Not Be Right': Scribble as Postdevelopmental Art. In M. Sakr and J. Osgood (eds.) *Postdevelopmental Approaches to Childhood Art*. London: Bloomsbury.

Dernikos, B. (2018). 'It's Like You Don't Want to Read It Again': Exploring Affects, Trauma and 'Willful' Literacies. *Journal of Early Childhood Literacy*. Online first.

Duhn, I. and Quinones, G. (2018). Eye-to-Eye with Otherness: A Childhoodnature Figuration. In A. Cutter-Mackenzie, K. Malone and E. Barratt Hacking (eds.) *Research Handbook on Childhoodnature. Springer International Handbooks of Education*. Cham: Springer.

Dyson, A. (2015). The Search for Inclusion: Deficit Discourse and the Erasure of Childhoods. *Language Arts Journal/National Council of Teachers of English*, 92 (3): 199–207.

Dockett, S., Einarsdottir, J. and Perry, B. (2009). Researching with Children: Ethical Tensions. *Journal of Early Childhood Research*, 7: 283–98.

Early Learning Coalition of Escambia County (2018). Results & Lessons Learned from the First Year of LENA Grow™ as part of ELC Escambia's 'Grow with Me' Initiative.

Ehret, C. (2019). Propositions from Affect Theory for Feeling Literacy through the Event. In D. E. Alvermann, N. J. Unrau and M. Sailors (eds.) *Theoretical Models and Processes of Literacy* (7th edition) (pp.563–81). New York: Routledge.

Ellsworth, E. (2004). *Places of Learning. Media, Architecture, Pedagogy*. London: Routledge.

Elwick, S. (2015). 'Baby-cam' and Researching with Infants: Viewer, Image and (not) Knowing. *Contemporary Issues in Early Childhood*, 16 (4): 322–38.

Escott, H. and Pahl, K. (2019). Learning from Ninjas: Young People's Films as a Lens for an Expanded View of Literacy and Language. *Discourse: Studies in the Cultural Politics of Education*, 40 (6): 803–15.

Evans, T., Hackett, A., Magaula, J. and Pool, S. (2018). What Parents Know: A Call for Realistic Accounts of Parenting Young Children. In K. Pahl and Z. Rasool (eds.) *Reimagining Contested Communities: Connecting Rotherham through Research* (pp.123–34). Bristol: Policy Press.

Facer, K. and Enright, B. (2016). *Creating Living Knowledge: The Connected Communities Programme, Community University Relationships and the Participatory Turn in the Production of Knowledge*. Bristol: University of Bristol/AHRC Connected Communities.

Favareau, D. and Gare, A. (2017). The Biosemiotic Glossary Project: Intentionality. *Biosemiotics*, 10 (3): 413–59.

Feld, S. (2012). *Sound and Sentiment. Birds, Weeping, Poetics, and Song in Kaluli Expression*. Durham, NC: Duke University Press.

Finnegan, R. (2002). *Communicating. The Multiple Modes of Human Interconnection*. London: Routledge.

Flewitt, R. (2005). Is Every Child's Voice Heard? Researching the Different Ways 3-year-old Children Communicate and Make Meaning at Home and in a Pre-school Playgroup. *Early Years*, 25 (3): 207–22.

Flewitt, R. (2006). Using Video to Investigate Preschool Classroom Interaction: Education Research Assumptions and Methodological Practices. *Visual Communication*, 5: 25–50.

Flewitt, R. (2013). *Early Literacy: A Broader Vision*. TACTYC occasional paper.

Flores, N. and Rosa, J. (2015). Undoing Appropriateness: Raciolinguistic Ideologies and Language Diversity in Education. *Harvard Educational Review*, 85 (2): 149–71.

Gallacher, L. (in press). From Milestones to Wayfaring: Geographic Metaphors and Iconography of Embodied Growth and Change in Infancy and Early Childhood. *GeoHumanities*.

Gallagher, M. (2016). Sound as Affect. Difference, Power and Spatiality. *Emotion, Space and Society*, 20: 42–8.

Gallagher, M., Prior, J., Needham, M. and Holmes, R. (2017). Listening Differently: A Pedagogy for Expanded Listening. *British Educational Research Journal*, 43 (6): 1246–65.

Gallagher, M., Hackett, A., Procter, L. and Scott, F. (2018). Vibrations in Place: Sound and Language in Early Childhood Literacy Practices. *Educational Studies: A Journal of the American Educational Studies Association*, 54 (4): 465–82.

Gershon, W. S. (2011). Embodied Knowledge: Sounds as Educational Systems. *Journal of Curriculum Theorizing*, 27 (2): 66–81.

Gillen, J. and Hall, N. (2013). The Emergence of Early Childhood Literacy. In N. Hall, J. Larson and J. A. Marsh (eds.) *Handbook of Early Childhood Literacy* (pp.3–17). London: Sage.

Gillies, V. (2007). *Marginalised Mothers. Exploring Working-Class Experiences of Parenting.* Oxon: Routledge.

Gillies, V., Edwards, R. and Horsley, N. (2017). *Challenging the Politics of Early Intervention: Who's 'Saving' Children and Why.* Bristol: Policy Press.

Grainger, K. (2013). 'The Daily Grunt': Middle-Class Bias and Vested Interests in the 'Getting in Early' and 'Why Can't They Read?' Reports. *Language and Education*, 27 (2): 99–109.

Gullion, J. S. (2018). *Diffractive Ethnography. Social Sciences and the Ontological Turn.* New York: Routledge.

Gurney, L. and Demuro, E. (2019). Tracing New Ground, from Language to Languaging, and from Languaging to Assemblages: Rethinking Languaging through the Multilingual and Ontological Turns. *International Journal of Multilingualism*. Available at: https://doi.org/10.1080/14790718.2019.1689982.

Hackett, A. (2014). Zigging and Zooming all Over the Place: Young Children's meaning making and moving in the Museum. *Journal of Early Childhood Literacy*, 14 (1): 5–27.

Hackett, A. (2016). Young Children as Wayfarers: Learning about Place by Moving through it. *Children and Society*, 30: 169–79.

Hackett, A. (2017). Parents as Researchers. Collaborative Ethnography with Parents. *Qualitative Research*, 17 (5): 481–97.

Hackett, A. and Somerville, M. (2017). Posthuman Literacies: Young Children Moving in Time, Place and More-than-human Worlds. *Journal of Early Childhood Literacy*, 17 (3): 374–91.

Hackett, A. and Rautio, P. (2019). Answering the World. Young Children's Running and Rolling as More-than-Human Multimodal Meaning Making. *International Journal of Qualitative Studies in Education*, 32 (8): 1019–31.

Hackett, A., Procter, L. and Seymour, J. (2015). *Children's Spatialities. Embodiment, Emotion and Agency.* London: Palgrave Macmillan.

Hackett, A., Procter, L. and Kummerfeld, R. (2018). Exploring Abstract, Physical, Social and Embodied Space: Developing an Approach for Analysing Museum Spaces for Young Children. *Children's Geographies*, 16 (5): 489–502.

Hackett, A., MacLure. M. and Pahl, K. (2020a). Literacy and Language as Material Practices: Re-thinking Social Inequality in Young Children's Literacies. Guest Editorial. *Journal of Early Childhood Literacy*, 20 (1): 3–12.

Hackett, A., MacLure, M. and MacMahon, S. (2020b). Reconceptualising Early Language Development: Matter, Sensation and the More-than-human. *Discourse: Studies in the Cultural Politics of Education*. Online First.

Hamilton, L. and Taylor, N. (2017). *Ethnography after Humanism, Power, Politics and Method in Multi-Species Research*. London: Palgrave Macmillan.

Hancock, R. and Gillen, J. (2007). Safe Places in Domestic Spaces: Two-Year-Olds at Play in Their Homes, *Children's Geographies*, 5 (4): 337–51.

Haraway, D. (2016). *Staying with the Trouble*. Durham, NC: Duke University Press.

Harding, S. (ed.) (1987). *Feminism and Methodology*. Milton Keynes: Open University Press.

Hargraves, V. (2019). The Posthuman Condition of Ethics in Early Childhood Literacy: Order-in(g) Be(E)ing Literacy. In C. Kuby, K. Spector and J. Thiel (eds.) *Posthumanism and Literacy Education. Knowing/becoming/doing Literacies* (pp.187–200). New York: Routledge.

Harrison, E. and McTavish, M. (2018). 'i'Babies: Infants' and Toddlers' Emergent Language and Literacy in a Digital Culture of iDevices. *Journal of Early Childhood Literacy*, 18 (2): 163–88.

Heath, S. B. (1983). *Ways with Words: Language, Life, and Work in Communities and Classrooms*. Cambridge: Cambridge University Press.

Hodgins, D. (ed.) (2019). *Feminist Research for 21st Century Childhoods: Common Worlds Methods*. London: Bloomsbury.

Hohti, R. and Tammi, T. (2019). The Greenhouse Effect: Multispecies Childhood and Non-innocent Relations of Care. *Childhood*, 26 (2): 169–85.

Holmes, R. and Jones, L. (2013). Flesh, Wax, Horse Skin, and Hair: The Many Intensities of Data. *Cultural Studies ↔ Critical Methodologies*, 13 (4): 357–72.

Holmes, R., Jones, L., Rossholt, N. and Anastasiou, T. (2015). Masticating 'Quality' and Spitting the Bits Out. *Contemporary Issues in Early Childhood*, 17 (1): 26–38.

Holmes. R., MacRae, C. and Arculus, C. (2019). 2-Curious: The Potential of Performance-Based Practice in Dialogue with Early Years Practice. *Impact. Journal of the Chartered College of Teaching*, September 2019 edition.

Holmes, R., Macrae, C. and Hackett, A. (2020). Introduction to Section 1: Thing-ness and the Power of Objects. In A. Hackett, R. Holmes and C. Macrae (eds.) *Working with Young Children in Museums; Weaving Theory and Practice*. London: Routledge.

Horton, J. (2018). For the Love of Cuddly Toys. *Children's Geographies*, 16 (4): 446–54.

Horton, J. and Kraftl, P. (2018). Rats, Assorted Shit and 'Racist Groundwater': Towards Extra-Sectional Understandings of Childhoods and Social-Material Processes. *Environment and Planning D: Society and Space*, 36 (5): 926–48.

Hultman, K. and Lenz Taguchi, H. (2010). Challenging Anthropocentric Analysis of Visual Data: A Relational Materialist Methodological Approach to Educational Research. *International Journal of Qualitative Studies in Education*, 23 (5): 525–42.

Hvit, S. (2015). Literacy Events in Toddler Groups: Preschool Educators' Talk about Their Work with Literacy among Toddlers. *Journal of Early Childhood Literacy*, 15 (3): 311–30.

Ingold, T. (2013). *Making. Anthropology, Archaeology, Art and Architecture*. London: Routledge.

Ivinson, G. (2018). Re-imagining Bernstein's Restricted Codes. *European Educational Research*, 17 (4): 539–54.

James, A. (1993). *Childhood Identities. Self and Social Relationships in the Experience of the Child*. Edinburgh: Edinburgh University Press.

Jeffrey, B. and Troman, G. (2004). Time for Ethnography. *British Educational Research Journal*, 30 (4): 535–48.

Jokinen, P. and Murris, K. (2020). Inhuman Hands and Missing Child: Touching a Literacy Event in a Finnish Primary School. *Journal of Early Childhood Literacy*, 20 (1): 44–68.

Joks, S., Østmo, L. and Law, J. (2020). Verbing meahcci: Living Sámi lands. *The Sociological Review*, 68 (2): 305–21.

Jones, S. (2013). Literacies in the Body. *Journal of Adolescent and Adult Literacy*, 56 (7): 525–9.

Jones, S. (2019). Diffracting: Human Limbs, Dead Birds, Active Books, and Bucking Horses: The Work to-Be-Made of Literacies in the Present. In C. Kuby, J. Thiel and K. Spector (eds.) *Posthumanism and Literacy Education. Knowing/Becoming/Doing Literacies* (pp.108–13). New York: Routledge.

Jones, L., Osgood, J., Holmes, R. and MacLure, M. (2014). (Re)assembling, (Re) casting and (Re)aligning Lines of De- and Re-Territorialisation of Early Childhood. *International Review of Qualitative Research*, 7 (1): 58–79.

Jones, S., Thiel, J., Da'vila, D., Pittard, E., Woglom, J., Zhou, X., Brown, T. and Snow, M. (2016). Childhood Geographies and Spatial Justice: Making Sense of Place and Space-Making as Political Acts in Education. *American Educational Research Journal*, 53 (4): 1126–58.

Kallifatides, T. (2001). *Ett nytt land utanför mitt fönster [A New Country Outside My Window]*. Viborg: Albert Bonniers.

Keene, A. (2011). *Baby Tepees Are Like, Totally, In*. (blog post). Available at: https://nativeappropriations.com/2011/04/baby-tepees-are-like-totally-in.html (accessed 11 June 2019).

Kohn, E. (2013). *How Forests Think: Toward an Anthropology beyond the Human*. Berkeley: University of California Press.

Kraftl, P. (2020). *After Childhood. Re-thinking Environment, Materiality and Media in Children's Lives*. London: Routledge.

Kress, G. (1997). *Before Writing: Rethinking the Paths to Literacy*. New York: Routledge.

Kraftl, P., Horton, J. and Tucker, F. (2012). *Critical Geographies of Childhood and Youth: Contemporary Policy and Practice.* Bristol: The Policy Press.

Kuby, C. (2017). Why a Paradigm Shift of 'More than Human Ontologies' Is Needed: Putting to Work Poststructural and Posthuman Theories in Writers' Studio. *International Journal of Qualitative Studies in Education*, 30 (9): 877–96.

Kuby, C., Thiel, J. and Spector, K. (eds.) (2019). *Posthumanism and Literacy Education. Knowing/Becoming/Doing Literacies.* New York: Routledge.

Kuby, C. R., Gutshall Rucker, T. and Kirchhofer, J. M. (2015). 'Go Be a Writer!': Intra-Activity with Materials, Time and Space in Literacy Learning. *Journal of Early Childhood Literacy*, 15 (3): 394–419.

Kuby, C. R. and Gutshall Rucker, T. (2016). *Go Be a Writer! Expanding the Curricular Boundaries of Writing with Young Children.* Melbourne: Hawker Brownlow Education.

Kuchirko, Y. (2019). On Differences and Deficits: A Critique of the Theoretical and Methodological Underpinnings of the Word Gap. *Journal of Early Childhood Literacy*, 19 (4): 533–62.

LaBelle, B. (2014). *Lexicon of the Mouth. Poetics and Politics of Voice and the Oral Imaginary.* New York: Bloomsbury.

Ladson-Billings, G. (2006). From the Achievement Gap to the Education Debt: Understanding Achievement in US Schools. *Educational Researcher*, 35: 3–12.

Lafton, T. (2019). Becoming Clowns: How Do Digital Technologies Contribute to Young Children's Play? *Contemporary Issues in Early Childhood.*

Laing, C. (2019). A Role for Onomatopoeia in Early Language: Evidence from Phonological Development. *Language and Cognition*, 11 (2): 173–87.

Lancaster, L. (2007). Representing the Ways of the World: How Children under Three Start to Use Syntax in Graphic Signs. *Journal of Early Childhood Literacy*, 7 (2): 123–54.

Lange, A. (2018). *The Design of Childhood: How the Material World Shapes Independent Kids.* London: Bloomsbury.

Lareau, A. (2003). *Unequal Childhoods. Class, Race, and Family Life.* Berkeley: University of California Press.

Leander, K. and Boldt, G. (2013). Rereading 'A Pedagogy of Multiliteracies' Bodies, Texts and Emergence. *Journal of Literacy Research*, 45 (1): 22–46.

Leddy, S. (2019). We Should All Be Reading More Ursula le Guin. Available at: https://theoutline.com/post/7886/ursula-le-guin-carrier-bag-theory

Le Guin, U. (1989). *The Carrier Bag Theory of Fiction. In Dancing at the Edge of the World.* New York: Grove Press.

Lenters, K. (2016). Riding the Lines and Overwriting in the Margins: Affect and Multimodal Literacy Practices, *Journal of Literacy Research*, 48 (3): 280–316.

Lewis, A. (2009). Silence in the Context of Child's Voice. *Children in Society*, 24 (1): 14–23.

Littler, J. (2018). *Against Meritocracy. Culture, Power and Myths of Mobility.* London: Routledge.

Lively, P. (1994). *Oleander, Jacaranda: A Childhood Perceived*. New York: HarperCollins.

Løkken, G. (2000). The Playful Quality of the Toddling 'Style'. *International Journal of Qualitative Studies in Education*, 13 (5): 531–42.

Luke, A. (1995). Text and Discourse in Education: An Introduction to Critical Discourse Analysis. *Review of Research in Education*, 21: 3–47.

Macdonald, S. (2001). British Social Anthropology. In P. Atkinson, A. Coffey, S. Delamont, J. Lofland and L. Lofland (eds.) *Handbook of Ethnography* (pp.60–73). London: Sage.

MacLure, M. (2009). Broken Voices, Dirty Words: On the Productive Insufficiency of Voice. In A. Jackson and L. Mazzei (eds.) *Voice in Qualitative Inquiry: Challenging Conventional, Interpretive, and Critical Conceptions in Qualitative Research* (pp.97–113). London: Routledge.

MacLure, M. (2013a). Researching without Representation? Language and Materiality in Post-Qualitative Methodology. *International Journal of Qualitative Studies in Education*, 26 (6): 658–67.

MacLure, M. (2013b). Brent's Misadventure: On the Event Status of a Behaviour Incident, AERA 2013.

MacLure, M. (2013c). 'The Wonder of Data'. *Cultural Studies ↔ Critical Methodologies*, 13 (4): 228–32.

MacLure, M. (2013d). Classification or Wonder? Coding as an Analytic Practice in Qualitative Research. In R. Coleman and J. Ringrose (eds.) *Deleuze and Research Methodologies* (pp.164–83). Edinburgh: Edinburgh University Press.

MacLure, M. (2016). The Refrain of the A-Grammatical Child: Finding Another Language in/for Qualitative Research. *Cultural Studies – Critical Methodologies*, 16 (2): 173–82.

MacLure, M., Holmes, R., Jones, L. and MacRae. C. (2010). Silence as Resistance to Analysis: Or, on not Opening One's Mouth Properly. *Qualitative Inquiry*, 16 (6): 492–500.

MacLure, M., Jones, L., Holmes, R. and MacRae, C. (2011). Becoming a Problem: Behaviour and Reputation in the Early Years Classroom. *British Educational Research Journal*, 38 (3): 447–71.

MacRae, C. (2011). Making Payton's Rocket: Heterotopia and Lines of Flight. *International Journal of Art & Design Education*, 30 (1): 102–12.

MacRae, C. (2012). Encounters with a Life(less) Baby Doll: Rethinking Relations of Agency through a Collectively Lived Moment. *Contemporary Issues in Early Childhood*, 13 (2): 120–31.

MacRae, C. (2020). 'Grace Taking Form': Re-animating Piaget's Concept of the Sensori-motor through and with Slow-Motion Video. *Video Journal of Education and Pedagogy*, 4 (1): 151–66.

MacRae, C. and Arculus, C. (2020). Complicité: Resisting the Tyranny of Talk in Early Childhood. *Global Education Review*, 7 (2): 43-57.

MacRae, C., Hackett, A., Holmes, R. and Jones, L. (2018). Vibrancy, Repetition, Movement: Posthuman Theories for Reconceptualising Young Children in Museums. *Children's Geographies*, 16 (5): 503–15.

Mannion, G., Fenwick, A. and Lynch, J. (2012). Place Responsive Pedagogy: Learning from Teachers' Experiences of Excursions in Nature. *Environmental Education Research*, 19 (6): 792–809.

Markstrom, A. (2010). Talking about Children's Resistance to the Institutional Order and Teachers in Preschool. *Journal of Early Childhood Research*, (8): 303–14.

Martin, A. D. (2019). The Agentic Capacities of Mundane Objects for Educational Equity: Narratives of Material Entanglements in a Culturally Diverse Urban Classroom. *Educational Research for Social Change*, 8 (1): 86–100.

Martín Bylund, A. (2018a). Minor (il)Literate Artworks: Inventive Processes of Biliteracy and the Role of Expertise in Early Childhood Bilingual Education. *Global Studies of Childhood*, 8 (1): 23–37.

Martín Bylund, A. (2018b). The Matter of Silence in Early Childhood Bilingual Education. *Educational Philosophy and Theory*, 50 (4): 349–58.

Markovits, D. (2019). How Life Became an Endless, Terrible Competition. September. Available at: https://www.theatlantic.com/magazine/archive/2019/09/meritocracys-miserable-winners/594760/

Mauthner, S. and Doucet, A. (2008). 'Knowledge Once Divided Can Be Hard to Put Together Again': An Epistemological Critique of Collaborative and Team-Based Research Practices. *Sociology*, 42 (5): 971–85.

Maybin, J. (2013). What Counts as Reading? PIRLS, EastEnders and The Man on the Flying Trapeze. *Literacy*, 47 (2): 971–85.

Mayes, E., Keddie, A., Moss, J., Rawolle, S., Paatsch, L. and Kelly, M. (2019). Rethinking Inequalities between Deindustrialisation, Schools and Educational Research in Geelong. *Educational Philosophy and Theory*, 51 (4): 391–403.

Mazzei, L. and Jackson, A. Y. (2019). Posthuman Literacies in a Minor Language: Expressions-to-Come. In C. Kuby, K. Spector and J. Thiel (eds.) *Posthumanism and Literacy Education: Knowing/Being/Doing Literacies* (pp. 170–4) New York: Routledge.

McKittrick, K. (2015). Yours in the Intellectual Struggle. In K. McKittrick (ed.) *Sylvia Winter. On Being Human as Praxis*. Durham, NC: Duke University Press.

Millei, Z. and Kallio, K. (2018). Recognizing Politics in the Nursery: Early Childhood Education Institutions as Sites of Mundane Politics. *Contemporary Issues in Early Childhood*, 19 (1): 31–47.

Miller, D. (1997). *Capitalism: An Ethnographic Approach*. Oxford and New York: Berg.

Mills, C. and LeFrancois, B. (2018). Child as Metaphor: Colonialism, Psy-governance, and Epistemicide, *World Futures*, 74 (7–8): 503–24.

Mitchell, K. and Elwood, S. (2012). Mapping Children's Politics: The Promise of Articulation and the Limits of Nonrepresentational Theory. *Environment and Planning D*, 30 (5): 788–804.

Morris, D., Collett, P., Marsh, P. and O'Shaughnessy, M. (1979). *Gestures. Their Origins and Distribution*. London: Book Club Associates.

Morrison, T. (1994). *The Bluest Eye*. London: Vintage.

Myers, C. (2019). *Children and Materialities. The Force of the More-than-Human in Children's Classroom Lives*. Singapore: Springer.

National Literacy Trust (2019). Chat, Play, Read. Department for Education campaign. Available at: https://www.youtube.com/watch?v=ovNfiLgmaPY

Nimmo, J. (2008). Young Children's Access to *Real Life*: An Examination of the Growing Boundaries between Children in Child Care and Adults in the Community. *Contemporary Issues in Early Childhood* 9 (1): 3–13.

Nursery World. (2019). *Thousands of Children Not Learning at Home*. 8 April. Available at: https://www.nurseryworld.co.uk/news/article/thousands-of-children-not-learning-at-home. (accessed 7 January 2020).

Nxamalo, F. and Brown, C. (eds.) (2020). *Disrupting and Countering Deficits in Early Childhood Education*. New York: Routledge.

Nxumalo, F. and Cedillo, S. (2017). Decolonizing Place in Early Childhood Studies: Thinking with Indigenous Onto-epistemologies and Black Feminist Geographies. *Global Studies of Childhood*, 7 (2): 99–112.

Nxumalo, F. and Ross, K. M. (2019). Envisioning Black Space in Environmental Education for Young Children. *Race Ethnicity and Education*, 22 (4): 502–24.

Nxumalo, F. and Rubin, J. C. (2019). Encountering Waste Landscapes; More-Than-Human Place Literacies in Early Childhood Education. In C. Kuby, K. Spector and J. Thiel (eds.) *Posthumanism and Literacy Education. Knowing/Becoming/Doing Literacies* (pp.201–13). New York: Routledge.

Nxumalo, F., Pacini-Ketchabaw, V. and Rowan, M. (2011). Lunch Time at the Child Care Centre: Neoliberal Assemblages in Early Childhood Education. *Journal of Pedagogy*, 2 (2): 195–223.

Olsson, L. (2009). *Movement and Experimentation in Young Children's Learning. Deleuze and Guattari in Early Childhood Education*. London: Routledge.

Olsson, L. (2012). Eventicizing Curriculum. Learning to Read and Write through Becoming a Citizen of the World. *Journal of Curriculum Theorising*, 28 (1): 88–107.

Olsson, L. (2013). Taking Children's Questions Seriously: The Need for Creative Thought. *Global Studies of Childhood*, 3 (3): 230–53.

Osgood, J. (2019). 'You Can't Separate It from Anything': Glitter's Doings as Materialized Figurations of Childhood (and) Art. In M. Sakr and J. Osgood (eds.) *Postdevelopmental Approaches to Childhood Art*. London: Bloomsbury.

Osgood, J. and Robinson, K. (2019). *Feminists Researching Gendered Childhoods. Generative Entanglmenets*. London: Bloomsbury.

Osgood, J., Albon, D., Allen, K. and Hollingworth, S. (2013). 'Hard to Reach' or Nomadic Resistance? Families 'Choosing' not to Participate in Early Childhood Services. *Global Studies of Childhood*, 3 (3): 208–20.

Pacini-Ketchabaw, V. (2012). Acting with the Clock: Clocking Practices in Early Childhood. *Contemporary Issues in Early Childhood* 13 (2): 154–60.

Pacini-Ketchabaw, V., Nxumalo, F. and Rowan, M. C. (2014). Researching Neoliberal and Neocolonial Assemblages in Early Childhood Education. *International Review of Qualitative Research*, 7 (1): 39–57.

Pacini-Ketchabaw, V., Kind, S. and Kocher, L. (2016). *Encounters with Materials in Early Childhood Education*. New York: Routledge.

Pahl, K. (2002). Ephemera, Mess and Miscellaneous Piles: Texts and Practices in Families. *Journal of Early Childhood Literacy*, 2 (2): 145–66.

Parr, A. (2010). *The Deleuze Dictionary. Revised Edition*. Edinburgh: Edinburgh University Press.

Patel, L. (2014). Countering Coloniality in Educational Research: From Ownership to Answerability. *Educational Studies*, 50 (4): 357–77.

Peterson, E. (2018). 'Data Found Us': A Critique of Some New Materialist Tropes in Educational Research. *Research in Education*, 101 (1): 5–16.

Phipps, A. (2019). *Decolonising Multilingualism. Struggles to Decreate*. Bristol: Multilingual Matters.

Phillips, L. G. and Bunda, T. (2018). *Research through, with and as Storying*. London: Routledge.

Pitt, J. and Arculus, C. (2018). *SALTMusic Research Report*, Youth Music. Available at: https://network.youthmusic.org.uk/saltmusic-research-report

Powell, S. and Somerville, M. (2018). Drumming in Excess and Chaos: Music, Literacy and Sustainability in Early Years Learning, *Journal of Early Childhood Literacy*, online first.

Rasmussen, K. (2004). Places for Children. Children's Places. *Childhood*, 11 (2): 155–73.

Rasmussen, D. and Akulukjuk, T. (2009). My Father Was Told to Talk to the Environment First before Anything Else: Arctic Environmental Education in the Language of the Land. In M. McKenzie, P. Hart, H. Bai and B. Jickling (eds.) *Fields of Green: Restorying Culture, Environment, and Education* (pp.285–98). Creskill, NJ: Hampton Press.

Rautio, P. (2013). Children Who Carry Stones in Their Pockets: On Autotelic Material Practices in Everyday Life. *Children's Geographies*, 11 (4): 394–408.

Rautio, P. (2019). Theory That Cats Have about Swift Louseflies: A Distractive Response. In C. Kuby, K. Spector and J. Thiel (eds.) *Posthumanism and Literacy Education. Knowing/Becoming/Doing Literacies* (pp.228–34). New York: Routledge.

Rautio, P. (2020). Post-Qualitative Inquiry: Four Balancing Acts in Crafting Alternative Stories to Live by. *Qualitative Inquiry*. Available at: https://doi.org/10.1177/1077800420933297.

Rautio, P. and Vladimirova, A. (2017). Befriending Snow. On Data an as Ontologically Significant Research Companion. In M. Koro-Ljungberg et al (eds.) *Disrupting Data in Qualitative Inquiry*. New York: Peter Lang.

Richardson, T. and Murray, J. (2017). Are Young Children's Utterances Affected by Characteristics of Their Learning Environments? A Multiple Case Study. *Early Child Development and Care*, 187 (3–4): 457–68.

Rousell, D. and Cutter-Mackenzie, A. (2019). The Parental Milieu: Biosocial Connections with Nonhuman Animals, Technologies, and the Earth. *The Journal of Environmental Education*, 50 (2): 84–96.

Rousell, D., Cutter-Mackenzie, A. and Foster, J. (2017). Children of an Earth to Come: Speculative Fiction, Geophilosophy and Climate Change Education Research. *Educational Studies*, 53 (6): 654–69.

Rowe, D. W. and Neitzel, C. (2010). Interest and Agency in Two- and Three-year-olds' Participation in Emergent Writing. *Reading Research Quarterly*, 45 (2): 169–95.

Rowsell, J. and Pahl, K. (2007). Sedimented Identities in Texts: Instances of Practices. *Reading Research Quarterly*, 42 (3): 388–404.

Saavedra, C. and Esquierdo, J. J. (2020). Platicas on Disrupting Language Ideologies in the Borderlands. In F. Nxumalo and C. P. Brown (eds.) *Disrupting and Countering Deficits in Early Childhood Education* (pp. 37–52). New York: Routledge.

Sakr, M. and Osgood, J. (eds.) (2019). *Postdevelopmental Approaches to Childhood Art*. London: Bloomsbury.

Schneider, J. (2002). Reflexive/Diffractive Ethnography. *Cultural Studies ↔ Critical Methodologies*, 2 (4): 460–82.

Schrader, A. (2012). The Time of Slime: Anthropocentrism in Harmful Algal Research. *Environmental Philosophy*, 9 (1): 71–94.

Schulte, C. (2019). Wild Encounters: A More-than-Human Approach to Children's Drawing. *Studies in Art Education*, 60 (2): 92–102.

Schulte, C. (ed.) (2020). *Ethics and Research with Young Children*. London and New York: Bloomsbury

Sheets-Johnstone, M. (1981). Thinking in Movement. *The Journal of Aesthetics and Art Criticism*, 39 (4): 399–407.

Singh, J. (2018). *Unthinking Mastery. Dehumanism and Decolonial Entanglements*. Durham, NC: Duke University Press.

Skeggs, B. (1997). *Formations of Class and Gender: Becoming Respectable*. London: Sage.

Smith, K. and Coady, M. (2020). Rethinking Informed Consent with Children under the Age of Three. In C. Schulte (ed.) *Ethics and Research with Young Children* (pp.9–21). London and New York: Bloomsbury.

Somerville, M. (2007). Postmodern Emergence. *International Journal of Qualitative Studies in Education*, 20 (2): 225–43.

Somerville, M. (2008). Waiting in the Chaotic Place of Unknowing: Articulating Postmodern Emergence. *International Journal of Qualitative Studies in Education*, 21 (3): 209–20.

Somerville, M. (2013). *Water in a Dry Land. Place-learning through Art and Story*. New York: Routledge.

Somerville, M. (2015). Emergent Literacies in 'The Land of Do Anything You Want'. In M. Somerville and M. Green (eds.) *Children, Place and Sustainability* (pp.106–25). Melbourne: Palgrave.

Somerville, M. (2016). The Post-Human I: Encountering 'Data' in New Materialism. *International Journal of Qualitative Studies in Education*, 29 (9): 1161–72.

Somerville, M. and Green, M. (2015). *Children, Place and Sustainability*. London: Palgrave.

Somerville, M. and Powell, S. (2018). Thinking Posthuman with Mud: And Children of the Anthropocene. *Educational Philosophy and Theory*, 51 (8): 829–40.

Springgay, S. and Truman, S. (2017). On the Need for Methods beyond Proceduralism: Speculative Middles, (In) Tensions, and Response-Ability in Research. *Qualitative Inquiry*, 24 (3): 203–14.

Springgay, S. and Truman, S. E. (2019). Counterfuturisms and Speculative Temporalities: Walking Research-Creation in School. *International Journal of Qualitative Studies in Education*, 32 (6): 547–59.

Stadlen, N. (2005). *What Mothers Do Especially When It Looks Like Nothing*. London: Piaktus.

Stengers, I. (2008). Experimenting with Refrains: Subjectivity and the Challenge of Escaping Modern Dualism, *Subjectivity*, 22, 38–59.

Stewart, K. (2007). *Ordinary Affects*. Durham, NC: Duke University Press.

Stirling, E., Billau, S., Batty, S. and Vallance, R. (2019). Textual Interface: A Design Fiction. In G. Brooks, H. Harriss and K. Walker (eds.) *Interior Futures*. Napa Valley, CA: Crucible Press.

Sundberg, J. (2014). Decolonizing Posthumanist Geographies. *Cultural Geographies*, 21 (1): 33–47.

Tammi, T., Rautio, P., Leinonen, R. and Hohti, R. (2018). Unearthing Withling(s): Children, Tweezers, and Worms and the Emergence of Joy and Suffering in a Kindergarten Yard. In A. Cutter-Mackenzie et al. (eds.) *Research Handbook on Childhoodnature*, Switzerland: Springer.

Tarc, A. (2015). Literacy of the Other; The Inner Life of Literacy. *Journal of Early Childhood Literacy* 15 (1): 119–40.

Thiel, J. (2015a). 'Bumblebee's in Trouble!' Embodied Literacies during Imaginative Superhero Play. *Language Arts*, 93 (1): 38–49.

Thiel, J. (2015b). Shrinking In, Spilling Out, and Living Through: Affective Energy as Multimodal Literacies. In G. Enriquez, E. Johnson, S. Kontovouki and C. Mallozzi (eds.) *Literacies, Learning, and the Body* (pp.106–20). New York: Routledge.

Thiel, J. (2020). Red Circles, Embodied Literacies, and Neoliberalism: The Art of Noticing an Unruly Placemaking. *Journal of Early Childhood Literacy*, 20 (1): 69–89.

Tizard, B. and Hughes, M. (1984). *Young Children Learning. Talking and Thinking at Home and at School*. London: Fontana Press.

Todd, Z. (2016). An Indigenous Feminist's Take on the Ontological Turn: 'Ontology' Is Just Another Word for Colonialism. *Journal of Historical Sociology*, 29 (1): 4–22.

Trafi-Prats, L. (2019). The Cucumber Party: For a Posthumanist Ethics of Care in Parenting. In C. Schulte (ed.) *Ethics and Research with Young Children: New Perspectives* (pp.129–46). London: Bloomsbury.

Trafi-Prats, L. (2019b). Carrying the Line with Sylvie: Drawing as an Immanent Predicate in Early Childhood Practice, National Art Education Convention, March 2019, Boston, USA.

Truman, S. (2019a). Inhuman Literacies and Affective Refusals: Thinking with Sylvia Wynter and Secondary School English. *Curriculum Inquiry*, 49 (1): 110–28.

Truman, S. (2019b). SF! Haraway's Situated Feminisms and Speculative Fabulations in English Class. *Studies in Philosophy and Education*, 38: 31–42.

Truman, S., Hackett, A., Pahl, K., Escott, H. and McLean Davies, L. (2020). The Capaciousness of No. Affective Refusals as Literacy Practices. *Reading Research Quarterly*. Available at: https://doi.org/10.1002/rrq.306.

Tsing, A. (2015). *The Mushroom at the End of the World. On the Possibility of Life in Capitalist Ruins.* New Jersey: Princeton University Press.

Tuck, E. (2010). Breaking up with Deleuze: Desire and Valuing the Irreconcilable. *International Journal of Qualitative Studies in Education*, 23 (5): 635–50.

Tuck, E. and McKenzie, M. (2015). Relational Validity and the 'Where' of Inquiry: Place and Land in Qualitative Research. *Qualitative Inquiry*, 21 (7): 633–38.

Tuck, E. and Ree, C. (2013). A Glossary of Haunting. In S. Holman-Jones, T. Adams and C. Ellis (eds.) *Handbook of Autoethnography* (pp.639–8). New York: Routledge.

Tuck, E. and Yang, K.W. (2014). R-Words: Refusing Research. In D. Paris and M. T. Winn (eds.) *Humanizing Research: Decolonizing Qualitative Inquiry with Youth and Communities* (pp.223–47). Thousand Oakes, CA: Sage.

Viruru, R. (2001). Colonized through Language: The Case of Early Childhood Education. *Contemporary Issues in Early Childhood*, 2 (1): 31–47.

Viruru, R. (2012). Postcolonial Perspectives on Childhood and Literacy. In N. Hall, J. Larson and J. A. Marsh (eds.) *Handbook of Early Childhood Literacy* (pp.18–34). London: Sage.

Vladimirova, A. (2018, April). *Children Reading Forest, Forest Writing Children.* Talk presented at the International Expert Symposium 'Language, Literacies and Materiality', Manchester Metropolitan University, Manchester, UK.

Walkerdine, V. (2017). Affective History, Working-Class Communities and Self-Determination. *The Sociological Review*, 64 (4): 699–714.

Walkerdine, V. and Lucey, H. (1989). *Democracy in the Kitchen. Regulating Mothers and Socialising Daughters.* London: Virago.

Wargo, J. (2018). Writing with Wearables? Young Children's Intra-active Authoring and the Sounds of Emplaced Invention. *Journal of Literacy Research*, 50 (4): 502–23.

Wargo, J. and Oliveira, G. (2020). What Constitutes Community? Ethnographic Perspectives on Adolescent and Adult Literacy Practice. *Journal of Adolescent and Adult Literacy*, 64 (1): 102–5.

Watts, V. (2013). Indigenous Place-Thought & Agency amongst Humans and Non-Humans (First Woman and Sky Woman go on a European World Tour!). *Decolonization: Indigeneity, Education and Society*, 2 (1): 20–34.

Weiss, E. (2016). Refusal as Act, Refusal as Abstention. *Cultural Anthropology*, 31 (3): 351–8.

Werrlein, D. T. (2005). Not so Fast. *Dick and Jane: Reimaginging Childhood and Nation in the Bluest Eye. MELUS*, 30 (4): 53–72.

Yamada-Rice, D. (2018). Designing Play: Young Children's Play and Communication Practices in Relation to Designers' Intentions for Their Toy. *Global Studies of Childhood*, 8 (1): 5–22.

Yoon, H. S. and Templeton, T. N. (2019). The Practice of Listening to Children: The Challenges of Hearing Children out in an Adult-Regulated World. *Harvard Educational Review*, 89 (1): 55–84.

Youngblood Jackson, A. (2016). An Ontology of a Backflip. *Cultural Studies ↔ Critical Methodologies*, 16 (2): 183–92.

Zembylas, M. (2019). From the Ethic of Hospitality to Affective Hospitality: Ethical, Political and Pedagogical Implications of Theorizing Hospitality through the Lens of Affect Theory. *Studies in Philosophy and Education*, 39: 37–50.

Zhao, S. and Flewitt, R. (2019). Young Chinese Immigrant Children's Language and Literacy Practices on Social Media: A Translanguaging Perspective. *Language and Education*, 34 (3): 267–85.

Zylinska, J. (2014). *Minimal Ethics for the Anthropocene*. Ann Arbor, MI: Open Humanities Press, an imprint of Michigan Publishing, University of Michigan.

Index

www.ingramcontent.com/pod-product-compliance
Lightning Source LLC
Chambersburg PA
CBHW050443280326
41932CB00013BA/2229